Manifestations of Grace

THEOLOGY AND LIFE SERIES

Volume 29

Manifestations
of
Grace

by

Elizabeth Dreyer

John —
What a pleasure to have
met. As the French say,
"Ayez courage!" All the best
Elizabeth Dreyer
March 1999

A Michael Glazier Book
THE LITURGICAL PRESS
Collegeville, Minnesota

A Michael Glazier Book published by The Liturgical Press

Cover design by David Manahan, O.S.B. Photo by CLEO Freelance Photo

ISBN 0-8146-5759-1

❧

To my Mother and Father,
Marie and Robert Dreyer,
with love and gratitude

❧

Table of Contents

Preface 1
Introduction 3

Part I: Setting the Stage 9
  1. Getting into the Act:
    Invitation to the Reader 10
  2. The Reflected Life:
    The Centrality of Experience 14
  3. Elements in a First Description of Grace 20
  4. Past Faulty Directions 26
  5. The Living Faith of the Dead:
    Tradition 33

Part II: Our Ancestors on Grace 39
  6. "Honey Pressed Down and Running Over":
    Hebrew Scriptures 43
  7. New Creation in Christ:
    Paul of Tarsus 54
  8. God the Divine Healer:
    Augustine of Hippo 65
  9. A Joyful Friendship:
    Thomas Aquinas 82
  10. "And All Shall Be Well":
    Julian of Norwich 104
  11. The Glory of the Cross:
    Martin Luther 126
  12. A Tug of War:
    Trent, Molinism and Jansenism 144

Part III: Grace Today 156
  13. The Passion of God:
    Grace as Self-Gift 161

14. The Human Person Fully Alive 170
15. In the Company of the Cosmos 190
16. "God Love Admiration":
    Grace in Literature 212
17. Conclusion:
    The Many Faces of Grace 236

Index 241

The priest was still on his way, and finally I was bound to voice my deep regret that such delay threatened to deprive my comrade of the final consolation of our church.... He then uttered these words ... And I am quite sure that I have recorded them accurately, for his voice, though halting, was strangely distinct:

"Does it matter? Grace is everywhere..."

George Bernanos
The Diary of A Country Priest

Preface

It is with pleasure and a good deal of fear and trembling that I undertake this book on grace. The closing words of Georges Bernanos' great novel, *The Diary of a Country Priest* have echoed down the years of my life since my college days: "Tout est grâce." Writing about grace in a more systematic way has been, therefore, both a new challenge and a coming home.

The goals of the book are modest, given the enormity of the topic. They include providing an opportunity for the reader (1) to become more aware of her/his own experience of grace; (2) to become familiar with some recent structures and methods in theology; (3) to gain a deeper knowledge and understanding of the tradition of grace; (4) to be challenged by, and to become free to embrace new developments and emphases that influence a contemporary theology of grace. In this task, I am indebted to the many distinguished theologians who have paved the way with their reflections and analyses of grace.

Theologians, no matter what the level of discourse, become vulnerable because they are constantly searching and on the lookout for better ways to speak about God. Edward Schillebeeckx reminds us of the experimental and hypothetical nature of theological statements that take seriously modern experience. It is by no means clear at the start which elements in new experience are important and which irrelevant; which are true to the gospel and which alien to it. But such uncertainties cannot deter us from the necessary task at hand.

Of course, the ultimate goal of theological discourse is to enhance our experience of God, our understanding and expression of grace as that experience which calls us to greater holiness and vitality—as a community and as individuals. More specifically, it calls us to be loved by and to love God and one another truly and in freedom.

First, I would like to thank Michael Glazier for the opportunity to write this book. I am also grateful to the Association of Theological Schools for a generous grant and to the Lilly Foundation, whose grant to the Washington Theological Union included funds for faculty research. Drs. Keith Egan, Walter Principe and David Reid offered valuable suggestions on the text, and students at the Washington Theological Union have assisted me in clarifying and communicating my thought. I also want to thank all those who offered moral support and encouragement for this project. Finally, I want to express gratitude to my husband, John Bennett, who, in addition to being an indefatigable editor, is an embodiment and a constant source of my awareness of the giftedness of grace in my life.

Introduction

Grace has many faces. Within the Christian community, grace is a familiar term for most Christians and a household word for the theologian. For some persons, it is a living reality in their daily lives; for others it is something they get when they pray or go to church; for professional theologians it is a technical term; and for still others it is a term they have heard, but one devoid of significance. Upon further reflection, one realizes that the horizons of grace are limitless. Grace encompasses all of Christian experience and theology—the mystery of God, the human community, the event of God incarnate in Jesus Christ, the church, the entire cosmos created and held in being by God.

One must also call attention to the list of illustrious theologians who have put their hand to the theology of grace—Augustine, Aquinas, Luther—and in our own day, Henri de Lubac, Piet Fransen, Henri Rondet, Karl Rahner, Judith Plaskow, Leonardo Boff, Juan Luis Segundo, to name but a few.

It is comforting to read John Macquarrie's comment in the Forward to Piet Fransen's *The New Life of Grace:* "There will never be too many books on grace, for grace is at the very heart of the Christian experience and, indeed sums it up in a single word."[1] The study of grace deals with questions of the relationship between God and the world, between God and persons. It examines our basic understanding of human existence and the ways in which we relate to the transcendent. Our queries about these issues are never-ending; our responses

---

[1]Piet Fransen, *The New Life of Grace*, trans. Georges Dupont. (New York: Desclee Co., 1969), p. ix.

never complete. The study of grace is a perennial one, challenging us in every age to reflect on and speak anew about the experience of God's presence in the world.[2]

As history moves forward, new questions emerge, persons have new experiences and new insights that must be brought to bear on religious experience. Further, language changes and the words describing grace a century ago may no longer be appropriate. "Actual," "habitual," "prevenient," and "sanctifying" are some of the terms once used to explain the different dimensions of grace. While some still use this terminology, others prefer to use language that is more in tune with contemporary experience. This book reaches for broader categories and new language as well as examines the ways of the past that have contributed to our understanding of grace. It is difficult to understand the present well without knowledge of the past.

In a similar way, great classics such as *The Divine Comedy* by Dante Alighieri or the plays of William Shakespeare need to be studied anew by each generation. As our presuppositions and horizons change, we experience the great themes of existence such as love, death, God, suffering, jealousy, and power in some similar, but also in different ways from our ancestors.

In the arena of faith, it is one God who offers us a graced existence, but the human community is ever in flux, changing position and perspective in both subtle and dramatic ways. All efforts to understand the ways of God's self-gift take place in time and history and therefore reflect constant movement. In each era, persons make judgments about ideas that are relative to their particular situation.

Geography is another important variable. Theologies are conditioned by situation and location. In the past, Christian theology was largely a European endeavor. But we have become aware of the serious problems created when one face of Christianity is imposed on all. Most recently, liberation

---

[2]For an analysis of recent literature on grace up to 1970 see Francis Colborn, "The Theology of Grace: Present Trends and Future Directions," *Theological Studies* 31(1970): 692-711. See also James Mackey, *The Grace of God, The Response of Man* (Albany, 1966); Gregory Baum, *Man Becoming: God in Secular Language* (New York: Herder and Herder, 1970).

theologians are doing theology out of the specific context of South and Central America, guarding against importing a brand of theology that is out of step with their experience. In a similar way, theologies of grace in China, Japan, Russia or Africa differ from one another in significant ways. For our purposes, we need to inquire about the meaning of grace in the context of North America, and even more particularly of experience in the United States. This is not intended to foster isolationism, but its opposite. An accurate grasp of our own situation frees us to be a contributing member of the global community.

Our understanding of grace is also conditioned by national, social, political and economic conditions. Grace may be experienced differently by the rich than by the poor and marginalized. The meaning of grace is also affected by personal characteristics—whether we are male or female; young or old; white, black, hispanic, or oriental. As we shall see, grace is discovered in the concrete circumstances of life, and thus its meaning is colored by the infinite variety of those circumstances.

Two analogies come to mind to illuminate this point. Ask several different people to write a short biography of your grandmother, and you end up with a variety of statements. There is only one grandmother, but she looks different depending on the eyes that perceive her. The neighbor down the street writes one story, the six-year old grandchild writes another, and the spouse of sixty years, yet another.

Similarly, if you were to write a biography of your grandmother at age six, twenty-six, fifty-six and eighty-six, there would be significant differences in emphasis, language, perhaps even format. And one can imagine yet a different account from an author writing fifty or even one hundred years later. That is why it is valuable periodically to reexamine the vital aspects of our faith. The grace you learned about in second grade may not be the grace that can serve you well today as an adult. It is futile to parrot a theology of grace in past terms that no longer relate to our experience.

Any and all understanding of grace is finite, relative and historically contingent. Therefore, it is wise to speak of grace in a cautious and tentative way, but speak of it we must.

Provisional judgments can serve as signposts both to a more complete truth of which we are as yet unaware and to an absolutely normative truth that lies beyond history. In addition, we can identify many common threads that, in general, can be applied to most theologies of grace. We recognize the tension between the one God and the many manifestations of that God's presence. It is our task to address this tension in creative ways without destroying either polarity.

But, in any event, the words of the theologian must emerge from the experience of the Christian community and then be tested by that experience. It is foolhardy to speak in absolute terms, knowing that some aspects of the past are no longer meaningful, and that the words we use today may no longer be useful to generations that succeed us.

Of all religious realities, it is imperative that grace be relevant to the truth of our daily experience. To the extent that religious experience becomes divorced from our daily lives and preoccupations, to that extent does it become boring, empty, routinized—and eventually dropped. Further, there is little sense in clinging to something out of ignorance or fear. But we do know there can be different levels of vibrancy in the life of faith. One aim of this book is to ask and respond to the question: How can we recover the fullness of grace in our daily experience, understanding, and language?

That fullness is possible only when we broaden our perspective beyond the horizon of Christianity. We need to be on the lookout for ways to talk about grace with believers of other traditions—Jews, Buddhists, Hindus, various forms of feminist expression, the American Indian traditions, etc. Second, we need to concern ourselves about how to live and act in a society some segments of which no longer believe in a reality beyond the present. Many in our world have no sense of God and are radically divorced from the stories and symbols that traditionally have put us in touch with the transcendent. Unlike earlier historical periods, we cannot presume that everyone acknowledges the transcendent dimension of life, or has a shared horizon of meaning or a common language to express it. We can't count on people to understand us when we talk about "grace."

While the majority of readers of theology books such as this one have a religious context (and the majority are also probably Christian), it is shortsighted to limit ourselves to this viewpoint. Awareness of belonging to a Christian community goes hand in hand with an awareness of belonging to a *human* community, one that includes diverse religious and secular perspectives. While this book is written primarily with the Christian community in mind, we cannot lose sight of the larger horizon. The viewpoint of this essay, valid in itself, is a partial one.

Since transformation in grace must lead to action for justice, peace, and dignity for *all* peoples, our participation in the life of grace connects us necessarily with persons across the globe. Events and policies in one country impinge directly and immediately on another. The web of interconnectedness becomes more complex with each generation.

This book addresses only a few of these issues, but one hopes that the reader will not lose sight of the larger horizon and be on the lookout for ways to integrate Christian perspectives with those that are different. As Christians, we have things to learn from, and things to contribute to, other visions of reality.

The following discussion is intended to broaden the concept of grace to make it more inclusive of the full range of human experience. The grace of God cannot be contained by nor limited to certain, preconceived channels. Every aspect of life— even sin—has the potential to become an experience of grace. Irving Singer suggests that regardless of what people call themselves, they fall into two classes: "those who believe that human nature is inherently good, and therefore capable of an ideal love, and those who do not.[3] This essay takes the former perspective, viewing creation as good and everyday life as the primary locus of grace.

In Part I, I address several preliminary topics that provide the groundwork for what follows. In Part II, I return to the past in order to look at several key figures in the discussion on grace. In addition to the biblical tradition, I examine

---

[3]Irving Singer, *The Nature of Love*, I (Chicago: University of Chicago Press, 1966) p. 342.

Augustine, Aquinas, Julian of Norwich, Luther, Trent, and selected modern developments. This helps us to see and understand our roots and also to realize that grace has indeed been understood differently in different historical periods. In Part III, I offer a vision of grace that I think can contribute to a renewed understanding of grace today. In some cases, this involves a recapitulation of age-old themes that still seem relevant. In others, new elements are introduced in order to correct past emphases that no longer seem helpful.

References

Heribert Mühlen, *Der Heilige Geist als Person* (Munster, 1967).

Patrick Fannon, "The Changing Face of Theology: Man in Nature and Grace," *Clergy Review* 52 (1967): 331-336.

Charles R. Meyer, "The Status of Grace Today," *Chicago Studies* 7 (1968): 27-51;

Edward Bozzo, "The Neglected Dimension: Grace in Interpersonal Context," *Theological Studies* 29 (1968): 497-504.

John W. Glaser, "Man's Existence: Supernatural Partnership," *Theological Studies* 30 (1969): 473-488.

Brian Kelly, "A New Approach to the Theology of Grace," *Irish Theological Quarterly* 34 (1967): 70-74.

David Burrell, "Indwelling, Presence, and Dialogue," *Theological Studies* 22 (1961): 1-17.

Karl Rahner, "Concerning the Relationship Between Nature and Grace," in *Theological Investigations* 1 (Baltimore, 1965): 297-318.

Part 1

Setting the Stage

> This communion with God through the Son in the Spirit is in fact a living communion that *can be experienced.*
>
> Edward Schillebeeckx
> *Christ*

Introduction

In order to facilitate our discussion on the history and meaning of grace, it is helpful at the outset to delineate several presuppositions and methodological concerns. Too often, we plunge into a subject without adequate attention to these issues or without attending to the reader's experience or thoughts on the topic. Therefore, in this section I address the following issues:

1) Getting into the Act: Invitation to the Reader
2) The Reflected Life: The Centrality of Experience
3) Elements in a First Description of Grace
4) Past Faulty Directions
5) The Living Faith of the Dead: Tradition

1

Getting into the Act:
Invitation to the Reader

Too often, one's encounter with theology is a purely passive one. We know that good listening and reading, although passive in some dimensions, require an enormous amount of engagement. Unfortunately, we rarely take the time or set up the structures that might enhance this more active participation. This is a serious omission since "insight" or the "Aha!" experience is directly dependent on the intensity of the learner's curiosity and search for answers. Too often education is based on answers to questions that no one has! But it is even more unfortunate when there are no questions to begin with. This is a sure recipe for becoming a dullard. The art of questioning, emerging out of a searching heart and mind, is one avenue to a vibrant and engaging life.

The desire to know is especially relevant to the theological enterprise. The reason for this lies in the scope of the study of theology. This scope can be described as a totality, or universal reality. The horizon of theology is the broadest possible one, encompassing all of reality. While other disciplines examine specific parts of reality, e.g., biology, psychology, anthropology, chemistry—theology examines reality in its totality. It has to do with ultimate reality and the ultimate questions that concern all of us.

It is hard to imagine a person who has no interest in or concern about the ultimate meaning of her/his existence. David Tracy argues that theology's task, always, is to articulate and respond to "existentially vital and logically odd questions."[1] Why am I here? Does my life have any ultimate significance? Why do the innocent suffer? Is there a God? Does this God relate to me and if so, how? Is there any order or plan to the cosmos and to my life? What is love? Does it matter whether or not I love well? What will happen when I die? These are the kinds of questions at the heart of the theological task.

Let us go one step further. Among the many subjects theology explores, grace is one that seems especially conducive to questioning and engagement. As we have noted, there is little in the life of a believer that is not related to grace. Since reflection on grace is reflection on the divine-human relationship, every aspect of life can be seen under the rubric of grace. Therefore, it is logical for anyone with interest in ultimate reality to be curious about this thing we call "grace."

One of the specific tasks of theology, therefore, is to ask questions about the contemporary experience of grace. When, where, and how do we encounter God? Out of this reflection, we arrive at language that expresses this experience. This language needs to be appropriate for our time, understandable and useful to the Christian community. It has to "ring true", as well as be convincing and persuasive to our ears and our hearts.

The next question is: How does one become engaged in this topic? For some, no prodding is necessary. They have already been thinking about this for years and have been searching high and low for any shred of insight into the meaning of God and grace in their lives. Others have no interest in the topic at all and no amount of inviting will budge them. These persons may posit the existence of a God, but are not curious about how this might impinge on their lives. Yet others have never thought of grace as such, but are open to learning something new and are ready to be engaged if only invited. The right invitation will vary from person to person. If the questions below do not suit you, make up your own. The point is to find out what you think about this subject and to uncover any questions that may be simmering beneath the surface of your

---

[1]David Tracy, *The Analogical Imagination*, (New York: Crossroad, 1981), p. 4.

consciousness—*before* you go on reading about it. Take a few moments to jot down answers to the following questions.

Questions

1. When you hear the term "grace", what words, ideas, images, thoughts come to mind? (Do not ponder long on this, but allow yourself to respond spontaneously. If nothing comes, do you know why?)

2. Have you ever experienced grace?

3. Choose one or two experiences and describe them, e.g., by asking:

   a) Who are the key figures?
   b) How did the experience make you feel?
   c) In what kind of circumstance were you?
   d) What did the experience tell you about yourself? About God?
   e) Did it affect your relationships with others? How?

4. Why do you think you remember this particular event?

5. Is the experience of grace rare or common for you?

6. Name three or four issues that you would include in a discussion about grace.

7. Does recalling your experience of grace raise any further questions?

After jotting down your responses, it may also be helpful to find out how others experience grace. You may discover commonalities, or perhaps find out that your experience of grace is quite distinctive from that of others. As we will see in the next section, your experience of grace is a very important element in the quest for greater understanding. This written record of some aspects of your experience can serve as a reference point when we examine how others in the Christian community have understood their experience of grace. In some cases, there will no doubt be common threads, but in others, you may diverge from the tradition or have different language or different emphases. This record can also be checked at the end of your study in order to see if and how your ideas and awareness of grace have changed or been deepened and reinforced.

Before proceeding, it might be helpful for me to mention my own questions, some of which fashion the shape of what is to come.

1. How *do* persons experience grace? Concretely, what does grace look like and feel like?

2. How is grace related to the human? What precludes us from experiencing grace in our everyday lives?

3. Whence comes people's basic security that allows them to take risks, e.g., for justice? Is that source reliable and more powerful than threatening forces, e.g., the possibility of a nuclear holocaust?[2]

4. Is grace a quality in God, and if so, what words or images best describe it?

5. Is grace a quality in humans and in the cosmos, and if so, what words or images best describe it?

6. How is grace related to freedom? Does grace influence our personal and corporate psychology, and if so, how?

With this preliminary exercise behind us, let us proceed to the next section, in which we discuss the important role of experience in theology.

---

[2]See Brian McDermott, *What Are They Saying About the Grace of Christ?* (New York: Paulist Press, 1984), p. 65.

2

The Reflected Life:
The Centrality of Experience

If someone were to ask you, "Do you have experience?" you would either respond with a speedy, "Of course!" or wonder in silence about a person who would ask such a question in the first place. But if you were asked to define experience, you would discover that the response is much less obvious. Experience is so basic, so primary that we take it for granted, and indeed, find it quite difficult to define or describe. John Shea describes experience as "the reciprocal flow between the self and its environments." The environments he names are self, family, friends, society and its institutions and the non-human environment, i.e., the universe.[1] In other words, experience is the interaction between ourselves and everything and everyone that is within and around us.

One can make further distinctions among the various kinds of experience. There is conscious experience of which we are aware as we go about our daily routine. There is unconsious experience that occurs for example in our dreams. And there is vicarious experience when I get some idea of what it is like to live in Africa from a friend who has just returned from there—even though I have never actually been there myself.

Until recently, human experience was not acknowledged as having a key role in theological pursuits. There was a strong need for certainty, and one does not have to reflect long on

---

[1]John Shea, *Stories of God*, (Chicago, IL: Thomas More Press, 1978), pp. 12-15.

human experience to know that it is filled with change, bias and error. The starting point for theology was God, but a God thought to be removed from the vagaries of human life. We also naively thought that we had access to God somehow *outside* of human experience. Now we realize that there is only one avenue to and from God and that is always *through* human experience. No matter what we say about God, it is said by humans, whose ideas and language are conditioned by a particular period in history, and by a particular socio-cultural matrix.

As a result of this historical consciousness, our language about God has become more careful, more tentative. We now realize that we are not capable of making absolute statements about God, that whatever we say about God, whatever images of God we use, are limited and finite and can only distantly approximate what God must really be like. The God we know in the human community is a *partial* realization of the totality of God. In this regard, one can call to mind persons of enormous sensitivity, and then try to imagine what the absolute fullness of that sensitivity must be like—a fullness that will always transcend our attempts to name and understand it—no matter how successful we may be.

Another result of this new consciousness is the choice by many theologians to take human experience as the starting point for doing theology. In the Roman Catholic tradition, Karl Rahner is an outstanding example of one whose theological system takes anthropology as its starting point. For Rahner, it is possible to talk about God from the starting point of humanity since the human person is one who by her/his very constitution is open to the totality of reality and therefore *as person*, open to the ultimate Mystery of God.

Any theological expression that is seriously out of touch with or divorced from the experience of the believing community should be called into question. Therefore, an important first question for theology has to be addressed to the community of faith, the "People of God", to use a phrase from the Vatican II documents: How is God present in our lives? Theologians then take the answers to that question in each generation, compare and contrast them with the content of the scriptures and the tradition and try to express the results in an ordered and clear way. If this articulation becomes stagnant and divorced from the ongoing experience of the community, then theology becomes dead, empty, and unreal, no longer able to speak to or help the community to grow in its relationship with God.

The questions in chapter one above are an example of using experience as a starting point. We are also aware that our theology has been built on a too narrow experiential foundation. For most of the almost 2,000 years of its existence, Christian theology has been based on the experience of only a few members of the community. Most Christian theology has been written by white, male, middle class, clerical, celibate, European males. This is only one perspective on religious experience. As our world becomes a global village, we are struggling to fill in the gaps in our theology by consulting the experience of women, blacks, hispanics, orientals, lay persons, poor and marginalized persons. Karl Rahner points to Vatican II as "the first major official event in which the Church actualized itself precisely as a *world Church.*"[2]

The task ahead is a challenging one, and it is clear that each and every voice is crucial if we are to create an authentic theology. To the extent that each of us refuses to reflect on and speak about our faith experience, to that extent is theology stunted and incomplete.

Structures of Meaning

In addition to the role of experience, there is yet another element that one needs to understand in order to do theology today. If theology's task is to enhance our understanding of faith experience, then we have to talk about meaning. What is the meaning of grace? What does it mean to be in relationship with God?

To begin, each of us might ask ourselves, What is the source of meaning? In some cases, this doesn't seem too difficult. Most of us are aware that many of our meaning structures

[2]Karl Rahner, "Towards a Fundamental Theological Interpretation of Vatican II," *Theological Studies* (1979): 717.

come from family, church and society, e.g., the meaning of work, or the meaning of leisure, or the meaning of child-rearing. But when it comes to religious issues, we may tend to forget that meaning is also mediated through the human community.

Just as the meaning of play, or exercise or learning is mediated through a particular community at a particular location, in a particular historical period, so too meaning about God and faith and grace is mediated through a specific community of persons. Too often, we think that religious meaning comes from "out there" somewhere, a *deus ex machina* breaking through to humans from the clouds.

But the Judeo-Christian God has chosen to reveal Godself *in* and *through* people and nature. This is why we spoke above about being tentative in our language about God. Since the meaning of God is always filtered through a specific human community, we have to inquire about that community and find out *who* is speaking about the meaning of grace. That meaning may differ in significant ways depending on who you are and where you live, whether you are wealthy or poor, male or female. This is also why it is important for all of us to pay attention to and speak about grace. The broader the experience considered in a theology of grace, the more truly does it reflect authentically the meaning of grace for that community.

It follows that a theology of grace is developmental. Just as my understanding of love changes as I move through the various stages of life from childhood, through adolescence to adulthood and old age, so does my understanding of God and of grace. The community's understanding also changes. The church's sense of grace in the nineteenth or the twentieth centuries differed from that in the thirteenth century. As we have seen, this requires that we keep writing about the meaning of grace, since meaning cannot remain static, ignoring the on-going changes experienced in history. It serves no purpose simply to rehearse a past theology of grace which tells of a union of God and the human person in terms which we cannot recognize in our own deepest experience.[3]

[3]Cornelius Ernst, *A Theology of Grace* (Notre Dame, IN: Fides Publishers, 1974), p. 64.

If grace has to do with one's relationship with God, and if for Christians, this God has been revealed in Jesus Christ, then we need to ask about the *meaning* of a faith encounter with Jesus. Those who actually met and followed Jesus had their understanding of the meaning of his coming. We have accounts of their encounters in which we read about this Jesus of Nazareth, but there is also the possibility of our meeting Jesus, really and personally today. This new kind of meeting involves a new kind of understanding and a new kind of meaning.[4]

This new meaning modifies and transforms the whole range of meaning and understanding of each other that we had before. "Those who turn to Jesus in faith become aware of new possibilities of meeting other people and understanding them. We may think of it as a new dimension of the world of meaning.... It is within this enlarged world of meaning, given in the experience of Jesus Christ in faith, that we wish to locate grace."[5]

Two alternatives to having a structure of ultimate meaning include those who say their meaning is finite, limited to this world and to history, and those who have concluded that there is no answer at all to the question of meaning. These latter either commit suicide, or live lives of quiet despair, convinced that there is no direction to life, no cohesive vision that helps to explain and give integrity to life's experiences.

This new thinking is a challenge to persons of all faiths. It is a call to all believers to pay attention to life, to reflect on its contours in the light of an encounter with deity—whether Christians, Jews, Buddhists, Moslems, Confucians, American Indians, etc. It is an invitation to make sense of our lives in light of both tradition *and* the truth of our experience.

Because grace has often been examined in abstract and theoretical categories that have prevented us from understanding its meaning in our everyday lives, and because the reality of grace is always revealed in the concrete circumstances of life, we need to describe grace from a perspective that is tangible and concrete.

[4]Ibid., p. 69.
[5]Ibid.

It is time now to venture an initial, approximate description of grace. This description is not intended to be all-encompassing or definitive, but rather to set some general parameters and to identify both a linguistic base and some basic presuppositions underlying the discussion to follow. It may also prevent us from pursuing a theology of grace in the chapters ahead based on misunderstanding about what it is, exactly, we are talking about.

3

Elements in a
First Description of Grace

It is difficult to decide what to put into a description of grace. I use the word "description" rather than "definition" because the nature of the task requires a category as open-ended as possible. The situation will frustrate those who like things clean, neat, organized and labelled. It will delight the person who is more comfortable with open boundaries, ragged edges and endless possibilities.

To support this approach, I cite two contemporary theologians, Cornelius Ernst—

> Grace becomes an open concept capable of embracing the whole of God's gift of [Godself to persons], and so capable of indefinitely various further particularization.[1]

and Leonardo Boff:

> We can never talk about grace in itself because it shows up in this particular thing or that particular thing. . . . Grace is not something isolated in itself that stands apart from other things. Grace is a mode of being that things take on when they come into contact with the love of God and are suffused with [God's] mystery. In that sense the whole world is related to grace.[2]

---

[1]Cornelius Ernst, *The Theology of Grace*, p. 29.

[2]Leonardo Boff, *Liberating Grace*, trans. John Drury (Maryknoll, NY: Orbis Books, 1979), p. 28.

If we understand grace to be a "mode of being", one can ask a number of further questions. Where does this mode of being originate? How does one receive it? In what does it consist? How does one live a life of grace? What specific qualities are visible in persons/things that are seen as being in contact with God's love? Can grace be lost? With these questions in mind, let us proceed to identify those elements that are most central to an initial and general understanding of grace. In Part III, we will be looking at some of the specific emphases in a contemporary doctrine of grace. But now our task is to present a general idea of what grace is, to identify those perennial qualities that characterize it, and to outline the main issues that contribute to a theology of grace.

Grace is Universal

If we see God as creator and sustainer of the cosmos, and if we subscribe to an open-ended notion of grace, we realize that nothing, *a priori* need be excluded from it. Every person, every reality has the potential to be touched by God's love.

Grace is Relational

Grace always involves relationships. The word "grace" initially points to the relationship between God and the world. Within this larger sphere, grace functions in a distinctive way in the God-human relationship. Of course, relationships with each other and with the world cannot be separated from the God-human relationship, and, in fact, are deeply affected by it. Initially, God is discovered in and through relationships among humans. One hears the Good News from the community into which one is born. Some persons experience God most tangibly in their relationships with others. Others find God in prayer and then make connections with their human relationships. Still others find God in the beauty of nature. While emphases differ, grace is a dialectical experience.

Since we are like and unlike God, any discussion about

grace must be careful to include both aspects. At times, theologians have been concerned primarily with the enormous differences between the divine and the human. Others, especially in some mystical traditions, have highlighted the closeness and the similarities. While we want to maintain the tension between the God who is transcendent and "Other" and the God who is immanent and closer to us than we are to ourselves, it is inevitable that we will favor one aspect over the other. This preference may result from what one has experienced and been taught about grace; it may be due to certain qualities in a given personality; or it may be a corrective response to a past over-emphasis in one direction.

If one thinks about all the dimensions involved in human relationships, one can get some sense of the breadth and complexity of grace. It involves issues of communication, intimacy, mutual knowledge and love, responsibility, commitment, alienation, separation, forgiveness, etc.

Grace is Corporate

Grace cannot involve only the individual and her/his relationship with God. Grace is open-ended. It operates in a variety of communities—in fact it has the potential to have meaning in all the communities to which we belong. This includes the family, the neighborhood, the faith community, the nation, the world and the cosmos. Grace can never thrive in isolation or solitariness. Indeed, one of its main functions is to connect, not to separate or set apart— to connect ultimately with the totality of reality and its trinitarian Creator.

God as the Source of Grace; Humans as Recipients

Who is this God who initiates a relationship with the cosmos and with the human community, who offers not merely life, love, and assistance, but God's very Self?[3] It is easy to see that

---

[3]In classical theology, grace, seen as the gift of God's Self to the world was called "uncreated grace". In this sense grace *is* God.

one's image of God influences the ways in which we experience, understand and talk about grace. If God is always looking over my shoulder to catch me doing something wrong, then it is hard to imagine grace as a generous, loving gift intended for my well-being.

The study of grace also has anthropology as a primary concern. Ideas about the make-up, desires and capabilities of human beings influence how we envision and talk about the divine-human relationship. If God is so different from humans, how is it possible to experience a shared life? In more traditional terms, this topic would be discussed as the relationship between the "natural" and the "supernatural". Such language may no longer be the most useful for a contemporary discussion of grace. This terminology did not appear in the official language of the church until the sixteenth century and is quite foreign to the way grace is portrayed in the scriptures.

God Initiates Freely

This is one of the most constant tenets in the doctrine on grace. I cannot think of a single theologian or church official who has held that the relationship between God and humans begins with human beings. It is always God who freely calls persons into being and holds them in existence with loving care. These divine actions come forth from a generous God who delights in giving gifts.

Attention to the authentic human experience of giving and receiving gifts will go a long way to further our understanding of grace. Grace is freely given, not something we earn or merit on our own. One who gives freely is not concerned about the balance of scales—I gave you two gifts, but you only gave me one—nor about demanding a certain kind of behavior of the one gifted. True gifts, freely offered, are signs of love, attention, valuing.

One who receives a true gift is often humbled and surprised at the care and generosity of the giver. One realizes that at a deep level, one is not worthy of the gift, especially of the gift of another in love and friendship. Gratitude follows quickly upon feelings of being undeserving—a simple, uncluttered response of "thank you."

The gift of grace is offered freely by God and we, in turn, are free to accept or reject it. The acceptance of grace enhances freedom, makes us free to love, free to see the world as touched deeply by God's love.

Sin and the Need for Grace

The presence of evil, selfishness and egoism is a part of daily experience. This experience of our lack of love awakens in us the need for grace. Since the community graced by God is a sinful one, grace takes on a new dimension. God continues to offer the gift in spite of our egoism and selfishness. The experience of love after transgression and forgiveness is different indeed from the love we know before the bond has been broken. Theologians talk of this graced existence as "salvation" or "redemption" or "justification".

As we shall see, sin is not the only context in which to talk about grace, but it is a central part of human experience relevant to any discussion of grace.

Consequences of Grace[4]

One also needs to ask about the effects of God's grace. While these effects are numerous, they include above all, (a) a participation in the very life and mystery of God (some theologians use the term "divinization"); (b) a life that is a visible celebration of the gracious love and goodness of God; (c) a transformation that leads one to act lovingly toward others and the world as God acts toward us; (d) an enhanced sense of connectedness or wholeness—within oneself, with others and with the universe; (e) confidence in the promise of full intimacy with God that is the final fulfillment of history.

This initial picture situates grace on a broad canvas. It also points to the complexity of the reality of grace. As a result,

---

[4]In classical theology, the effects of grace in human persons were known as "created grace" to distinguish it from the uncreated gift of God's self to the world.

there are many legitimate vantage points from which to view grace. These perspectives or emphases vary from one historical period to another. Some are contrary to the original spirit of the Christian message. But even among those positions that have been considered faithful to that message, there is much diversity—as we shall see in Part II.

In addition to this overview of the primary aspects of grace, it is important to be aware of some of the unhelpful ways in which the Christian community has thought about grace in the past. Knowing the faulty directions of the past allows one to be on guard lest these ideas on grace unconsciously block the possibility of living the life of grace to the fullest.

4

Past Faulty Directions

As we view the past from our present vantage point, we see that not all earlier conceptions of grace are viable today. Past categories and language about grace grew out of specific socio-historical conditions. We look at various examples of this in Part II. In their own time, certain ideas about grace were seen to be the most effective and to make the most sense. But now, since our situation has changed, we realize that some of these former ways of understanding grace have either been misunderstood or are no longer helpful. They are no longer in harmony with our experience and so prevent us from living the fullness of grace.

Often modifications of the past are a matter of a change of emphasis. In some cases, we find ourselves returning to an understanding of grace of a much earlier period—one that has since been discarded or fallen into disuse. The reality of grace encompasses many elements, and different elements need to be highlighted in different historical periods, depending on the needs of the time. Doctrine about grace always has a context and must be seen in relation to what is happening in a given historical period. For example, if there are persons of influence in the faith community or in the society who support a position of total autonomy of the human person from God, then the doctrine of grace should change to meet this challenge, emphasizing the role that God plays in the divine-human relationship. One can imagine the opposite case as well.

Let us, then, identify some of the ways in which we do *not* want to understand grace today.

Strict Separation of Nature and Grace

The West is undoubtedly more guilty of this error than the East. The Western practice of taking distinctions to their limit can result in a false separation. Grace is then viewed in terms of exclusive either/ or disjunctions that do not do justice to the complexity of human existence. In some disciplines, such a method is appropriate. In others it is not. In a theology of grace one wants to give full attention to the rigorous dictates of reason *and* to the multifarious ways in which grace expresses itself concretely.

Realities that contain a surplus of meaning require this. One thinks of falling in love or heroic courage and their expression in poetry or music. One can agree with Pascal that the heart has its reasons that reason does not know. What we are suggesting, however, is the avoidance of a facile reductionism on either side of the equation. We want to use reason to its fullest possible capacity, realizing that this does *not* mean making an absolute distinction between the divine and the human in such a way that the points of connection become dim or even impossible.

Reifying Grace

One consequence of Christianity's appropriation of philo-sophical categories from the Greek tradition is the reification of grace. Grace is understood as a thing, something almost physical, something to be quantifiably measured and mechan-ically transmitted. In this view, grace is a "thing" quite distinct from nature. This error leads us to the "banker's" image of grace. Good deeds merit grace that can then be put in a bank account for future use.

Reifying grace also leads to relating nature and grace in unhelpful ways, e.g., piling one on top of the other like grease rising to the top of a pot of soup.[1] Another more extreme

---

[1] The technical theological term for this view is "extrinsicism".

position disallows any connection at all between the two. Nature displaces grace or vice versa, since two "things" cannot occupy the same space at the same time. Finally, we may separate nature and grace by attributing all the activity of grace either to God or to humans, rendering one or the other superfluous.

However, if we understand grace as divine self-communication, these dichotomies become radically inappropriate. Karl Rahner suggests a more unified way of viewing nature and grace:

> The strictly theological concept of "nature" therefore does not mean a state of reality, intelligible in itself and experienced by us separately on top of which an additional higher reality would be superimposed. Nature is rather that reality which the divine self-communication creatively posits for itself as its possible partner in such a way that in relation to it that communication does and can remain what it is: a free and loving favour. . . . The difference between nature and grace must be understood on the basis of the radical unity of God's free self-communication as love.[2]

Over-emphasis on the Transcendent

Past formulations of the doctrine of grace have consistently emphasized the transcendent, at times at the expense of the human. Natural values were treated as having little or no consequence. There seemed to be a fear that if the human were given a significant role on the stage of grace, then somehow God would necessarily be reduced in stature. This kind of thinking may be the result of the tendency to separate nature and grace in an absolute way. This error can lead to a theology that gives mere lip-service to the event of incarnation, and it can contribute to a loss of confidence, dignity and responsibility in members of the faith community.

---

[2] *Sacramentum mundi*, s.v. "Grace."

Over-emphasis on Sin

This position suggests that God relates to the human almost exclusively as a result of our sinfulness. In this view, God is found in failure rather than in success, in sorrow rather than in joy, in weakness alone rather than in strength. This stance keeps the focus on the narrow, even boring, reality of human sinfulness, and away from God and the dazzling brilliance of the grace God offers.

An over-emphasis on sin has also produced an attitude of legalism in which believers ask inappropriate questions like How far can we go and still remain in God's favor? Still more discouraging has been the choice on the part of church leaders and theologians to honor such questions. These questions and answers diminish the expansiveness and the profound truth of grace, creating a narrow and constricting understanding of grace that falls dangerously short of its power and mystery.

An exclusive focus on sin, or an erroneous concept of sin can lead to what Walter Brueggemann calls "underliving."[3] Believers are prevented from living the fullness of the life of grace, celebrating the joys of life with God and embracing their relationship with God and others in trust and accountability.

Extreme Abstraction

The tendency to make grace a "thing" or to see God far removed from the daily round of human living has led to a theology of grace characterized by extreme abstraction. Especially after Trent, the theology of grace seems to have lost contact with human experience. Karl Rahner understands the theology of grace as that part of theological anthropology that deals with the human person as redeemed and justified. We should not speak in the abstract about grace, but about *persons* endowed with grace.[4] This understanding makes it harder for

---

[3] Walter Brueggemann, *In Man We Trust* (Atlanta: John Knox Press, 1972).

[4] *Sacramentum mundi*, vol. 2, p. 422.

theologians to remove themselves from the concrete experience of grace in persons' lives.

This form of abstraction appears when philosophical categories, meaningful in one period of history are retained after they have lost that meaning. We experience this problem today when we look at the language of grace used in an earlier time. Medieval expressions, categories, and distinctions often do not help us understand grace today. Talk about grace as "supernatural", "prevenient", "concomitant", "actual", and "habitual", is no longer adequate to the ways in which we find God in religious experience. Preoccupation with doctrine resulted in talk *about* grace. There was little evidence of grace itself, of the experience of grace and its presence in the world.[5] We understand ourselves in a more wholistic sense and our approach to grace is more synthetic than analytic.

Extreme Individualism

The emergence of a worldview in which the individual began to take precedence over corporate identity can be traced to the tenth and eleventh centuries. The switch to a growing sense of individual identity was evident on many fronts—in law, in monasticism, in the universities. This cultural trend perdured throughout the centuries, signalled in dramatic ways in the French and American Revolutions and in the Enlightenment. Most recently in America, this trend has been called into question. Some judge that we have gone too far in this direction and are in danger of losing our sense of community, seen by some as the "glue" of a society.[6]

The tradition of the spiritual life is no exception. Too often grace was seen as a private affair between the individual and God. Piet Fransen says of past theologies of grace: "Influenced by an atmosphere of dominant individualism, the theology and preaching of recent centuries presented grace all too

---

[5]Leonardo Boff, *Liberating Grace* (Maryknoll, NY: Orbis Books, 1976), p. 5.

[6]See Robert Bellah, et al. *Habits of the Heart: Individualism and Commitment in American Life.* (Berkeley, CA: University of California Press, 1985).

frequently as not more than an enriching of the individual life of the soul."[7]

Two unhelpful corollaries of this view of grace include seeing grace as a static rather than as a dynamic entity, and emphasizing the interior aspects of grace to the exclusion of any external effects. The former error is corrected if one looks at grace as relational, since one needs only to refer to the experience of being in relationship with another to see its extraordinarily dynamic qualities. The latter position becomes modified when one looks at grace in a more communitarian sense. The experience and understanding of grace need to come out of belonging to a community, and the fruits of grace are discerned in terms of action on behalf of the many communities of which we are a part.

False Images of God

Finally, an inadequate theology of grace can lead to false images of God—a problem that leads, in turn, to truncated and/or crippling concepts of the human person. A theology of grace that emphasizes God's power and activity to the exclusion of human cooperation can lead to an image of God as "Big Daddy" or "Mr. Fix-it"—someone who may then seem to treat humans in capricious or puzzling ways. This God will receive praise when things go well, but such a God also gets blamed when things go poorly, or when one is faced with inexplicable suffering.

Such an image may also support irresponsibility or feelings of powerlessness in human persons. If nothing we say or do matters, why bother? When we set up false connections—or in the extreme, eliminate any connections at all—between God and ourselves, we begin to feel like pawns or lose interest altogether.

In a theology that reifies grace, God can become the "Almighty Banker" and we industrious Americans set out to

---

[7]Piet Fransen, *Divine Grace and Man*, Trans. Georges Dupont (New York: New American Library, 1965), p. 90.

work with a vengeance, earning income and storing up reserves to insure a seat in the eternal kingdom. A false sense of self-sufficiency or a disposition of self-righteousness are the fruit of such an image of God.

Conclusion

With our present desire to view the human person in a wholistic manner, many of these past understandings of grace are found lacking. We realize that it is no longer possible to adhere to a strict separation of nature and grace. Many may even want to discard the vocabulary of nature and grace so that our language would more accurately reflect the organic and concrete ways in which we experience ourselves, others and therefore, God. We value maturity and do not want to continue in an eternal adolescence in our relationship with God. We experience ourselves as interconnected members in a global community and eschew a theology of grace that has a privatized sense of "me and God" at its center. A viable theology of grace today will have to take these factors into consideration.

Let us proceed now to an examination of the role of tradition and of several outstanding figures who have influenced theologies of grace down to the present.

5

The Living Faith of the Dead: Tradition

In a recent essay entitled, "American Memory," Lynne V. Cheney argues that inadequate teaching of history in U.S. public schools is putting at risk our national character, dissolving the sense of nationhood that is our civic glue and threatening to condemn our nation to perpetual infancy.[1] Surveys show that two-thirds of America's 17-year-olds cannot locate the Civil War in the correct half century. The results of forgetting history are embarrassing at best and at worst, equivalent to what an enemy might do to destroy a nation.

It is legitimate and important to understand the world in which we live. But our understanding of that world can only be scattered and partial if it lacks knowledge of the events and ideas that brought this world into being. Anthropologists, studying primitive societies have identified tradition as the glue that brings cohesiveness to a clan or a tribe.[2] Custom is often the vehicle by which tradition transmits itself—particular ways of preparing food, or rituals accompanying rites of passage. Often the most intense arguments between newly married partners occur over such issues. "But this is the way we *always* did it," whether it be Thanksgiving, Christmas or childrearing, is an oft-repeated phrase. And who is not touched by the famous opening song from the play "Fiddler on the Roof"—"Tradition"?

[1]Lynne V. Cheney, *American Memory*. (1987).

[2]Jaroslav Pelikan. *The Vindication of Tradition* (New Haven, CT: Yale University Press, 1984), p. 6.

The study of history can also be a liberating activity. It allows one to see the range of positions on an issue, to comprehend the reasons for them, to be moved and inspired by history's ideals, and to struggle to overcome its pitfalls and illusions. In fact, wisdom suggests that it is foolish to treat the past lightly. Present achievements have that very past as their foundation.[3] "By including the dead in the circle of discourse, we enrich the quality of the conversation."[4]

But we must also be alert to unintelligent attitudes toward tradition. Many persons both within and outside of the Roman church have the impression that tradition is a static, monolithic, homogeneous entity. In this view tradition becomes a narrow confining force that is to be rejected. Sometimes our actions do reflect stasis, but a closer look at the historical record produces a contrary impression. In fact, tradition is teeming with movement, diversity and often with internal conflict of one sort or another. We have seen that the dynamism of history requires repeated analysis of the past from the ever new perspectives of the present.

There are others who make an idol of tradition, making the preservation of the past an end in itself. This position "claims to have the transcendent reality and truth captive and encapsulated in the past, and it requires an idolatrous submission to the authority of tradition, since truth would not dare to appear outside it."[5] Holders of this view see the past as an idyllic time to which they long to return. In both these views, tradition is regarded as a homogeneous mass. In the former it is regarded as totally negative; in the latter, it is all rosy. The rosy view overlooks or quickly by-passes the crises and tensions of past eras. Signs of nostalgia appear in the trappings of talk about "the good old days" or of horror at the hopeless depravity of the present age. However, one is surprised to find similar, almost identical laments in the documents from almost every age. The long view of history does afford us the possibility of judging one era more war torn and destructive than another.

---

[3]George Will, "Learning from the Giants," *Newsweek*, (Sept. 14, 1987): 96.

[4]Jaroslav Pelikan, *The Vindication of Tradition*, p. 81.

[5]Ibid., p. 55.

But every age has its fierce critics and prophets of gloom. Pelikan captures this difference between "tradition" and "traditionalism"⁶ when he says, "Tradition is the living faith of the dead, traditionalism is the dead faith of the living. ...it is traditionalism that gives tradition such a bad name."⁶

Christopher Lasch offers an alternative view. He suggests a conversational relationship with the past, one that seeks neither to deny the past nor to imagine a false picture of it. He invites us rather "to enter into dialogue with the traditions that still shape our view of the world, often in ways in which we are not even aware."⁷ It is important to note that in this dialogue, instead of simply addressing the historical record, we need to grasp the ways in which it addresses us. This need not imply an unquestioning attitude toward authority, nor universal agreement. As we have said, a close look at tradition reveals conflict as well as consensus. In fact, it is tradition that allows us to disagree without resorting to the sword.⁸ "Part of the value of tradition is that it commemorates past achievements (critically) and makes us all parties to those achievements." It is a betrayal of tradition to use it to enforce conformity to a rigid set of values.⁹

The values attached to knowing our historical past also apply to country, church, family and personal history. Any account of what grace means and how it operates in our lives requires, then, consideration of the tradition. In terms of grace, our past includes giants of thought like Augustine, Aquinas, Luther and Karl Rahner. It also includes the ways in which ordinary believing persons have allowed God to grace their lives for millennia. Evidence for the latter is scarce and difficult to interpret. The more common route, which we take here, is to look at the positions of major figures. But we do not need to divorce the understanding of grace of great thinkers from the experience of the common person. Indeed, the theologians

---

⁶Ibid., p. 65.

⁷Christopher Lasch, "The Communitarian Critique of Liberalism," *Soundings*, 69 (1986): 66.

⁸Ibid., p. 67.

⁹Ibid., p. 71.

we examine, although specialists, lived in society, enjoyed its benefits, and suffered from its shortcomings, just like everyone else.

The Historian's Task

One task of history is to mediate this tradition. The historian is the "middle person" between the past and the present. She tries to bring the past into the present in a meaningful way. But this tradition is not something "out there" upon which to gaze and about which to make judgments. What happened then is part of a process that ends up with us *now*. On the one hand, we mediate the tradition by making intelligent decisions about it, but on the other hand, the tradition mediates us, i.e., our understanding of the tradition forms the basis of our own development. We are always in the stream of this process and development. At each stage in history, new information emerges. We need to be on the lookout for, and open to, this new data, and be willing to see how the tradition is changed by new information or experience. I agree with Henri Rondet when he says, "despite the clarifications worked out in the course of the ages, the theology of grace remains 'open-ended'" and the return to tradition and reflection on it "can be the most valuable stimulant for the mind that seeks an understanding of the faith."[10]

Different positions on grace, as well as other theological, intellectual and cultural movements, like all living things, are born, live out their allotted lifespan, and come to a close.[11] Weaknesses within each system hasten their demise and changes in history render a given position obsolete. The rise and fall of theological positions are a given of history. But this phenomenon does not therefore consign past thought to the rubbish heap forever.

---

[10]Henri Rondet, *The Grace of Christ: A Brief History of the Theology of Grace*, trans. and ed. Tad W. Guzie, (Westminster MD: Newman Press, 1967), xix. Original edition, 1948.

[11]Gerald A. McCool, "Neo-Thomism and the Tradition of St. Thomas", *Thought* 62 (June 1987): 131.

There is also the familiar phenomenon of the "eternal return" in which great currents of thought come back into relevance after periods of eclipse. Platonism rose again in Middle Platonism, in Plotinus, in medieval, Renaissance and seventeenth-century Platonism and in our own time, in the thinking of Alfred North Whitehead. Augustinianism arises so regularly it is as if it were always with us, and Kantianism has returned for several encores.[12] Of course, the return involves change and alteration to accommodate present concerns. Further, this change includes fresh interpretations and methods of discernment—the ability as a community to use what is helpful and recognize what is harmful, to see what fits into a new system and what doesn't. At times the recovery of aspects of the tradition enrich the present, but recovery also has the potential to narrow ideas and practice, to impoverish rather than enhance what has been handed down.

The historical question is twofold: (1) understanding a text, or a person, or an event in its own space and time; (2) figuring out what, if anything, it might mean today and how it adds to or detracts from our own faith life. The historian needs to remain faithful to the past data that are at hand as well as to activate her imagination and her attention to the depths of present human experience. It is often difficult to "cross over" to a text that is hundreds of years old, to imagine what life was like in the time of Augustine, or Aquinas, or Luther. The historical task requires an openness to differences and great attention to the socio-cultural information that is available. For very early periods, this kind of evidence is often quite slim.

It may be easier to understand this dynamic on a smaller scale, the understanding of which can then be applied to the wider canvas of history. The enormous strides in psychological knowledge have made us acutely aware of the influence of family history and of the importance of early childhood in our lives. We now know how deeply and in some cases irrevocably our past dictates who we are and what we make of our lives.

It may be curiosity, but more often it is a crisis that forces us

---

[12]Ibid.

back to that past to discover its contours and to become more aware of how it inhibits present behavior. Since the past cannot be changed and since it has such an overwhelming hold on our present, we struggle to raise the material from the unconscious to the conscious level, to marshal its positive energy, and by negotiation, to minimize its destructive tendencies. The determination and hope for change spring eternal. Just as unconsciousness can have a negative influence in our personal and familial lives, so too, when applied to our faith lives, it can deprive us of health, maturity and the fullness of life that grace promises.

We hope to have shown here that it is possible and desirable to discover connections between the past and the present. In significant ways, whether I know it or not, the experience and thought of persons like Augustine, Aquinas and Luther do impinge on the well-being (or lack thereof) of my faith life. The history of grace takes place on a continuum and all of us are on it. For good and ill, our lives and the lives of our ancestors in the faith are intimately intertwined.

In Part II, we examine some of the highlights of this history of the meaning of grace. The words of Teresa of Avila, written to her sisters in the sixteenth century, come to mind: "It is a shame and unfortunate that through our own fault we don't understand ourselves or know who we are. Wouldn't it show great ignorance, my daughters, if someone, when asked who he was didn't know, and didn't know his father or mother or from what country he came?"[13] The choice is ours whether to become conscious participants in the faith story that is ours or to remain unconscious victims.

---

[13]Teresa of Avila, *Interior Castle*, 1.1.2.

Part II

Our Ancestors on Grace

What you have as heritage,
Take now as task;
For thus you will make it your own!
Goethe, *Faust*

Human beings are worth something because their memories
are their own. They are the point of departure for new
options, for new marks they can imprint in the body of
time.
Juan Luis Segundo
Grace and the Human Condition

Introduction

With these perspectives on the tradition in mind, and having heard arguments in favor of the wisdom of the past, let us plunge into the task. The limits of this essay allow only a brief examination of the highlights of the history of grace, enough to whet the reader's appetite, sending her to the library to read the original material and other commentators to see for herself.

In the following chapters, we try to be sensitive to the socio-historical milieu of each figure. We point to some of the factors impinging on the various positions on grace. What were the influences, the disagreements, the vested interests of the authors that caused them to take the particular position they did? Second, we examine the authors with an eye to the key questions we've identified in any theology of grace, especially the ways in which they understand the relationship between the divine and the human. In the life of grace, what role does God play, what role is given to humanity? Is there a balance or does one party have a monopoly in the process? If both God and human persons have a role, how is that discussed? in what arenas does each operate? How do the varying functions relate to one another?

We will examine the theology of grace in the Bible—both the Hebrew Scriptures and Paul in the New Testament—in Augustine, Aquinas, Julian of Norwich, Luther and Trent. A note of explanation is in order, since, to my knowledge, Julian of Norwich has never been included in any formal treatment on grace.[1] The biblical material, Augustine, Aquinas and Luther are important because of their enormous influence on the way we have thought about grace for centuries in the Western Christian tradition. I include Julian for another purpose—to recover a strain in the tradition that has been neglected and is too often forgotten. She was an anchoress, a solitary in England during the fourteenth century, whose theology of grace in many ways, was very traditional in its view of God as the main actor in the divine-human relationship. What is distinctive about her theology is her vision of the human person which is unusually positive. Her anthropology contrasts markedly with most of the tradition that preceded her and with much of the theology of later periods as well. Her theology is included since it provides a needed balance in our understanding of grace today.

---

[1] Susan Thrift Mahan has treated Julian's anthropology in a dissertation at Marquette University, Milwaukee, Wisconsin, 1987: "The Christian Anthropology of Julian of Norwich."

Let us begin then, with the writings of the oldest of our ancestors in the Judeo-Christian tradition, the Hebrew scriptures. The journey begins in Jerusalem, with the community from which Jesus emerged and out of which he spoke his message.

Biblical Foundations

INTRODUCTION

As we have seen, it is a perennial concern of theology to ground itself both in the tradition and in present human experience. A particularly important part of that tradition is the biblical account of the originating story of Christianity— including its foundations in the Hebrew Scriptures and the early accounts of the life, death and resurrection of Jesus and the development of the church recorded in the New Testament.

One always needs to take into account the latest discoveries of biblical scholars as they interpret the meaning of the text in its own time as well as its meaning in the present situation. Any doctrine of grace must investigate the substance of the biblical message and flow from it, acknowledging as well the differences in time, categories of intelligibility, and language that separate a past century from the twentieth. An example may be instructive here.

In his book, *Christ*, Edward Schillebeeckx states that the New Testament reveals the exodus characteristic as an essential quality of the Jewish-Christian community. But the *form* that this exodus has to take must continually be discerned anew, in freedom, within one's historical circumstances. Despite the differences between God and humans, he says, we are no longer bound to the Middle-Platonic two-storey universe, nor to the hyperbolic way the New Testament expresses its apocalyptic sentiments. But to be faithful to the tradition, each community must find its own specific form of the exodus as a consequence of a renewed, and yet abiding, eschatologically oriented experience of grace. "New Testament Christianity can only be a model indirectly, and not directly."[2] It is not our aim here to give a thorough analysis of all the issues involved in an account of the biblical notion of grace. But we will try to sketch the broad contours of the meaning of grace in the Hebrew scriptures and in Paul.[3] This is a process of re-membering (*anamnesis*). But this kind of remembering is not just a matter of reminding oneself what happened in an earlier time. Schillebeeckx says it well:

> It is a return to the past in narrative with an eye to action in the present. God "reminds himself" of his earlier saving acts in and through new acts of liberation. So Christian faith is a remembrance of the life and death of the risen Jesus through the practice of becoming his disciples—not through imitating what he has done but, like Jesus, by responding to one's own new situations from out of an intense experience of God.[4]

[2] *Christ,* (New York: The Seabury Press, 1980), p. 561.

[3] It is accurate to say that the entire New Testament is concerned with grace. However, we focus on Paul, since his is the most overt and systematic treatment of grace.

[4] Ibid., p. 641.

6

"Honey Pressed Down and Running Over": Hebrew Scriptures

The Hebrew Scriptures: Introduction

Theology today is divided into specialties. Among the most prominent are biblical, historical, cultural, moral and systematic theologies. Methodologies also differ depending both on the theologian and the topic to be studied. But no matter what the starting point or method of any particular project, it is important to connect theological understanding and expression with its roots in religious experience. In the case of the Christian community, those roots go back a long way to the origins of the biblical account of the Hebrew nation and God's dealings with this people.

The mindset, worldview, culture and accepted meaning of persons living in 1200 B.C. and of persons living in the late twentieth century couldn't be more diverse. At times it is a strain to connect these two worlds and yet it is important to do so. Just as we are inevitably and irrevocably connected with our roots and ancestors, so too as Christians we are connected with our foremothers and forefathers in the faith.

It is in this spirit that we examine past understandings of grace. We do not intend to defend the past blindly and absolutely, nor to force narrowly conceived links between then and now. What we can do is mine the past to discover elements that seem to be irrelevant or even antagonistic to our experience and those that can indeed enhance our graced lives today—elements that both comfort and confront us as we grapple with the meaning of grace.

For Christians, talk about grace can be so exclusively filtered through the New Testament that the reality of the Hebrew experience is obscured. Further, the idea that the theological notion of grace is essentially Christian[5] cannot be maintained even in the narrowest linguistic sense. Let us turn, then, to the world of the Jewish community.

The Hebrew worldview differs in significant ways from our own. For example, it did not include the distinction, familiar to us, between nature and history. The Hebrew language has no equivalent to our term, "nature". God was fully present in nature. The voice of God was heard in the thunder. The hand of God was visible in both rescue and pestilence. The breath of God was the animating force giving life to humans. Therefore, we need to leave aside for a moment our modern ideas about grace in order to enter as fully as possible into the worldview of the Hebrew community.

Most studies on grace in the Hebrew scriptures focus on vocabulary. Although there is no Hebrew word for "grace" as we use that term today, there are three words found in the Hebrew scriptures that can be related to the idea of grace. These are *hen, hanan,* and *hesed.* Scholars often examine the meaning of these words in the Hebrew scriptures and then trace them as they are translated in the Septuagint and eventually in the New Testament. While this is an important foundation for any understanding of grace, it can be limiting, since the reality of grace permeates all of Hebrew experience and is not located in a single term or event.

Therefore, in addition to a short summary of the meaning and development of these three Hebrew words, we will look at some of the broad contours of the meaning of grace in the Hebrew scriptures under various headings or images that capture some of the central elements in Hebrew experience and understanding of grace. This material is presented from

[5] Henri Rondet, *The Grace of Christ*, p. 20.

two perspectives: ways in which grace applies to God, the giver of grace; and ways in which it applies to human persons as the recipients of grace. Several of these characteristics overlap, e.g., the freedom with which Yahweh offers grace results in freedom in the recipients. Others will be distinctive to one or the other perspective. But let us turn first to a brief overview of the meaning of the Hebrew terms related to grace.

Hen[6]

The term *hen* means "favor", or "charm", "attractive-ness", "elegance". *Hen* focusses on that attitude or disposition that wins favor, especially from superiors. Its original setting may have been the court, in which case one would say that a subject would win the favor (*hen*) of the king, or that the king would show favor (*hen*) to the subject. This term does not refer to a quality of the king, but always of the one in the inferior position. In the Septuagint, *hen* is translated *charis*, e.g., "But Noah found favor (*hen/charis*) in the eyes of the Lord" (Gen 6:8).

Most often, *hen* points to a social attitude rather than to an individual quality, and also includes the action that flows from such an attitude. In the Hebrew Scriptures, the term is seldom used in a theological sense, but it foreshadows the later idea of grace inasmuch as it refers to relationships—especially those relationships in which one person is favorably disposed to another. Relationship is a central element for the Israelites whose lives revolve around their covenant with God.

Hanan

Hanan, the verb from which *hen* is derived, means to be gracious or to show mercy to another. *Hanan* occurs often in the Psalms and refers to God's gracious concerns for persons, especially for those who are in need. As with *hen*, the emphasis

---

[6]I rely in this section on the following studies, all of which are recommended for further study: Edward Schillebeeckx, *Christ*, (New York: The Seabury Press, 1980), 86-111 ; *Sacramentum mundi*, 1968, s.v. "Grace," by Klaus Berger; *The Interpreter's Dictionary of the Bible*, 1962, s.v. "Grace", by C.L. Mitton.

in the term *hanan* is on action rather than simply on an inner disposition. These terms highlight doing something rather than being someone, although the two dimensions cannot ultimately be separated from one another. In the Hebrew scriptures, *hanan* is used both in a secular sense with no overt religious meaning, and at times with religious content. As with *hen* its context is that of relationship. Schillebeeckx describes the meaning of *hanan* in a number of ways. *Hanan* implies the approach of one person to another; one person's turning toward another; the attention one pays to another; the kindness behind a gift or a present; a response with all one's heart to a crying need or a lack in another; forgiveness, graciousness, as when a victor in battle spares the vanquished.[7]

In its religious meaning, *hanan* occurs sixty times in the Hebrew scriptures, forty of which refer to God and twenty-six of which appear in the Psalms. Since the book of the Psalms is Israel's prayer book, we can conclude that talk about God's graciousness often took place in the context of communication with God. *Hanan* frequently occurs in prayers of petition, prayers in which a suffering and needy person calls out to God for relief. "Be gracious to me, O Lord, for I am languishing" (Ps 6:2). "Turn to me and be gracious to me, for I am lonely and afflicted" (Ps 25:16). "Incline your ear, O Lord, and answer me; for I am poor and needy. Be gracious to me, O Lord " (Ps 86: 1, 3).

The intensity of these prayers presupposes confidence in God. One does not pour out one's grief and request aid if there is no hope of receiving help. The Israelites knew that God was a God who would give them a hearing and that God's promises of assistance were trustworthy. This assistance came in all forms—strength in weakness; forgiveness for sin; healing from illness—spiritual, physical, psychological; rescue from the enemy—within and without; freedom from trouble and anxiety. These prayers reflect the concrete realities of life. They are not abstract, detached expressions of theological themes, but impassioned pleas, emerging out of the very heart of human experience.

[7] *Christ*, pp. 86-87.

As Schillebeeckx says so well, *hanan* in the Hebrew scriptures connotes a free gift, an expression of God's graciousness to Israel. The word is sometimes used in connection with "the face of God" which shines upon a person who is blessed and has found favor in God's sight (Gen 33:10; Num 6:25). The term calls forth the image of God and Israel setting out together (Ex 33: 12-33), knowing each other's names, with God's face turned toward Israel.[8]

Hesed

This third term is not related to the same root as *hen* and *hanan*, but is often used as a substantive form of the latter word. While *hen* and *hanan* are translated with the Greek *charis* in the Septuagint, *hesed* is usually translated with the Greek *eleos* which means "mercy." *Hesed* is like *hen* and *hanan* in that it points to action as well as to an attitude of kindness; it refers to what extends beyond strict obligation or duty; it suggests mutuality in relationship. *Hesed* reflects a generous giver who gives freely, openly, superabundantly, unexpectedly, with no regard for self. "The Lord, the Lord, a God merciful and gracious, slow to anger, and abounding in steadfast love and faithfulness, keeping steadfast love for thousands, forgiving iniquity and transgression and sin" (Ex 34:6-7).

Hesed is often connected with other terms that nuance and add new dimenions to its meaning. It is linked with *'emet* which means faithfulness or reliability; with *rahamin*, which means tender, almost vulnerable love—the kind we read about in Hosea. *Hesed* refers to God's graciousness to persons but is not attributed to persons as they relate to God. Rather it is a quality that should serve as a model for relationships among humans. God's *hesed* is a model for the ways in which the Israelites should treat one another.[9] Other responses to God's *hesed* toward Israel include thanksgiving and praise for the gifts of this merciful and kind God.

To sum up, then, *hesed* is the mercy, forgiveness and loving

[8] Ibid., p. 89.

[9] Ibid., p. 98.

kindness of God. It is mutual, surprising or unexpected, abundant and overflowing beyond our imagining, faithful, reliable, something that can be trusted no matter how dire the circumstances. It is this loving God who initiates and shows mercy to God's chosen people. Israel responds with joy, gratitude and praise to their God.

The experience of grace changes and takes on new aspects as it is expressed in the New Testament and in the later tradition. But as we shall see, some of the basic realities reflected in the language of *hen, hanan* and *hesed* remain at the heart of the meaning of grace even to the present.

With this brief etymological survey as background, let us turn to some of the broader ideas and images that might bring us closer to the Hebrew experience of grace. Since the Israelites understood all that was given and everything that happened to them as the fruit of God's loving mercy and faithfulness in the covenant as grace, it will be impossible to give a comprehensive treatment. But it is possible to sketch some of the major components of the Hebrew experience of grace, with one eye on the integrity of the experience as it is expressed in the scriptures and the other on the experience and needs of the contemporary believing community.

The Hebrew Image of God

Who is this God who gives grace, whose face turns toward Israel in generosity and kindness? What characteristics are revealed in the text of the Hebrew scriptures?

The first quality we might mention is freedom. God's actions on behalf of Israel are not necessary, not coerced, and not earned by something Israel has done. God freely chooses to reach out to Israel, to grace the people in many ways, and to stand by them always.

Second, God is gracious. Often in the texts, graciousness is linked with several other qualities—mercy, compassion, constancy, long-suffering, (Num 14:18; Joel 2:13; Jonah 4:2; Neh 9:17). "But thou, O Lord, are a God merciful and gracious, slow to anger, and abounding in steadfast love and faithfulness. Turn to me and take pity on me" (Ps 86:15).

This God is also reliable, one upon whom Israel can count. God's faithfulness is rock solid, perduring throughout the generations (Ex 34:7; Is 26:4). It is a love that lasts despite ingratitude and infidelity (Hos 2:19-20). The objects of God's graciousness are especially the needy, those who are weak and poor and oppressed in any way (Prov 14:31; 28:8). These call out to God and their prayer is heard. They are rescued from horrors of all kinds, many of which are described in vivid detail (Ps 22:6-21).

Forgiveness is another trait often mentioned in the texts. "I will forgive their iniquity and I will remember their sin no more" (Jer 31:34). God does not treat the sin of Israel as it deserves to be treated. This God does not nurse anger or grudges, or take an accusing stance toward the people. God's love is strong and wins out over an attitude of handing out the sinner's just deserts, of demanding an "eye for an eye" (Ps 103:8-14).

This regard for another is contrary to many ordinary ways of thinking and acting. These actions are surprising. They cause us to sit up and take note, to ponder on this God who is so ready to forgive and to allow the sinner to begin anew.

Fourth, this God is generous. This generosity, evident in a ready forgiveness, extends to many other spheres as well. It is an overwhelming generosity, hard to fathom in a world of strict rules governing mutual rights and obligations. "You anoint my head with oil, my cup overflows. Surely goodness and mercy shall follow me all the days of my life" (Ps 23:5-6). God is a gift giver, one who continually offers good things for the welfare of the people. God's gifts included the call to Israel to be the chosen people; God's actions in the Exodus, in the giving of the land, the punishment of enemies, and of course in the Law, the embodiment of God's presence to Israel. God's grace was the source of happy marriages, healthy children, abundant crops, a full table, and so many of life's simple joys, so precious to those who experience them. In the spiritual realm, grace brought about renewal of life and of the covenant, regeneration and a new heart (Jer 31:31).

These generous actions on Israel's behalf are not cold or indifferent, but reflect a tender care. We are all familiar with the story of Hosea and with the image from Isaiah—"Can a woman forget her sucking child, that she should have no compassion on the child of her womb?" (49:15). And again, "The Lord is gracious and merciful, slow to anger and abounding in steadfast love. The Lord is good to all, and God's compassion is over all that God has made" (Ps 145:8-9).

The reverse side of grace is punishment. The covenant demands accountability. The Hebrew terms for "favor" that appear so frequently, for example, in the Psalms, are almost totally absent from the prophetic literature. The prophets are concerned more with failure than with favor in the people and speak of judgment and punishment for Israel's refusal to follow in God's ways. But even in the prophets, there are islands of relief from the judgment and one has the sense that the *hesed* of God wins over judgment:

> "A new heart I will give you, and a new spirit I will put within you; and I will take out of your flesh the heart of stone and give you a heart of flesh. And I will put my spirit within you, and cause you to walk in my statutes and be careful to observe my ordinances. You shall dwell in the land which I gave to your ancestors; and you shall be my people, and I will be your God" (Ez 36:26-29).

These qualities describe a God who is in relationship with the people. The God of Israel is not a loner, but rather one who chooses to get involved, to turn toward the people, to become intimately engaged in their lives and to stick by them in all kinds of circumstances. In some inexplicable way, God finds the people attractive, grace-ful and is drawn to them. God experiences tenderness and loving care for this people in spite of their sinfulness and failings. The people find favor in God's eyes and God is extraordinarily gracious to them. In fact, this relationship is so intimate that if one were to ask Israel, "Who are you?" they would respond, "We are the people married to Yahweh." And if we were to ask God, "Who are you?" God would respond, "I am the one who is married to Israel."[10]

[10]From a lecture given by Walter Brueggemann at St. Louis University, Summer, 1974.

Israel's Response to God's Actions

God's graciousness elicits a variety of dispositions and responses from Israel. Even before we talk about an active response, we see that because of God's gracious gesture towards the human community, the people have a grace-fullness, an attractiveness in God's eyes. No matter what happens, ultimately the people find favor before the face of God that is turned toward them.

God's graciousness encompasses all of reality and its effects are evident from the originating event of creation. In the Genesis story, women and men are created in God's image. God's presence makes human persons attractive and appealing. This charm and pleasantness in humans perdure in God's eyes in all circumstances, even when the gifts of grace are rejected or abused.

In God's free gifts of grace to Israel, Israel becomes free itself. It is free to accept or reject the graces offered, and if accepted, the people are given freedoms of all kinds. Freedom from sin, from self-preoccupation, from holding grudges, from anxieties about their lives, from the oppression of enemies. They become free to love and be merciful to others as God has been to them.

God's gracious action is perceived as a call. God turns toward Israel and invites them to be a holy people, to enter into a covenant that will insure and direct the mutual commitment God initiated. The call and response provide the framework for this relationship that is worked out in the small and momentous events of Israel's concrete daily existence. As we saw above, God's grace itself is a gift and is the source of many gifts that show God's kindly disposition toward this people. God is the source of happiness, of the joys and pleasures that life may offer to Israel. The gifts are concrete and real to them, and their response takes several forms. We will mention two.

Israel responds to God's *hesed* through repentance and by living in an upright way. God's relationship with the Israelites is characterized by love, generosity, mercy and justice. When this is experienced, one wants spontaneously to turn or return to God, to repent of one's ungrateful ways. In addition, God's dealings with the Israelites become the model for the way in which they should treat one another. They are to be faithful and true in their dealings with each another (Gen 24:49). In the book of Ruth, Naomi also makes the connection in reverse. She says to her two daughters-in-law: "May the Lord deal kindly with you, as you have dealt with the dead and with me..." (Ruth 1:8). When the Israelites wonder about what they should be like or how they should act, they have the ways of the covenant before them, and a merciful God whom they can emulate in their relationships with each other. A high standard of love is expected, one which bears fruit in an ethical way of life.

Second, the Israelites respond to God's gifts of grace with gratitude, praise, celebration and joy. The realization and acceptance of God's abundant giving is acknowledged and celebrated in song and dance. Jeremiah tells how God will build Israel up again. God says, "Again you shall adorn yourself with timbrels, and shall go forth in the dance of the merrymakers (Jer 31:4). The psalmist says, " But I will sing of your might; I will sing aloud of your steadfast love in the morning. For you have been to me a fortress and a refuge in the day of my distress" (59:16). Isaiah speaks of how God comforts Israel: "Joy and gladness will be found in her, thanksgiving and the voice of song" (51:3).

One primary locus for this celebration is the liturgy. The community comes together to give thanks and sing the praises of this God who does marvelous things. "O give thanks to the Lord, for the Lord is good; for God's steadfast love endures forever" (Ps 107:1; 136).

The total experience of grace recorded in the Hebrew scriptures is built upon some important presuppositions. The Israelites know the God we described above. They know that this God is quick to forgive and never tires of reaching out to hold them up. They know they can count on the promises offered and they rely on God's strength. The word often used to express the fact that God is watching out for us is providence. The Israelites trusted that they were in the hands of a caring, personal God who wished them well. They had confidence and depended on their God.

A second presupposition is that the Israelites were aware of their failures and their sinfulness. They knew they did not always respond well to God's gifts of grace—a knowledge that made them aware of how much they were *in need* of God. The experience of suffering, of need, of oppression, coupled with their trust in God's promises and power led to the kind of prayer we find in the Psalms.

It is not difficult to reflect on one's own experience in order to identify some of the same dynamics recorded in the Hebrew scriptures. One can recall perhaps being offered a gift—the spontaneous, generous gesture from someone in whose eyes we find favor. We are surprised, astounded by the generosity. It makes us feel known and appreciated and yet in some sense unworthy of so magnanimous a gesture. Gratitude wells up and the urge to "kick our heels" in joy, to celebrate, to tell everyone about it comes over us. Or perhaps we are on the giving end, taking the initiative to give gifts to someone who is in need or attractive to us.

In addition to becoming familiar with the story of the chosen people, it is reflection such as this that can help us get in touch with and understand in some way the experience of the Israelites and their God. We can become more alert to the dynamic of grace in our lives and to our response to it—or the lack thereof. Each person will experience grace in a unique way that flows out of the kind of relationship she has with God, with herself and with other persons. For the Hebrews of the covenant, grace was God's free, unlimited, unsolicited, unaccountable love.

7

New Creation in Christ:
Paul of Tarsus

We move now into the world of the New Testament. Here we find no radical discontinuity from the Hebrew conception of grace as God's favor to the world, but now the reality of grace is filtered through the experience of the death and resurrection of Jesus and is located in the particular historical and cultural milieu of the early Christian community. For the early Christians, grace remains a free gift of a generous God (1 Cor 15:10; Eph 3:7; 2 Cor 6:1); and it still concerns the relationship between God and the human community.

It is not possible here to provide a systematic treatment of grace in the entire New Testament. We will concentrate on Paul, keeping in mind that what we find in Paul is not unlike the concepts of grace in other New Testament authors. On the one hand, none of the biblical writers, including Paul, develops the theme of grace in as systematic a way as do later writers in the tradition. On the other hand, even though the other New Testament authors do not use the term *charis*, the entire text is suffused with and motivated by the experience of Jesus, as the graced gift of God. Kingdom, discipleship, miracles, Word, light, life, truth—all have to do with grace.

If we were to focus exclusively on the Greek term for grace, *charis*, we find that Paul uses the term twice as often as all the other New Testament writers combined. *Charis* is not found at all in Matthew, Mark, 1 John, 3 John or Jude. In the gospel of John, the term occurs four times, all in the Prologue, and Luke uses it six times. In contrast, Paul uses the term one hundred and one times in his letters. We will look at ways in which Paul develops his idea of grace and at several primary characteristics that give us a sense of Paul's understanding of the experience of grace. In examining Paul's treatment of grace, we ask about the identity of God and the ways in which God relates to the human community in Paul's eyes. This relationship is primarily one of call and response which will be the prism through which we look at Paul's understanding of the graced life.

Grace in Paul: The Context

Because Paul does not have a "tract" on grace, the reader in search of the meaning of grace in Paul is drawn into the wider context of Paul's writing and the experience behind it. In fact, experience becomes a major category of interpretation, just as it was for our analysis of the Hebrew Scriptures.[1] Paul's experience of the risen Lord was no ordinary one. In contemporary psychological language, one could call it a "peak experience". Or if we were to capitalize on the image of Paul's conversion, we could talk about it in terms of falling to the ground in the midst of a light flashing from heaven. At any rate, Paul's experience of grace is not of the "business as usual" type. In observing the variety of ways in which Paul talks about his experience of grace, it is not difficult to sense the deep feelings conveyed by the text. Paul is enthused, passionately involved, intense. His entire world has been turned upside down as a result of his encounter with the risen Lord.

Other factors also influenced Paul's understanding of grace. As the early Christian community moved away from Judaism, it struggled to understand itself in the light of its Jewish past. Because of this situation, Paul contrasts grace with the law, struggling to build a bridge between two worlds. The law is good, but it is not the source of our justification, which comes

---

[1]We might recall here the exercise for the reader with which we began. The reader's experience may provide tools that would be of assistance in "crossing over" into Paul's experience.

only through faith in Christ (Gal 2:16). Second, Paul sees grace in terms of redemption or salvation—important categories in the Jewish community. Christians saw Jesus as the embodiment of the Messiah awaited by the Jewish community.

There were yet other forces that influenced Paul's doctrine of grace. The Pharisees and the Stoics placed great emphasis on ethical effort, on the centrality of human activity for the good. In contrast, Paul's point of departure is the utter gratuity of God's action in everyone, beginning with his own experience. He takes a strong position upholding grace as a totally free and unmerited action of God toward humans.

Finally, in response to the extreme spiritualizing tendencies of the Platonists, Paul situates grace squarely in the milieu of history—grace refers to his own apostolic calling, to a realm that embraces the whole of humanity in its history, to the concrete communities to which he ministers, and even to the collection of money for the poor in Jerusalem. Each community is the body of Christ in a real and concrete way, and the fruit of grace takes on flesh in the specific gifts of each person, given in grace for the benefit of the whole community. Paul's grace is no abstract, other-worldly phenomenon.

Meanings of Grace

One of the first things one notices in reading Paul's letters is that the term *charis* appears often in his greetings and farewells. The phrase, "Grace to you and peace from God our Father and the Lord Jesus Christ", becomes a refrain in many of the letters. Grace is from God and also from, through and in, Christ; it is connected with peace; it is a wish that Paul offers to the members of the early communities.

Paul also connects grace with his own call to apostolic ministry and with that of other Christians (Rom 11:5; 1 Cor 15:10; Gal 1:6, 15). The call is to belong to God (Rom 1:6), to be saints (1 Cor 1:2), to possess every spiritual gift of action, speech and knowledge (1 Cor 1:5). Not only does grace make Paul an apostle, but it also gives him whatever qualities he will need to minister effectively.

Grace in Paul is especially connected with *action*. The community under grace lacks no gift (1 Cor 1:7)—service, exhortation, teaching, miracles, healing, prophecy, money for the poor in Jerusalem, governance, tongues, and above all love (Rom 5:5).

In these salutations, Paul often moves from talk about grace to talk about thanks and praise. Paul's experience of grace consists significantly in his response to having received such a gift. He immediately moves to expressions of glory to God (Gal 1:5; 2 Cor 1:3) and thanksgiving (1 Cor 1:4; Rom 1:8).

Grace, for Paul, is not limited to specific gifts or dispositions. In fact, grace provides the total ambiance in which Christians live. Grace is the context in which and by which the Christian is able to live a life pleasing to God.

But above all, for Paul, grace is about God. Grace is not some entity or product of God. Rather *grace is God* in God's creative graciousness. "Ever since the creation of the world his invisible nature, namely his eternal power and deity, has been clearly perceived in the things that have been made" (Rom. 1:20). *Grace is God* in God's freedom. *Grace is God* in God's acceptance and embrace of a sinful and unworthy people. "For I am not ashamed of the gospel: it is the power of God for salvation to every one who has faith..." (Rom 1:16). *Grace is God* in God's steadfast love and in God's generous gift of Jesus. "God is faithful, by whom you were called into the fellowship of his Son, Jesus Christ our Lord" (1 Cor. 1:9). *Grace is the dynamism of God*, the active and effective power of God bringing aid to God's people. "He is the source of your life in Christ Jesus, whom God made our wisdom, our righteousness and sanctification and redemption" (1 Cor. 1:30). Grace is God *doing* for people.

Grace is the risen Christ

The single most important aspect of Paul's understanding of grace is that it is actualized in the cross and resurrection of Jesus. The active power of God becomes a reality in Christ. Christ is the *charis* of God. It is Jesus in his obedience, in his self-emptying and in his poverty (2 Cor 8:9), but above all, it is the Christ of the resurrection. Grace is Jesus loving us in his death and the Christ of the resurrection. Grace is also the continuing activity of Christ in the world in every age and in every corner of the world.

Finally, this divine activity can reproduce itself in human life, especially in our relationships with one another and with the world. *Grace is the Christian person, living and acting in the Spirit.* Grace is accepting the acceptance of God which, in turn, allows the gracious activity of God to be reenacted continually in history. Gracious talk imparts grace to others (Eph 4:29; Col 4:6); generosity helps those in need (1 Cor 16:3; 2 Cor 8:4); visiting one another brings grace and pleasure (2 Cor 1:15); Christians preach Christ, not themselves (2 Cor 4:5); the reconciliation of God is active in the community (2 Cor 5:18); we are created for good works (Eph 2:10); grace extended to others results in thanksgiving that gives glory to God (2 Cor 4:5). We turn now to look more closely at the identity of the One who bestows such gifts on the community.

An Inclusive God

The gift of Jesus Christ supercedes any narrow, elitist or exclusive understanding of redemption. Because grace is the result of God's infinite, undeserved and merciful generosity in Jesus Christ, Paul sees no reason why the Gentiles should not be admitted to the church. Further, they need not be subjected to the dictates of the Jewish law, but may become members of the community on the basis of faith or trust alone. As Paul travels from one community to another, one can almost hear the refrain behind the text: "There seems to be no reason to exclude this group of people from the church." Everyone is called to the fullness of a graced life.

Another kind of inclusivity is pointed to by Cornelius Ernst in his *Theology of Grace.*[2] Ernst notes a progression in Paul's thought from Romans to Ephesians. In Romans, Paul uses

[2]Ernst, *The Theology of Grace* pp. 24-29.

grace as an adverbial expression qualifying God's gracious actions. The fruit of this action is a realm, a regime, an economy or a dispensation which embraces all of humanity in its historical course. The emphasis is on the human community and its history. In Ephesians,[3] however, Ernst notes the cosmic focus, the solemn, liturgical style. The horizon has expanded considerably and the reader is invited into the celebration of a giver who is more than cosmic, and of an order that is all-embracing. "'Grace' here is clearly still a 'realm' or 'regime', but now it is a regime which gives a quality and a character to a kind of cosmic spring and summer, flowering and harvest in Christ. 'Grace' becomes the quality of the apocalypse of the plenitude of the eternal God in the temporal dispensation of creation, redemption and recapitulating fulfilment. Grace is the transcendent heart of the universe."[4]

The language of grace in Paul undergoes an extension which allows us to review the whole of the revelation of God in Jesus Christ from the vantage point of grace.[5] Grace becomes an open concept capable of embracing the whole of God's gift to the human community, and so capable of unlimited diversification and particularization.[6] Paul thinks of the grace of God taking on flesh in a variety of ways. It gives us a new life; it confers various gifts; it inspires persons to new ways of thinking and living. The idea is not to itemize these gifts in a quantitative way and call one of them "grace". Rather, grace "qualifies the whole of God's self-communication as a gift beyond all telling." It "indicates a wholly new dimension of relationship between God and creation, a transposition of the relationship between Creator and creature into a new mode."[7] We will make use of this idea in Part III where we will look at ways in which grace becomes meaningful in today's world.

---

[3] Most scholars agree that Ephesians was not written by Paul himself, but that it represents a faithful and mature development of Pauline thought.

[4] Ernst, *The Theology of Grace*, p. 26.

[5] See Colossians 1:1-13: "Of this you have heard before in the word of the truth, the gospel which has come to you, as indeed in the whole world it is bearing fruit and growing. . . " (1:5-6).

[6] Ernst, p. 29.

[7] Ibid.

The God Who Gives Life in Christ

It is the life, death and resurrection of Jesus that saves. "For if while we were enemies of his Son, much more, now that we are reconciled, shall we be saved by his life" (Rom 5:10). The term "in Christ" becomes almost a refrain in Paul's letters. To live "in Christ" is to be changed, to be filled with life. The context in which we live, the very breath we breathe has been changed. The rule of death has been conquered and replaced by a rule of life. "If, because of one man's trespass, death reigned through that one man, much more will those who receive the abundance of grace and the free gift of righteousness reign in life through the one man Jesus Christ" (Rom 5:17). The love and mercy of this God are so great that even when we were dead through our failings, God gave life forever, making "us alive together with Christ (by grace you have been saved), and raised us up with him, and made us sit with him in the heavenly places in Christ Jesus, that in the coming ages he might show the immeasurable riches of his grace in kindness toward us in Christ Jesus" (Eph 2:5-7).

Life, for Paul is connected with acquittal (Rom 5:18). We are made righteous and as "sin reigned in death, grace also might reign through righteousness to eternal life through Jesus Christ our Lord" (Rom 5:21). In baptism, we are buried with Christ into death, so that through Christ's being raised from the dead, we too are able to walk in the newness of life (Rom 6:4). How might one connect this death/life motif to contemporary experience?

Life and death are universal human experiences. Each of us has our own sense of what is life-giving and what is death-dealing in our lives. Initially, one might think of physical life and death. Biologists, physical scientists, anatomists and medical personnel deal daily with the complex systems of life—breathing, blood circulation, the nervous system, etc. Artists and poets, those who pay close attention to reality, portray with subtle contours and bold, broad strokes the human form. And each of us, at different moments, has been aware of being alive, of the sound of our heartbeat, of the ability to breathe, to walk, to see. We also live with death, the death of relatives, friends and loved ones; the slow death of illness or age; the death of lying and hypocrisy; the death of phoniness and egoism.

What does it mean to be a human person, fully alive? Again, the responses will be legion. For some it is the ability to run a marathon, to give birth to a child, to provide for one's family. For others it might be the experience of learning, of playing the piano, of singing or painting a picture. For still others it is the chance to comfort the sick, to nurse the dying, to abandon selfishness in service to one's neighbor. For many it is the gift of loving well and of being loved.

Death, of course, is the opposite experience. It is sin and stasis and selfishness. Death is fear, cowardice, illusion, ignorance and disdain for others. But through grace, death can become the door to life. The dying that grace embraces is dying to sin and selfishness so that the life of God might reign in our being. The awareness and acceptance of our being dead in sin leads to repentance and forgiveness. God is the one who wants us fully alive. Grace is this well-wishing God.

The God Who Liberates in Christ

Another way to talk about life is to use the language and images of freedom. For Paul, all persons need of liberation. All have sinned, all are slaves, caught in the web of law and works (Rom 6:14-18; 7:4-6; 11:6). All stand in need of forgiveness. Paul juxtaposes the image of slavery with that of the sons and daughters of God. "For all who are led by the Spirit of God are children of God. For you did not receive the spirit of slavery to fall back into fear, but you have received the spirit of children" (Rom 8:14). Not just individuals, but the whole of creation is caught in slavery. In grace "the creation itself will be set free from its bondage to decay and obtain the glorious liberty of the children of God" (Rom 8:21).

Converted from Judaism, Paul writes about the Law in ways that underline the reality he knew as grace. For Paul, the Law is good and holy, but it merely reveals to humans their inability to live by it. The Law serves to uncover our unfreedoms, to show us that on our own we are powerless over evil and conflicted in the deepest recesses of our wills (Rom 7:19).

Freedom from the Law, from sin, from death—these "freedom froms" allow one to embrace the "freedom fors." Grace empowers us to be free to choose life, to choose to love well, to hate evil, to live in the Spirit of God, which means self-sacrifice and laying down our lives in love. For Paul, grace frees us to follow the way of the Lord and live "in Christ".

Once again, it is helpful to reflect on one's personal experience of bondage and freedom in order to get a more concrete sense of grace. All over the world we are in bondage to attitudes of racism and sexism. The poor cry out for freedom to enjoy the necessities of life. On the personal level, we experience slavery to alcoholism, to inordinate wealth, to destructive relationships. All persons can profitably reflect on the ways in which they experience the slavery of darkness and death. The responses will be infinite, but anything that one allows to become an idol becomes a slave master—no matter how grandiose or insipid the object might be. In strange ways we become co-conspirators with the forces that enslave us.

Grace is the call, the invitation to abandon our enslaving ways and to live in the trust and freedom offered by God to every creature. Too often the prospect of greater freedom terrifies us. What would a life lived in the freedom of God be like? One would be forced to give up petty bickering, complaining and ingratitude in order to embrace a life of joy, thanksgiving, praise and genuine love. But experiences of authentic freedom keep the attractiveness of the call to grace before us. God's gracious action in Christ has indeed freed us from the weight of sin forever. We are to live no longer as slaves but as friends of God (Jn 15:15).

God the Gracious Benefactor

Throughout Paul's letters, grace is seen as a gift. Grace is not our doing, but a gracious gesture of God toward us (Rom 5:15; Eph 2:8). The gift is completely gratuitous, since there is nothing we have done, nor could do, to earn or deserve it. The motive seems to be disinterested love, pure and simple.

Paul also seems quite sure about the superabundance of grace. In his analogy of Christ as the second Adam, Paul emphasizes the difference between Adam and Christ. The free gift of Christ is not like the trespass of Adam. They are not comparable realities. If many died through Adam's trespass *"much more* have the grace of God and the free gift in the grace of that one man Jesus Christ abounded for many"(Rom 5:15). Sin abounds and the Law was given to increase our sense of sin even more. But no matter how prevalent or powerful sin may be, it cannot win out over grace (Rom 5:20).

God is not your ordinary benefactor. God is able to provide every blessing in abundance, so that we may always have enough of everything and be able to provide for every need in abundance (Rom 9:8). God's grace is a grace that surpasses our wildest imaginings (Rom 9:14). Paul speaks of God's graciousness as "immeasurable riches" (Eph 1:7; 2:7).

This theme of superabundant grace is supported throughout the entire New Testament. Jesus' whole ministry can be said to exemplify generosity beyond measure. Stories from that ministry drive the point home in numerous ways—the prodigal son, the workers in the vineyard, the woman caught in adultery, the stories of Zacchaeus and Lazarus. The stories challenge us to act in like manner. As recipients of grace, we are to give to others as God gives to us. Luke takes this a step further "...give, and it will be given to you; good measure, pressed down, shaken together, running over, will be put into your lap" (6:38).

As one begins to reflect on and take seriously this beneficent God, it appears more and more absurd to think of rejecting such graciousness or receiving the gifts of grace in vain. Certainly Paul does not want to get in the way of gifts (2 Cor 6:3), and he implores his readers not to accept the gift of reconciliation in Christ in vain (2 Cor 6:1). One outcome of accepting grace is that we become co-benefactors with Christ, giving to others as he gives to us.

Paul talks about grace as movement from one state to another. The cross and resurrection of Christ, the gifts of a generous God, make possible the journey from death, sin and darkness to life and light; from Law to grace; from slavery to the freedom of the children of God. This movement is called conversion (*metanoia*) or transformation. The call to change is offered to everyone—women and men of every race, creed and color. And everyone is free to respond to the call, to move toward light and freedom or to choose to remain dead. Paul's discussion of grace is reminiscent of the familiar statement in Deuteronomy: "See, I have set before you this day life and good, death and evil" (Deut 30:15). But for Paul, the point of conversion is not primarily ethical or confessional. Rather, an affirmative response to the call of grace causes one to experience life and all of reality as fresh and new.

From this brief exposure to grace in the scriptures, one begins to get a "felt sense" of the contours, depth and magnitude of God's grace as it was perceived by God's people. Perhaps one also begins to make connections with specific experiences in one's own life—experiences that are appropriately called "graced". It is possible to cross over into the lives of our Hebrew and later, Christian ancestors in the faith, to feel with them the power, the joy, the challenge, the shock of God's activity in their lives. As we proceed to look at later interpretations of grace, it is important to remember that each author is using the scripture as a touchstone from which s/he attempts to re-interpret the reality of grace in his or her own time and culture.

8

God the Divine Healer:
Augustine of Hippo

By the time of Augustine (354-430), the theological debate on grace had gone through several stages and had become more focussed. The writers of the first two centuries continued to stress the biblical connection between grace and a new life of righteousness. But as Christianity begins to use the categories of Greek philosophy, theologians start to talk about grace in terms of "divinization". They argue that if the Logos is God and the Logos sends the Spirit into the world, who must also be God, then indeed the human person, in faith, is capable of participating in the very nature of divinity.

In the West, the discussion about grace took a different turn, away from a more cosmic understanding to one that centered on the individual in history; away from an emphasis on divinization toward an interest in moral behavior. Just as Paul's discussion on grace was influenced by the circumstances of his time, so were the later discussions on grace, whether in the East or West, shaped by the atmosphere and currents of the time, especially those that seemed to threaten the truth of the gospel. Paul emphasized the utter gratutity of grace in order to confront the Hebrew connection between grace and the fulfillment of the Law. Irenaeus struggled against the elitist and ahistorical position of the Gnostics in favor of a broader understanding of grace that included the human person's free, historical acceptance of a free gift of God.

Augustine's doctrine of grace is no different. It is clear from his writing that Augustine's ideas on grace changed quite dramatically during his lifetime. One of the major factors responsible for this change was Augustine's confrontation with Pelagius. Since Augustine's thought has had such an enormous influence on later thinking on grace, one can say that the primary aspects of a theology of grace in the West stem in large measure from this fourth century dispute. Let us try to catch a glimpse of what it was like to live in the Roman Empire in the fourth century.

The Fourth Century

By the fourth century, the Roman Empire had been in decline for over a hundred years.[1] Human effort to restore it to its original vigour failed repeatedly. Internal decay and military disasters weakened the socio-political structure. Barbarians threatened from the North, well-organized and warlike Persians from the East. Taxation was forever on the increase, and inflation afflicted the poor, creating a chasm between them and the affluent who were bent on ever greater accumulation of property. The Christianization of the Empire by Constantine in the early fourth century resulted in masssive conversions that lacked depth and commitment. It is not difficult to imagine the confusion, sense of threat, and deep insecurity that must have attended this situation.

Augustine's North Africa was also under siege. It was no longer alive with its earlier expansion and prosperity, but had become stagnant.[2] The wealth of Africa had moved elsewhere. Those on the land experienced extreme poverty. The prosperity of those in the cities often depended on luck or the whim of those with position and power. Insecurity and pessimism was a feeling familiar to many. One of Augustine's opponents from southern Italy, Julian of Eclanum, would point to African pessimism as an influence on Augustine's theology that was foreign to the milieu of the Italian churches.[3] Two leading

---

[1]See Charles Norris Cochrane, *Christianity and Classical Culture* (London: Oxford University Press, 1940), p. 380f.

[2]See Peter Brown, *Augustine of Hippo* (Berkeley: University of California Press, 1967), p. 19f.

[3]Henry Chadwick, *Augustine*, (Oxford: Oxford University Press, 1986), p.111.

ecclesial figures active in the midst of this change and decay were Pelagius and Augustine of Hippo.

Pelagius

Who was Pelagius? In fact, we know little about him. He was a provincial from Britain who spent a significant part of his life in Rome among wealthy, cultivated, influential Christians. We know he wrote letters, a commentary on Paul's letters, and a work entitled *On Nature*. In 411, Pelagius stopped in North Africa for a short visit before sailing to Palestine. By this time, Augustine was already writing against some of the teachings of Pelagius' followers, but it was not until 415 in *Nature and Grace* that Augustine points directly at Pelagius as a dangerous enemy of orthodoxy, especially of the doctrine on grace. In fact, Pelagius had claimed the support of Augustine, among others, for his doctrine in his work, *On Nature*. Augustine realized that Pelagius was "a figure whom he could no longer continue to treat with distant respect as a celebrated holy man, while politely overlooking theological disagreements."[4]

The weaknesses in Pelagius' theology of grace lay in his positing the possibility of a power-not-to-sin in human persons. He saw Christianity primarily in terms of law, and the demand of obedience to this law of God was like an "icy puritanism", devoid of comfort, and with little allowance for human frailty. Peter Brown notes further, "Like many reformers, the Pelagians placed the terrifying weight of complete freedom on the individual; he was responsible for his every action; every sin, therefore, could only be a deliberate act of contempt for God."[5] However, there are elements of the received tradition about Pelagius that are not true to his thought. It is not true that Pelagius denies the necessity of grace. Nor does he teach that persons may attain salvation by their own unaided nature.[6]

---

[4]Robert F. Evans, *Pelagius: Inquiries and Reappraisals*. (New York: Seabury Press, 1968), p. 89.

[5]Peter Brown, *Augustine of Hippo*, p. 350.

[6]Ibid., pp. 92, 109.

Are there not some elements in Pelagius' thought that if retrieved, might be helpful additions to a contemporary theology of grace? I will mention four: (1) the call to a mature faith; (2) Pelagius' positive anthropology; (3) his emphasis on community and the universality of the call to the fullness of the Christian life; (4) the centrality of baptism.

1. Pelagius' idea of the Christian life was that each person was capable of living a perfect life in response to God's demand for unquestioning obedience. Pelagius' sole definition of a Pelagian was that s/he was an "authentic Christian", one who was different from those who were Christian in name only.[7] Wary of "cheap grace", he wanted people to know that it was possible "to reach the stars" of the Christian life. He minimized tendencies toward passivity, toward an attitude that said, "Let God do it all"—an attitude that could lead to indifference and irresponsibility.[8] He combatted the tendency in human nature to remain a child, to be taken care of, to leave the responsibilities of right living to others. He issued a call to Christian maturity, to grow and develop into the fullness of adulthood in faith. In this aspect, Pelagius reminds us of the saints and mystics whose desire that all persons reach the heights of holiness caused them to exhort, to goad those around them to the heights of union with God. Pelagius was a fiery reformer, stirring his listeners to the heights of perfection. One convert to Pelagius' position wrote, "When I lived at home, I thought that I was being a worshipper of God.... Now, for the first time, I have begun to know how I can be a true Christian...."[9]

2. The center of Pelagius' thought on grace was his vision

---

[7] Many had become Christian out of political expediency or to accommodate a spouse in a mixed marriage.

[8] Peter Brown identifies in Roman society in the fourth century a tendency among certain groups to create an elite way of life marked by high standards of excellence— an aristocratic elite who set themselves apart from the ignorant crowd. "Behind the counsels of perfection of Pelagius, we can sense the high demands of *noblesse oblige* and the iron discipline of a patrician household." "Pelagius and His Supporters: Aims and Environment," in *Journal of Theological Studies* 19(April, 1968), p. 97.

[9] *Ep. "honorificentiae tuae"*, 2, Caspari, p. 8: *Patrologia latina*, (PL) Supplement, 1690-91. Cited in P. Brown, "Pelagius and His Supporters", p. 101.

of the human person as one whose dignity lies precisely in being a special creation of God. For Pelagius, nature was created in the image and likeness of God, thus susceptible to the possibility of attaining perfection. Because of these factors, he had great confidence in human ability to attain perfection. Pelagius puts in relief the independence and freedom of the human person, not in opposition to God, but as the privileged gifts of God as generous creator. Grace was manifest in a special way in human freedom, a gift of God that enabled persons to opt for the good. This freedom remained intact and was not destroyed by original sin. For Pelagius, the forces weakening freedom were located outside the person in society and could, therefore, be overcome.

Further, Pelagius disagreed with the doctrine of original sin that posited irreparable damage to the human capacity for good. For him, the very make-up of human nature as God's creation made it possible to grow in the spiritual life. Nature was basically good, a position that gave rise to a very optimistic outlook. His spirituality was one that encouraged everyone to be strong, capable, able-bodied Christians. He wanted the Christian to shine in the eyes of the world. In 418, in the midst of the Pelagian controversy, one of Pelagius' brilliant followers, Julian, bishop of Eclanum in sourthern Italy, rose to defend the church against what he considered to be Augustine's errors. The defense was entitled, "The Five Praises", and reveals the thrust of a message that strikes the modern reader as particularly appealing—praise of creation, of marriage, of God's law, of free will, and of the hard won merits of the holy ones of old.[10]

3. For Pelagius, religious heroism was the responsibility of everyone and could not be left to an elite group. "For Pelagius and the Pelagian the aim always remained not to produce only the perfect individual, but above all, the perfect religious group."[11] Pelagius did not put his primary emphasis on the individual, but rather insisted that the full demand of the Christian life, with all its rigor, should be imposed on every

[10] *Patrologia latina* xlviii, 509-526. Cited in Brown, *Augustine of Hippo*, p. 362.

[11] Peter Brown, " Pelagius and His Supporters", p. 102.

baptized person. "Surely", queries Pelagius, "it is not true that the Law of Christian behaviour has not been given to everyone who is called a Christian?. . . . There can be no double-standard in one and the same people."[12]

However, even though the goal of reform was aimed at a rather wide group in the church, the Pelagian church, with its extreme demands, would never include more than a minority of Christians. In contrast, Augustine's church would have room for all kinds of persons in Roman society. The mediocre or those on the fringe would not be excluded, making way for a church of the majority—the church that indeed was embraced in the condemnation of Pelagius.

4. Pelagius does away with the hierarchical divisions that create an elite (the early ascetics) who are called to one kind of Christianity, and a plebeian class, called to a less difficult and less glorious way. From this vantage point, baptism becomes the central identifying mark of the Christian, and conversion from past bad habits becomes the central building block of the Christian life. In the Italy of the late fourth century, adults embraced baptism as the entry into a life aimed at perfection. For Pelagius, baptism effected a complete restoration of the original state of humans and suppressed the effect of the habit of sin.

Augustine's doctrine of original sin made sin such a powerful force that baptism seemed impotent in the face of it. Julian, the Pelagian bishop of Eclanum, opposed Augustine's doctrine. In Julian's view, to accept the ideas of Augustine would be to encourage whole congregations, who had only recently nerved themselves to enter upon the drastic commitment of Christian baptism, to settle back into the moral torpor of confirmed invalids."[13] In his refutation of Pelagius, Augustine sees baptism as merely a superficial "shaving" of sin. It left the Christian with roots and stubble that would only too soon grow again.[14]

[12]*De divitiis*, vi. 3, Caspari, pp. 32-33. PL Supplement 1387. Cited in Brown, "Pelagius and His Supporters", p. 102.

[13]Apud Aug. *Op. Imp.* ii. 8 and iv. 114. Cited in Brown, "Pelagius and His Supporters", p. 109.

[14]*II Epp. Pelag.* I. xiii. 26. Cited in Brown, "Pelagius and His Supporters", p. 109.

For the Pelagians, since sin had not inflicted total destruction on human nature, the possibility of conversion was not improbable or remote. Baptism did indeed bring about a "new creation." Sinful behavior could be reversed and discipline was the way to nurture and sustain this goodness throughout the Christian life.

Conclusion

While Pelagius' theology of grace does not adequately consider the weaknesses of the human condition nor the need for compassion, it has much to recommend it. Since most of what we know of Pelagius' thought is filtered through Augustine, one needs to sort out the facts of Pelagius' thought from the "Pelagianism" that formed in Augustine's mind.[15] But since Augustine's doctrine of grace was so influenced by what he perceived as dangers in the thought of Pelagius, Christianity in the West has viewed Pelagius in an almost exclusively negative light, preventing us from exploring the legitimate and useful ideas that his thought provokes.

While he couldn't match Augustine's ability to penetrate the reality of the human situation, he was trying to shore up the practice of the Christian life in an affluent milieu characterized by unthinking, mediocre behavior. He wanted Christians to be seen as models in the eyes of the Roman world. "Pelagianism had appealed to a universal theme: the need of the individual to define himself, and to feel free to create his own values in the midst of the conventional, second-rate life of society."[16]

From our vantage point today, it is possible both to be clear about the dangers that exist in certain aspects of Pelagius' approach, and also to be open to those positive strains in his thought that have been obscured. Modern scholarship has relieved us of the need to look at Pelagius as the "bogeyman" when we talk about grace.

[15]Brown, *Augustine of Hippo*, p. 345.
[16]Ibid., p. 347.

> . . . there is little room for the caricature of Pelagianism first sketched by Augustine and often repeated by modern scholars: there is no out-and-out 'naturalism' in Pelagius, for the simple reason that the man who has recovered his natural capacity to act, inside the Christian church, is discontinuous with any 'natural' man outside the Church.[17]

Pelagius sees grace operating in a variety of ways. God operates in the Mosaic law and in the faith of Abraham as well as in the law of Christ. Grace is present in baptism and is also a help in the struggle to do good works and to follow the law. But perhaps the most distinctive way in which grace operates in Pelagius' thought is in the act of creation. He affirms the freedom and goodness that are essential dimensions of the human person because she has been made in the image and likeness of God.

We return to these issues in Part III, but now let us look at Augustine's theology of grace.[18]

Augustine[19]

Augustine, the "Doctor of Grace", needs no lengthy introduction. He is a figure that looms large on the canvas of Christian history. Augustine was born in Thagaste in Africa (today Souk Ahras in Algeria) in 354 of a poor family, who sacrificed to give him a classical education—one of the few avenues to success for the poor. He was educated in Carthage, and would soon become a well-known orator. His education had developed in him "a phenomenal memory, a tenacious attention to detail, and an art of opening the heart.[20]

---

[17]Brown, "Pelagius and His Supporters", p. 103.

[18]In his book, *The Experience and Language of Grace*, Roger Haight advocates a creative use of the tension between Pelagius and Augustine and underlines the importance of integrating aspects of both positions into a total view of the Christian life. They need not be set in rigid opposition to one another. (New York: Paulist Press, 1979), p. 42.

[19]The reader is encouraged to read Books VIII to X of the *Confessions* as preparation for this section.

[20]Peter Brown, *Augustine of Hippo*, p. 38.

Well-known are his attachment to his mother, Monica; the abandonment of his beloved consort of fifteen years; his love for his illegitimate son, Adeodatus who dies at a young age; his intense need for and delight in his friends; the influence of Ambrose, bishop of Milan; his conversion to Christianity; his voluminous writings; his call to priesthood and his deep involvement with the church as bishop of Hippo.

Augustine's theology of grace is found scattered throughout his writings, most of which were written in response to pastoral issues that emerged in his church.[21] It is possible to trace the development in Augustine's own thought on grace and also to see the differences between his theology of grace and the understanding that he had inherited from the tradition.

In the 390's, during his battle with the Manichees,[22] Augustine wrote two commentaries on Paul's letter to the Romans.[23] In these works, the roles of human choice and divine influence appear more complex than in his earlier writings, although he does emphasize the necessity of God's divine call and grace for salvation. In these earlier writings, Augustine's thought is not completely dissimilar from that of Pelagius, i.e., the human person contributes toward her/his salvation through the free choice of faith. However, Augustine becomes growingly alarmed at the ramifications for a theology of grace inherent in what he understands Pelagius to be teaching. In response to the Pelagian position, Augustine emphasizes the extreme damage done to human nature by original sin, and the subsequent need for total and absolute reliance on the grace of Christ for redemption. Less than two

---

[21] Grace is more directly addressed in the following works: *On Free Will* (388); commentary on Psalm 118 (119), (392); *Confessions* (397); The Anti-Pelagian Writings (411-); *On the Spirit and the Letter* (412); *On Nature and Grace* (413); *On the Grace of Christ and On Original Sin* (418); *Against Julian* (421); *On Grace and Free Will* (426); Epistles 140, 146, 185.

[22] A system of thought to which Augustine was initially drawn, that posited an extreme dualism between matter and spirit. One focus of attention in this sect was the existence of evil. Convinced that evil could not exist at the hands of a beneficent God, they posited a separate, equally powerful evil force—the Kingdom of Darkness that invaded the Kingdom of Light.

[23] Their titles are *Propositions from the Epistle to the Romans,* and *Unfinished Commentary on the Epistle to the Romans.*

years later in his letter to Simplicianus, Augustine reverses his position, eliminating any idea of human merit in the process of redemption.[24]

The church's understanding of grace before Augustine, while not completely uniform, did share a basically common outlook. J. Patout Burns suggests that in this common understanding, the church held that God had created human nature with an inalienable capacity to choose good and reject evil. Whatever the effects of Adam's sin, human nature retains its capacity for good. Since God does not require the impossible, everyone must be able to do the commanded good and avoid the forbidden evil. This common doctrine "limited the role of divine grace to clarifying true good and evil, facilitating what can be done by natural power and forgiving the failures of those who repent."[25] The Christian is aided in this task by the revelation of God's love and forgiveness, by the example of Christ and the saints, and by the promise of reward and the threat of punishment.[26]

Building on the Platonic tradition, Augustine introduces a new interpretation of Paul's epistles.[27] He calls into question both human autonomy and the human person's capacity to choose the good. He sees the human capacity for clinging to the good as radically impaired, no longer capable of the slightest contribution toward salvation.

Augustine's theology of grace is grounded in experience and takes charity as its center. The tenacity of his reflection on his life (seen most vividly in the *Confessions*), results in the powerful and universal appeal of his thought. He has examined with brutal honesty the labyrinthine ways of the human psyche and hardly a reader exists who does not see herself reflected in his words. On the other hand, his theology has been so dominant

[24]Paula Fredriksen Landes. *Augustine on Romans* (Chico, CA: Scholars Press, 1987), p. x.

[25]J. Patout Burns, "Grace: The Augustinian Foundation," in *World Spirituality*, Vol. 16 (New York: Crossroad Publishing, 1986), p. 332-333.

[26]Ibid.

[27]I rely here on the article cited above by J. Patout Burns, "Grace: The Augustinian Foundation."

that in some ways his piece of the truth has been universalized, at times to the exclusion of other viewpoints. Because Augustine's theology is so intimately connected with his personality and life experience, it also has its limitations. His feelings of utter powerlessness to do the good are only one dimension of human experience that gives rise to reflection on grace. In Part III, we will look at grace from other perspectives as well.

Some of the weaknesses of Augustine's theology of grace have come to the fore in our discussion on Pelagius. Augustine gave unwarranted weight to original sin and its effects. Human nature is devoid of grace in itself, even to the extent that unbaptized infants are condemned along with those not predestined by God for eternal life. Guilt predominates and human independence and freedom are minimized. Augustine's theology could encourage mediocrity, since the excuse of lifelong convalescence is readily available. Grace becomes the exclusive domain of God in Christ, and sin is given a power that too thoroughly eclipses the grace of creation. Obscured is Irenaeus' "glory of the human person fully alive" as a legitimate locus of grace. Adam's sin is passed on to others through the sexual act, a position that led Augustine to justify intercourse as the good use of an evil, a position that is violently at odds with contemporary understandings of the goodness of sexuality. For all his brilliance—reading his books causes one to be blinded by it—Augustine was a man of his times, influenced by the forces around him, limited by his own demons. But let us examine those central apsects of his understanding of grace that have born the test of time, and continue to be a lively resource for us.

We focus on the *Confessions*, since it may be argued that this text contains the fullest and most attractive expression of Augustine's views on grace, even though the term "grace" is seldom used.[28] The *Confessions* is written in the form of a prayer, a direct address to God that begins, "You are great, O Lord, and greatly to be praised: great is your power and to

---

[28]Cornelius Ernst, *Theology of Grace*, p. 40.

your wisdom there is no limit." In harmony with the biblical record we have examined above, and on which he depends so heavily, Augustine's talk about grace is above all, talk about the greatness and generosity of God. But Augustine introduces novelty into the discussion by adding a profound analysis of the human person. The subtleties of the human psyche under grace are laid bare in an incomparable and compelling way. In his discussion on memory in Book X, Augustine says:

> Men go forth to marvel at the mountain heights, at huge waves in the sea, at the broad expanse of flowing rivers, at the wide reaches of the ocean, and at the circuits of the stars, but themselves they pass by. (X. 8. 15)

Let us turn, then to some of the hallmarks of Augustine's theology of grace.

1. As one reads the *Confessions*, one is struck by the extent to which Augustine is in touch with, and relies on, his experience. As we have seen in Part I, all theology is related to experience in one way or another. But few theologians have left such an extensive record of this particular aspect of their theology. Eleven years after his conversion, Augustine reflects on his entire life *in the light of his discovery of God.* His memory makes this possible:

> There too I encounter myself and recall myself, and what, and when, and where I did some deed, and how I was affected when I did it. There are all those things which I remember either as experienced by me or as taken on trust from others.... 'I will do this or that,' I say to myself within the vast recess of my mind, filled with images, so many and so great, and this deed or that then follows (X. 8.14).

His careful attention to the human psyche resulted in a convincing portrayal of the complexity of human motivation. Doing the good was not the consequence of a simple, straightforward decision of the will. Augustine had experienced Paul's frustration at doing the evil he abhorred and failing to do the good he willed. Augustine's penetrating analysis of human psychology has been one of the hallmarks of his appeal through the centuries. One reads the *Confessions* as if it were a mirror, reflecting not only the ambiguous, struggling aspect of human freedom one recognizes in oneself, but also the liberating grace that ultimately saves us from eternal confusion. Augustine's brutal honesty and the way he trusts his own experience of grace invites the reader to do the same. Augustine elicits from us the desire and the courage to pay attention to the truth of our own stories of the ways we experience grace, and to trust that experience, whatever shape it may take.

In reading the *Confessions*, one is struck above all, by the intensity of Augustine's personality and thus of his experience. His journey is all-consuming, passionate and convincing. He also appeals to a breadth of experience in order to convince the reader of what he is saying.[29] The level of feeling that emanates from these pages draws the reader into the circle of Augustine's search for God and his conversion. It is difficult to read the *Confessions* without being touched, without feeling the pull toward transformation. Augustine wants others to know and experience the delight he has found in the Christian God. In his *Retractiones*, written toward the end of his life, Augustine looked back on the *Confessions* and said, "as for me, they still move me, when I read them now, as they moved me when I first wrote them."

2. For Augustine, feeling plays an important role in the act of choice. His experience of the complexity of feelings helps Augustine to give a probing account of the human choice of the good. Freedom was not simply a matter of knowing what to choose, as Pelagius held, but involved loving and feeling as well. Peter Brown says, "The *Confessions* are, quite succinctly, the story of Augustine's 'heart', or of his 'feelings'—his *affectus*.[30] But since we are unable of ourselves to order our

---

[29]Augustine appeals to experience in many of his writings. One of the most cited examples is found in his *Commentary on John*, 26. PL 35.1608.

> Show me a lover, and he feels what I am saying. Show me someone who desires, who is hungry, who wanders thirsting in this desert, sighing for the fountain of his eternal homeland; show me one such and he understands what I am trying to say.

[30]*Augustine of Hippo*, p. 169.

affections, it has to come from God. For Augustine grace was a gift that introduced order into hopelessly disordered affections. Augustine knew firsthand that delight was the only affective force that could move the will to action. Grace made possible a delight in the good, that in turn, made possible good choices. We choose what we love, but without God, it is not possible to love the right things.

When knowledge and love are in harmony, it is impossible to resist the good. One is drawn irresistibly toward the good by the overwhelming pleasure one finds in it. The graced person is drawn or lured by the sheer pleasure of the object of her love.[31] Above all, Augustine's theology of grace is a theology of love.

3. The *Confessions* also reveal Augustine's experience of the omnipresence of grace. God's concern, presence and activity in his life knew no bounds. As Augustine traced the details of his life, ostensibly to show the utterly pervasive nature of sin, the reader realizes that the flip side reveals the pervasiveness of grace. Augustine realized that he would not even exist unless he were in God and God in him (I.2.2). God's grace-filled providence reached into every corner of Augustine's being—in the womb (I.7.12), at the breast (I.6.7), in childish petulance and rivalries (I.6.8; I.7.11), in language (I.8.13), in the mischief of adolescence (I.19.30; II.4.9).

At first one reads with incredulity the story of such wanton evil in a child—even to its life in the womb! But gradually, one realizes that for Augustine, God's care is so limitless, so total, that no corner of his existence, no matter how inconsequential, escapes the loving attention of this wonderfully powerful God. The power of God's grace is so strong that even his most intransigent habits of sin cannot prevail against it.

The reader of the *Confessions* senses Augustine's relief. His experience tells him that on his own, there is no hope, no way out of the morass of selfishness and sin. God alone makes this possible. Augustine experiences this rescue in the same profoundly intense way in which he experienced the hopelessness

---

[31]See *Expositions on the Book of the Psalms*: Ps. 118.

and power of sin. The rescue is brought about through any number of mediations—primary among them for Augustine is his mother, Monica. But it is God who saves Augustine from sin. The powerful love of God is experienced by Augustine as pure, unadulterated, and undeserved gift.

The awareness of such loving concern on the part of a generous God can have but one result. The realization of the power and the unlimited extent of grace breaks forth in a hymn of thanks and praise, in a life of joyful gratitude for the graces offered and made available by God in Jesus Christ. The *Confessions* echoes thanks and praise from cover to cover. The one who was lost has been found, and the meaning of Augustine's life, in all its detail, is revealed, after his conversion, in the light of God's graces to him.

4. Grace, for Augustine is above all, medicinal. The extreme disorder in human nature caused by sin results in the constant need for healing. In Book IV, Augustine cries, "I raged, and sighed, and wept, and became distraught, and there was for me neither rest nor reason. I carried about my pierced and bloodied soul, rebellious at being carried by me, but I could find no place where I might put it down" (IV. 7.12). While today we may not want to focus on this aspect of grace as exclusively as Augustine did, we must admit that it is one of the primary ways in which we experience grace. For Augustine, the first step is to come to know that we are wounded. Once we are aware of our wounds, we begin to feel the need and the desire to be healed, to be made whole.

This desire for healing is a leitmotif in Augustine's understanding of grace. No matter what one's condition in life, it is possible to want God, to yearn for the healing touch of the divine hand. Augustine's experience of total incompleteness and helplessness emerges in his passionate longing for the grace of God's presence in his life. Augustine's capacity for passionate loving was immense. In reading the *Confessions*, one gets the sense that there was little Augustine did not love passionately. He loved the world, he loved women, he loved language, he loved the theatre, he loved his male friends—all with a rare intensity.

His love for the world was so great that he was always on

the verge of making idols of the objects of his love. This explains why he had to repudiate so many of the things that had been attractive to him once he discovered the Christian God. God had to be the sole object of his affections. In Book XII of the *Confessions,* Augustine says,

> Speak in my heart, with truth, for you alone speak thus. . . . I will enter into my chamber and there I will sing songs of love to you, groaning with unspeakable groanings on my pilgrimage, and remembering Jerusalem, my country, Jerusalem, my mother, and you who over her are ruler, enlightener, father, guardian, spouse, pure and strong delight, solid joy, all good things ineffable, all possessed at once, because you are the one and the true good (XII.16.23).

And again in Book X:

> You have sent forth fragrance, and I have drawn in my breath, and I pant after you. I have tasted you, and I hunger and thirst after you. You have touched me, and I have burned for your peace (X. 10. 38).

Many people today find God precisely *in* the things Augustine felt compelled to reject. But Augustine does call us to fan the flame of our own yearning for God, a flame that often goes unrecognized, or even gets put out in a predominantly Christian culture in which God's presence can be taken for granted. Perhaps it never even occurs to many of us that it is possible to *want*, to *desire,* to *long passionately* for the graceful presence of God.

This emphasis on grace as healing undergirds Augustine's sense of the developmental or progressive nature of grace. While grace makes conversion possible, even a profound change of heart does not eliminate the damage that exists in the very core of our being.

> Alas for me! Lord, have mercy on me! Alas for me! See, I do not hide my wounds. You are the physician; I am a sick man. You are merciful; I am in need of mercy. Is not "the life of man upon earth a trial?" . . . Is not the life of man upon earth a trial, without any relief whatsoever (X.28.39)?

Books VIII and IX of the *Confessions* detail the transforming effects of grace in Augustine's life, but Book X reminds us that convalescence is a constant state this side of heaven. The road of grace is a road of slow and never-ending progress against the strong force of sinful habit that builds up over the course of a lifetime.

Augustine thus sets the main lines of the discussion on grace that will perdure into the Middle Ages and beyond. God will remain the mighty creator, the munificent giver of all graces, the physician who heals the wounds of sin. The human person, unable to do much to cooperate with God, remains almost exclusively the passive receiver of grace. But the image of the human person will take on other aspects different from Augustine's, who saw the human person ineluctably entangled in the persistent, debilitating, and bleak web of sin.

9

A Joyful Friendship: Thomas Aquinas[1]

We move now from the fourth to the thirteenth century. This leap does not suggest that no one in the intervening centuries wrote about grace. Indeed, it has been acknowledged that in one way or another, all religious experience and theology are concerned with grace. The monastic writers (e.g., Richard of St. Victor, Bernard of Clairvaux, Aelred of Rievaulx) and visionaries (Marie of Oignies, Hildegard of Bingen, Elizabeth of Schönau) of the twelfth century, provide an especially rich resource for a theology of grace. But the limits of space demand that further inquiry be left for another time.

The Medieval Setting

The thirteenth century witnessed extraordinary developments on several frontiers. In many ways, the foundations for these developments had been laid in the twelfth century, a century often spoken of as the renaissance of the Middle Ages. Geographical centers included Chartres, Oxford, and later Paris. The period was characterized by discoveries in nature, physics and natural science, a revival of the classics, and great apostolic fervor in the church. Life was of a piece and reflected a high degree of integration of the sacred and the profane:

---

[1]Recommended reading to accompany this chapter: *Summa theologiae:* Ia-Iae, qq. 109-114; *De veritate,* q. 24; *Summa contra Gentiles,* book 4, chs. 17-21.

> Not only are religious and secular pieces found side by side,
> set to the same music, in the same books, but they often had
> the same author who sang the joys of earth and the joys of
> heaven to the same tune in almost the same breath.[2]

Nature and the human person were related as macrocosm to microcosm. The spiritual treatises of the time contained both the inwardness of Augustinianism and the consciousness of physical principles and a materialist outlook. There was a balance between grace and nature and an intimate physical and spiritual relationship between the human person and the universe. Persons had a ready disposition to relate their natural human experiences to the sphere of the sacred. The ordinary and familiar were means of opening oneself to the spiritual and the divine. However, this outlook was not without opposition, especially from the monastic communities that continued to emphasize a contempt for the world—a tension that perdured into the thirteenth century.

The thirteenth century was an age of intense evangelical fervor. Francis and Dominic founded their orders; the Augustinians and Carmelites experienced a renewal of life and ministry in their orders. It was also an age of reason, of systematization, and of sustained study of the bible. Virtually all the masters of theology wrote commentaries on various books of the bible and the first concordances appear at this time.

Most important for our discussion of Aquinas' theology of grace was the reintroduction in the West of the works of Aristotle. Aquinas, though a singularly traditional thinker, was also a great innovator.[3] He appropriated the scientific, metaphysical approach of Aristotle and fused it with the Augustinian, neoplatonic strains of Pseudo-Dionysius and John Damascene. The schoolmen imported categories from rational analysis of secular phenomena into interpretations of

---

[2]Charles Homer Haskins, *The Renaissance of the Twelfth Century* (Cambridge, MA: Harvard University Press, 1957), pp. 170-171.

[3]Bernard Lonergan, "Aquinas Today: Tradition and Innovation", in *A Third Collection*, edited by Frederick Crowe (New York: Paulist Press, 1985), p. 51.

sacred doctrine. Someone from the monastic tradition like Bernard of Clairvaux, following in the footsteps of the Fathers, had relied almost exclusively on categories from biblical language and from experience to talk about God. School masters such as Thomas were also capable of waxing eloquent using biblical imagery and language.[4] However, in the newly developed genres such as the *summae* and disputed questions, they transposed these subjective descriptions into categories worked out by philosophers in their objective analysis of reality.

This change in worldview and the subsequent changes in the way theology was done led to both gains and losses. The schoolmen expressed their experience of God in a language that was clear, objective, logical, and in a system in which each piece was carefully fitted to the whole. Scholasticism put the intellectual currents of the day at the service of theology, thus adapting the Christian tradition to the medieval world. In this process, however, the personal, subjective fervour so evident in earlier theological language was obscured. One can get a sense of the difference from the following passages:

Bernard:

> For his living, active word is to me a kiss, not indeed an adhering of the lips that can sometimes belie a union of hearts, but an unreserved infusion of joys, a revealing of mysteries, a marvellous and indistinguishable mingling of the divine light with the enlighted mind, which, joined in truth to God, is one spirit with him.[5]

---

[4]Examples from Thomas can be found in his biblical commentaries, sermons and hymns. Commenting on Psalm 39, Thomas writes:

> "My heart glowed within me," that is, the warmth of charity was roused up in my heart, Prov. 6: "Can we hide fire in our bosom so that our garments do not burn?" So we cannot hide God's words when our hearts are inflamed with charity, Ps 119:140. (*Postilla super psalmos*, 38:4).

[5]Bernard of Clairvaux, *On the Song of Songs*, I (Spencer, MA: Cistercian Publications, 1971), p. 9.

Aquinas:

> I answer that nothing can act beyond its species, since the cause must always be more powerful than its effect. Now the gift of grace surpasses every capability of created nature, since it is nothing short of a partaking of the Divine Nature, which exceeds every other nature. And thus it is impossible that any creature should cause grace. For it is as necessary that God alone should deify, bestowing a partaking of the Divine Nature by a participated likeness, as it is possible that anything save fire should enkindle.[6]

In large measure, Aquinas is a faithful interpreter of Augustine. The basic foundations of Christian theology in the West laid by Augustine remain intact—creation and the human person as good; original sin as the cause of serious damage to the integrity of the human person; the resulting need for healing and redeeming grace. Aquinas differs from Augustine (1) in his strong emphasis on the transcendence of the final end; (2) in his choice to locate original sin in the disordered will rather than in disordered concupiscence; (3) in his synthesis of Aristotelian philosophy and Christian theology; (4) and in the central role he gives to Aristotle's notion of nature in his theology of grace.

Aquinas in History

Aquinas' innovations proved to be threatening to the traditional way of doing theology. Already in 1277 (he died in 1274), a number of his theses were condemned in Paris. Theologians such as Bonaventure and John Peckham were concerned that the scholastic method relied too heavily on human reason, with a resulting diminishment of God. Others thought that the utter mysteriousness of God was compromised by a too heavy reliance on philosophical categories to

---

[6]Thomas Aquinas, *Summa theologiae*, I-II, q. 112, a 1.

explain the Christian message. In addition to the condemnation, many of Thomas' interpreters misunderstood his thought. We now know that later circumstances caused scholars to impose emphases on Thomas' thought that are not actually present in his text.[7]

Because of the depth and importance of his thought, scholars in every generation return to Thomas' theology and use it as a springboard for their own thought. In our own time Etienne Gilson (d. 1978) and Marie-Dominique Chenu have tried to retrieve the original thought of Thomas behind the many layers of accretion of the last six hundred years. Modern theological method has permitted a more accurate glimpse of Thomas' theology on its own terms than was possible in earlier generations. Finally, scholars today as diverse as Karl Rahner (d.1986) and Bernard Lonergan (d. 1986) take Aquinas as their inspiration. Let us attempt now to sketch the major contours of Thomas' theology of grace and to examine its strengths and weaknesses in light of a contemporary understanding.

Aquinas on Grace

Thomas Aquinas' treatment of grace is found throughout his corpus. In addition to his analysis of grace in the *Summa theologiae,* I-II, questions 109-114, one could profitably consult the related issues of predestination (I. q. 23-24); the divine missions (I, q. 43); the grace of the angels (I, q. 62); the creation of Adam (I, q. 95); the infused virtues (I—II, q. 62-65); the new Law (I—II, q. 106); charity (II—II, q. 23); the grace of

---

[7]For example, the reduction of grace into the categories, "habitual" and "actual" is not found in Thomas. Also the extreme focus on justification and merit, issues of the Reformation, are not present. Third, Thomas never taught that the soul has a natural finality due to creation that was separate from a super-added finality due to being elevated to the order of grace. Cajetan (d. 1534) and Robert Bellarmine (d. 1621) had discussed the hypothetical "state of pure nature" to meet the problems raised by the Reformation. The Jesuit, Suarez (d. 1617), then incorporated this position into his own post-Tridentine scholasticism. Such positions were put forward in the context of later developments and read back into Thomas. See Henri de Lubac, *The Mystery of the Supernatural,* trans. Rosemary Sheed (New York: Herder & Herder, 1967). French original, 1965.

Christ (III, q. 8); and the effect of the sacraments (III, q. 62, 69, 79).[8] His scriptural commentaries, especially those on Romans and Ephesians are also invaluable resources for his thought on grace.

The over-arching plan of the entire *Summa theologiae* takes the form of a double movement. All things come forth from God in the beginning and return to God in the end. The common Latin phrase for this approach is *exitus-reditus*. For our purposes here, we need only say that for Thomas, grace is primarily the graciousness of God issuing in the gifts of grace, i.e., the means by which all things return to God, to whom all being is ordained. The gifts of the Holy Spirit, in particular, have a predominant role.

We will divide the material under the following headings: (1) Image of God; (2) Nature and Grace; (3) Healing and Elevating Grace; (4) Grace as Deification.

Image of God

God as Source of all Activity. For Aquinas, all activity and perfection have their source in God. Creatures exist and act according to the plan of God's providence. As we shall see, for Thomas, human beings never act independently of God, even though Aquinas does make distinctions among the different forms of God's help that are needed depending on the kind of human activity being considered. Everyone seeks God under the common notion of good, and everything seeks to be like God in its own way. But our turning toward God results from God having turned toward us.[9] Ordinarily, when Thomas spoke of grace, he was referring to those gifts given to persons— what he called "created grace". However, this created aspect of grace is not to be cut off from the notion of grace as "un-created", i.e., God's very love and being. Thomas views grace above all as the first gratuitous gift of God, given out of the

---

[8] Henri Rondet, *The Grace of Christ,* pp. 209-210.

[9] *Summa theologiae* I-II, q. 109, a. 6.

abundance of God's merciful love. Grace in persons is the outcome of God's mercy, and God alone is its cause.[10]

God's Love. For Aquinas, grace is primarily an effect of divine love. God's love involves not only an act of the divine will but also implies a certain effect of grace—it is by God's love that we are made good. He distinguishes between a common sense of love, in which God loves all things that exist and by so loving gives things their natural being; and a special love, in which God draws the rational creature above the condition of its nature to a participation in the divine good. By this second, special love, God wishes for us the eternal good which is none other than God's very self. In this context, Aquinas often uses the New Testament image of adoption. Grace makes us the adopted children of God and therefore heirs to God's Kingdom. Grace refers not only to the gift of eternal happiness, but is also related to many other of God's gifts to us.[11]

God as Friend. In his treatise on grace in the *Summa*, Aquinas gives us some clues about the way he images God. In Q.109, he asks whether persons can fulfill the commandments of the Law on their own. His answer is no, but in his response to the second objection he speaks about how God assists us in fulfilling the Law. In the second argument, Aquinas quotes Jerome (d. 419-20) who says that God would not give a law that it was impossible to fulfill. Therefore, it is possible for humans to fulfill the Law on their own. In his reply to this objection, Aquinas suggests that the necessary presence of divine assistance does not cancel out human effort. He cites Aristotle's *Ethics* which says, "What we can do through our friends, we can do, in some sense by ourselves." One way in which Aquinas looks on the cooperation between God and human persons is to look upon God analogically as friend— God works with us as a friend might, helping to bring about the desired effect, but in a way that does not negate our own contribution.

---

[10] *Summa*, I-II, q. 112, a. 1.

[11] Ibid., q. 110, a. 1, ad 3.

The Role of the Holy Spirit. In Part III of the *Summa*, Aquinas discusses Christ as the mediator of God's grace. Christ possesses the fullness of all grace and the source of all grace is the glorified humanity of Christ.[12] But in Part I-II, in the section on grace, he speaks of the indwelling of the Holy Spirit in us as an effect of grace.[13] He quotes 1 Cor. 3.16: "Know you not that you are the temple of God, and that the Spirit of God dwells in you?" By a kind of personal seal, the Holy Spirit (and Christ) give us, through grace, the gifts of love and wisdom—and understanding and counsel with relation to the intellect—for our enjoyment.[14] The functions of the Holy Spirit are to move and to protect, functions which operate both in the initial reception of grace and extend beyond to ensure our continued good and to keep us from sin. Further, the grace of the sacraments comes principally by the power of the Holy Spirit.[15] Neither does the Holy Spirit act in isolation, but in communuity with God and with the Son.

Later, Thomas makes a distinction between the grace that makes us pleasing to God and gratuitous grace.[16] It is through the first kind of grace that persons are united to God. Through gratuitous grace, ordained to the common good of the entire church, one person cooperates with another in order to lead the other to God. This activity on behalf of another is specifically the work of the Holy Spirit. Thomas quotes 1 Cor. 12.7 in this regard: "And the manifestation of the Spirit is given to every person for utility", i.e., for others.

---

[12]*Summa*, III, q. 7.

[13]See also the *Summa contra Gentiles*, Book 4, chs. 19-22. Thomas connects every inclination of the will and of the sensible appetite—whose origins come from love—with the Holy Spirit. The Holy Spirit is also the principle of the creation of things and to the Holy Spirit is attributed dominion and life. Thomas cites John 6:64, "It is the Spirit that quickeneth"; and Ezechiel 37:5, "I will send Spirit into you, and you shall live." The Creed professes belief in the Holy Spirit, the "giver of life". All of these gifts are the fruit of grace.

[14]*Commentary on the Sentences,* I, d. 14, q. 2 a. 2; d. 15, q. 4, a. 1.

[15]*Summa*, q. 112, a 1, ad 2.

[16]Ibid., q. 111, a. 1. Aquinas quotes John 3.5: "Unless one be born again of water and the Holy Spirit s/he cannot enter into the kingdom of God."

Nature and Grace

Aquinas takes Aristotle's notion of nature and makes it a central tenet of his theology of grace. Nature, for Thomas is a stable reality, a system that is created by God in an orderly and logical way with its own internal dynamism, laws, and structures. Each aspect of being is ordained to an end and has, by nature, the means to accomplish that end. For example, the function and goal of the eye is to see and so the nature of the eye is such that the goal of seeing is able to be accomplished. The consistency in the nature of the human person is not due to nature in itself, but rather to the end for which it is intended— an end that is supernatural. The *telos* or goal of human life is God and it is this final purpose that gives order and orientation to nature. Thomas chooses to explain the life of grace in terms of nature and its operations. He does not see these two realms as equal, but he does see parallels between the principles of nature and of grace. Grace is a quality in the soul that brings about the transformation of human nature that is needed in order for human persons to fulfill the totality of their existence which is conformity to Christ in the Spirit, i.e., union with God.

Since Thomas used the integrity of human nature as a way to understand grace, he held that in order for an act to belong to a person, it had to be elicited through that person as a principle of operation, integral to human nature. He shifts Augustine's emphasis on God acting directly in us to an emphasis that tries to preserve the integrity of human oper- ations. Grace, therefore, is seen as a habit, as a form that is infused in the soul. Grace is a permanent quality or disposition. Grace transforms human nature into a new creation that then operates in a way that enables it to attain its godly end. Instead of an exclusive emphasis on grace as healing, Aquinas intro- duces the idea that grace is primarily elevating, raising human persons in a way that establishes proportionality between their natural reality and their divine end.

We see then, that Thomas understands grace as a justifying, habitual gift or habit. In the natural order God informs nature and provides for virtues that serve as principles of action that incline nature to its own proper movements. Similarly, in the realm of the supernatural, God informs and gives supernatural qualities to accomplish supernatural movement. Grace is a kind of quality or permanent habit, a hold God has on one's very being. Its presence (called by later writers "actual grace") results in a renewed nature.

As we have seen, Aquinas' method leads him to maintain a profound unity between nature and grace, between spirit and matter. Without eschewing the radical discontinuity between the divine and the human, Aquinas' theology reveals a startling continuity between them. By analogy and by participation, the human person, who remains *one* person and *one* center of thought and action, operates harmoniously in the spheres of the human and of the divine. Human persons are moved and they act; grace forms them and they form themselves. The virtues that accompany grace are gifts of God, but they also require human cooperation.[17]

In the generations that followed Aquinas, theologians, nervous about connecting the activity of God too closely with the structure and functions of nature, emphasized the absolute freedom of God to act out of love. They feared that the use of Aristotle to explain grace resulted in a kind of determinism that tied God in a limiting way to the stable order of nature. There were also questions about how grace could transform nature ontologically into a new being without threatening human freedom. The Jesuit Molina (d. 1600) sought to correct this problem by referring to grace as an attracting force that moved the will to act. The Jesuits Francisco de Suarez (d. 1617) and Robert Bellarmine (d. 1621) reacted against this position, since they thought that it did not sufficiently protect God's role.

The discussion about grace continually collapses the tension between the powers of God and those of the human person or sets them in opposition to each other. If humans are given credit for graced activity, then it appears that God is *necessarily* diminished. The search continues to structure the inquiry about grace in ways that do justice both to God and to the human

---

[17]Henri Rondet, *The Grace of Christ,* p. 224.

person who is God's creation.

Thomas' solution is to speak analogically about the roles of God and of persons. God and humans do not cause grace in the same way, but this does not prevent Thomas from maintaining that both God and persons are free agents who cause graced effects, each acting with a fullness in their proper order—divine and human. Thomas does not see this as a competition, but as cooperation in which God guarantees the very freedom of the human agent. This viewpoint provides an important resource for a contemporary understanding of grace.

Healing and Elevating Grace

Aquinas both continues and modifies the Augustinian tradition that sees grace as a healing force. Thomas adds the distinction between the state of nature before sin—a state which did not require healing grace —and human nature after sin, which does. But the reason for the utter gratuity of grace is no longer sin, as Augustine held. Rather, it is the disproportion between persons in their natural state and the final end for which they were made that requires supernatural elements. For Thomas, grace makes right the inner relationship of the soul to God and through this process, gradually rights the relation of one's psychic drives, body, and world to the inner self. Grace first has an impact on the inner orientation of persons through justifying faith, and gradually embodies this inner transformation, bringing it to fruition by means of outer human acts, and eventually completes it in final salvation.

As the soul is the higher principle, bringing the body to perfection, so the entire person is brought to its final perfection through infused virtues and the gifts of the Holy Spirit, necessary to close the gap between the natural desire of humans to see God (their only true final end which is supernatural), and the inability of unaided human nature to achieve this end.[18]

[18]See Walter Principe, *New Catholic Encyclopedia*, s.v. "Destiny, supernatural," "Vocation to Supernatural Life," and "Obediential Potency."

Thus, we see how Thomas retains an Augustinian understanding of grace as healing or restorative, but he places greater emphasis on elevating grace—the center of his synthesis.

Deification

The Greek tradition places deification at the center of its theology of grace in a way that western theologies do not. This Greek tradition provides a rich resource in which one can more fully appreciate the contours of deification as the primary effect of God's grace in the human person. At the center of this view of grace is the deified Christ—the Christ of the transfiguration and resurrection—with whom and through whom the whole person, body and soul becomes deified. In this regard, scholars point to Thomas' reintegration of the resurrection of Christ into his theology of redemption. In his own time, Thomas was unique in his stress on the active causality of Christ's resurrection in our continuing Christian life and in our own resurrection—body and soul.[19] This theology of deification teaches the possibility of a consummation of the earthly life of faith in a supernatural, ecstatic vision and love of God on earth, within the framework of ecclesial spirituality.[20]

The Greek Fathers, like Augustine, are interested in the psychology of liberation and divinization and do not pursue the metaphysical approach to grace taken by Aquinas. But the roots of the idea of deification are deeply embedded in the tradition and appear in the West as well as in the East under a variety of forms. Let us see how Aquinas deals with deification as an effect of grace.

---

[19]See *Summa*, III, q. 56. Some scholars see Thomas' emphasis on the resurrection as an authentic recapturing of Paul's theology of the resurrection.

[20]Some of the more important references on this topic include: V. Lossky, *In the Image and Likeness of God* (Tuckahoe, 1974) eds. Erickson and Bird; John Meyendorff. *St. Gregory Palamas and Orthodox Spirituality* (Crestwood, NY: St. Vladimir Seminary Press, 1974); George I. Mantzaridis, *The Deification of Man: St. Gregory Palamas and the Orthodox Tradition* (Crestwood, NY: St. Vladimir Seminary Press, 1984).

The term used most by Aquinas in this context of deification is "participation" —what we might call "sharing." In his treatise on grace in the *Summa*, Thomas refers to human *participation* in God (or sharing in God's life) four times. Grace is participation in the divine goodness; participation in the divine nature; participation in the divine love. In the human power of intellect, we participate in divine knowledge through the virtue of faith and the gifts of wisdom, understanding, counsel and knowledge; in the power of will, we participate in the divine love through the virtue of charity and the gifts of piety and fear of the Lord. In the emotional life, through the virtues of moderation (temperance), courage (fortitude), great-heartedness (magnanimity), meekness and humility, the passions and sense appetites are ordered by grace. For Thomas, grace transforms the *whole person from within.* In a similar way, the nature of the soul participates in the divine nature after the manner of a likeness, through a certain regeneration or re-creation.[21] As we have seen, the sole source of this deifying participation is God.

In some ways, one can say that Aquinas' entire theology is teleological, i.e., he examines and understands all of reality as it relates to its proper, final goal. It is this final end that dictates how each created reality functions. While union with God had always been the goal of the Christian life, Aquinas employs the idea of *telos* as a metaphysical principle upon which he builds his theological system.

In his treatise on the last end,[22] Aquinas posits that all persons have the same, single, final end that is desired by all. That end is happiness. This final happiness is not found in wealth, honors, fame, power, bodily good, pleasure—or any created good. Rather, the final happiness of persons is found in the vision of the uncreated Good which is God. God is happiness by God's very essence, but human persons are happy by participation in that essence. In fact, through participation in God, human persons are called *gods* in a certain sense as well.[23]

[21]*Summa* I-II, q. 110, a. 4.

[22]*Summa*, I-II, qq. 1-22.

[23]*Summa* I-II, q. 3, a. 1, ad 1.

There is another dimension to deification that Aquinas discusses in his treatise on the virtues. The relevant virtue here is charity.[24] Aquinas does not use the terms "deification" or "participation" here, but rather the term "communion" to describe the intimate relationship between God and humans that is effected through charity. He says, "Charity signifies not only the love of God, but also a certain friendship with God. This implies, besides love, a certain mutual return of love, together with mutual communion." He quotes the first letter of John to support his position: "Persons who abide in charity, abide in God and God in them" (1 John 4.16). Aquinas goes on to note that this friendship with God that is characterized by a certain intimate conversation is begun here and now in human life through grace, and will be perfected in the future life by glory.

Finally, one can point to Aquinas' frequent use of the image of adoption to describe the divine-human relationship.[25] As generous and infinitely good, and in addition to creating us in God's own image, God freely chooses to admit human persons to the divine estate. This means that we are invited to share in all the good things of God, to enjoy divine happiness. In fact, Aquinas states that we are adopted by all the persons in the Trinity, an adoption that takes place through the gift of grace, making us new creatures, able to participate in the very life of the trinitarian God.

The goal of grace, then, for Aquinas, is a *personal* sharing in the mutual indwelling of the three divine *persons* in an intimate relationship of knowledge and love. The dynamic sharing of life within the Trinity is the source of human conformation to the image and likeness of the three persons. Through grace-filled, Spirit-directed activities, human persons are called to a vision of, and a sharing in, the loving, joyful life of a personal God—Mother/Father, Son and Spirit.

---

[24]*Summa* I-II, q. 65, a. 5. See also the *Summa contra Gentiles*, Book 4, chs. 21-22.

[25]Aquinas speaks of adoption in many places throughout his corpus. The reference used here is in the treatise on the mystery of the Incarnation. *Summa*, III, q. 23, a. 1.

Critique

A. PROBLEM AREAS

Often Aquinas is critiqued, not on the grounds of the content of his theology of grace, but on the scholastic method in general, or on later aberrations in the use of that method, or on the language he uses, or even on the basis of a misunderstanding of his theology. At times, such critique stems from a reaction within Catholicism to the officially imposed hegemony of St. Thomas on Roman Catholic theology. Some Protestant critique has come as a result of seeing Thomas as a willing participant in the medieval, "papist" understanding of merit that is seen to erode the Protestant principle of *sola fide*. Here we will name several legitimate problems that have come to light in recent years—issues that need to be considered in any serious reappropriation of Aquinas' theology of grace.

1. Lack of Existential Concreteness

Thomas' use of an objective, scientific method with set categories and abstract interrelationships can result in a breakdown when it is applied to the existential living out of a graced life. Rondet allows that Thomas' moral theology, for example, reveals psychological acuteness, but that he pays too little attention to the problems raised by the psychology of justification. He suggests that Thomas simply did not fully possess the phenomenology of his metaphysics.[26] When one asks specific, concrete questions about how Thomas' system would become enfleshed in the Christian life, one encounters some of the vagueness in his terms. He does not always succeed in accounting theoretically for the actual, complex structure of human experience.

I think we can presume that Thomas was seriously engaged in the processes of his own spiritual journey toward union with God, and that his theological thought was integrated with this lived experience at some level. One can only regret that we

---

[26] *The Grace of Christ*, p. 232-233.

are not left with more evidence of the ways in which Thomas applied his theology of grace in his own life and in the lives of those who no doubt sought his counsel.

2. Language

Today, readers of Thomas have to struggle with the metaphysical, technical, scholastic language that houses his theology of grace. (We have noted that his biblical commentaries are often an exception.) It is abstract, dry, and can appear to be static. "Instead of being understood as the power and force of God working in human personality, in a person's willing and action, grace began to be thought of in the technical metaphysical and ontological categories of nature and habit."[27] Such categories are the antithesis of the rich symbolic, polymorphic language of poetry—the language preferred by many today as the more adequate way to talk about the mysterious workings of grace in our lives. Ideally, we need both poetic and more rigorous philosophical language to satisfy our hunger to talk about and understand the fullness of graced reality.

3. Grace as Static

Third, some critics think that Thomas' theology of grace leads to a mechanistic understanding of grace. If the analogue is the ordered, stable structure of human nature, then grace too can be understood in a way that eliminates the possibility of the many surprising ways in which God deals with the human. However, I believe this criticism should be aimed at misinterpretations of Thomas rather than at Thomas himself. If anything, Thomas' theology of grace is suffused with dynamic movement.[28]

---

[27]Haight, *The Experience and Language of Grace*, p. 73.

[28]There is a legitimate question to be raised about Thomas' metaphysics as it leads to an image of God as the "unmoved mover." Persons today hunger for a way to talk about God that is more dynamic and changing. Process thinkers have struggled with notable success to portray a God who, while capable of change, remains God.

4. Dualism

A fourth critique centers around the juxtaposition of the terms natural and supernatural—a problem that didn't exist for Augustine. (Augustine does, however, use the terms nature and grace.)As we have seen above, use of these terms can suggest a dualistic system that bifurcates the experience of grace into two separate elements, with God as an extrinsic source and the human person as a passive recipient. Separation of nature and grace has led to other dualistic categories such as religious/temporal; sacred/profane, etc. Again we suggest that such criticism is more appropriately aimed at misinterpretations of Thomas or at later scholasticism. For Thomas God is most intimately present in the deepest level of our being and activity, and through grace is *newly* and more *personally* present because of God's love and choice of us as friends.

5. No Historical Consciousness

Finally, as a product of the medieval worldview, Thomas does not do justice to the claims of history. While he recognizes historical development, e.g., from the patristic period to his own time, he views grace in a metaphysical way that does not adequately take account of historical consciousness. Today we view grace as embedded in a specific time and culture and any statement about grace will reflect the particularity of experience which becomes the starting point for theology. Contemporary metaphysics is challenged to account for diverse experiences and conceptual frameworks, without succumbing to an absolute relativism.

B. ENDURING STRENGTHS

1. Reason

Aquinas introduced reason, illumined by faith and the gifts of the Holy Spirit enlightening the mind, as a key factor in the theological task, and therefore in one's understanding of grace. He introduced clear distinctions between reason and faith, but his purpose was not to see them as separate entities, but rather as partners working together in mutual support. Reason helps one to see that faith and grace are intelligible realities. In this regard, Aquinas uses as an example persuasive teaching. One particular form of grace is that which allows one person to cooperate with and assist another in the journey to God. The use of reason in persuasive teaching can be an effective means to that end. In order to teach well, three things are required: first, one must possess the fullness of knowledge of divine things; second, one must be able to *confirm or prove* what is said, since without this appeal to reason words carry no weight; and third, one must know how to present what he knows to his hearers.[29] On a more general note, Thomas also advocates the use of reason in the realm of faith: "For though it is not in our power to know by ourselves the things of faith, nevertheless, if we do what we can, that is to say, if we follow the guidance of natural reason, God will not fail to give us what is necessary to us."[30]

Through his emphasis on reason, Aquinas brings the discussion about grace into the broader forum of human intellectual endeavor. He was concerned implicitly with an ordered approach to theology. This approach can be related to our present efforts at doing theology. As in the thirteenth century, so modern theology is in need of a broad and coherent basis. To the extent that grace is experienced within the human community, so this experience and its effects are susceptible to human analysis and inquiry. Thus the possibility is enhanced for discussion about grace in a wider community—beyond that of persons who experience grace in a homogeneous fashion. In many ways, Aquinas stands as a symbol in our tradition, challenging us to use our God-given reason to understand the divine-human relationship and to relate the broader world of intellectual inquiry to our experience of faith.

2. Anthropology

Second, Aquinas advocates what might be called a positive

[29]*Summa*, I-II, q. 111, a. 4.

[30]Disputed question, *De Veritate*, q. 14, a. 11, ad 2m.

anthropology. Due to the use of Aristotle's metaphysics, ethics and psychology, the doctrine of grace in the late thirteenth century took a markedly anthropological turn. Perhaps Aquinas is best known for his appropriation of Aristotle's hylomorphic theory in which the soul is seen as the form, the animating principle of the body. Aquinas sees the human person as a spiritual-physical unity. The human being is not composed of two separate substances, body and soul; she is one substance in which two component factors can be perceived. The body or the soul alone is incomplete. The soul depends on the body for its particular natural characteristics and for the sense data that leads to understanding. The body needs the soul as its animating principle. All human activity is ascribed to the human person as a whole. When we feel, it is the whole person who feels, not the soul alone nor the body alone. Similarly, we cannot understand something without the soul, but it is the person who understands.[31]

Since, for Aquinas, the body allows the soul to attain the perfection of its nature and vice versa, the body is not seen as a hindrance to the life of the soul, the way so many before him viewed the body/soul relationship. This wholistic anthropology has important ramifications for a doctrine of grace. The gift of Godself is given to the whole person, and is intended to enhance the life of that person. The renewed person created by grace involves a totality, not just a spiritual, immaterial dimension.

Thomas emphasizes the wholeness and integrity of the human person without denying the reality of original sin. As we have seen, for Thomas, sin weakens one's inclination to virtue, but does not completely destroy it nor can sin destroy the constitutive principles of human existence.

In addition to the grace of being created, Adam is endowed from the first instant of his creation with the grace that makes possible participation in the very life of God (*Summa* I, q. 95; II-II, q. 5). For Thomas, the question of grace is no longer situated, as it was with Augustine, in the context of the original

---

[31]Frederick Copleston, *Thomas Aquinas,* (New York: Barnes & Noble, 1976) [1955], p. 160.

fall, but rather in that of the ordination of human persons to a supernatural end beyond their natural capacity. Thomas also widens the net of grace, explaining that infidels and persons living before Christ were able to be saved (*Summa,* I—II, q. 98. a. 2).

For Thomas, human persons pursue their final supernatural end right along with the various temporal ends proper to their human nature. There is an interdependence between the two orders. They are not at war with one another or pasted one on top of the other. They are related in ways similar to the ways in which the soul and body are integrated.[32] There is also in Thomas' theology of grace, a sense of the cooperation between God and humans. Even though it is the Spirit that makes such cooperation possible, Thomas sees human activity as having a function in the redemptive process. Freely chosen gospel activity has a positive role in the journey toward union with God. This perspective gives a certain dignity to the integrity of the human person, created by God and in God's image. It also accounts theologically for that aspect of human experience that reflects a sense of wholeness, of competence, of creativity, of ability and willingness to live the Christian life in a mature and responsible way.

Conclusion

From the Fathers of the early church to Augustine and down to the Middle Ages, theologians looked at reality essentially in terms of union with God.[33] There was little place in this worldview to look upon or value things as purely natural, earthly phenomena. Human activity either brought one closer to union with God or it did not. For some, pagans and unbaptized infants suffered the same fate. Likewise there was possible only one kind of grace—a grace that justifies, that

[32]Rondet, *The Grace of Christ,* p. 218.

[33]For this section I found helpful an article by Jean-Marc Laporte, "The Dynamics of Grace in Aquinas: A Structural Approach," in *Theological Studies* 34 (1973): 203-226.

makes acts meritorious for heaven. However, within this system, a lingering question continued to be expressed: What about the good deeds of pagans? Can they be written off with a sweep of the hand? Don't the scriptures and the early writings in the church give evidence of the godless preparing themselves by their own activity for justification? What about Paul's speech on the Areopagus about the unknown God of the Greeks?

The medieval period saw a shift in theology intended to accommodate this question more adequately. It first emerges in the work of Philip the Chancellor (c. 1225), and comes to full flower in Aquinas. The pressure of this question led to a distinction between two types of good activity: meritorious activity and good activity that is not yet meritorious. A similar distinction in grace also emerges: the grace of justification that heals and makes meritorious acts possible;[34] and another kind of divine assistance, not grace in the true sense but something that enables sinful persons to act in their own power. Grace remains gratuitous because those receiving it are unworthy of it. But, one may ask, what about the grace received in the Garden by Adam and Eve before sin? Ultimately, Thomas answers that grace is gratuitous because it is supernatural, i.e., it makes it possible for human persons to reach an end that is beyond their power.

As a result of this shift, meritorious activity is seen as an activity radically beyond the powers of human nature. Grace becomes a supernatural, elevating reality, changing human nature in its deepest ontological structures. In time, it was necessary to deal with nonmeritorious activity in a similar manner within the natural scope of human power. "The moral impotence of man, unable to avoid sin without grace, is now seen in its ontological dimension. It stems from man's inability to fulfill himself even connaturally without healing grace.

---

[34]True grace is further distinguished into *gratia gratis data*, referring to charismatic gifts given in a transitory way, usually for the good of the community and *gratia gratis faciens*, the grace that is offered to all persons—grace that heals and elevates as one progresses on the personal, dynamic journey to perfect union with a personal, trinitarian God.

Habitual grace is then understood to heal man as well as to elevate him."[35] Aquinas expresses this position in its fullness: the healing power of grace now relates precisely to nature on the one hand and to the elevating supernaturalizing function of grace on the other.

According to Rondet, the Thomistic synthesis "is nothing other than the Augustinian synthesis, but rethought in terms of a doctrine which explicitates the absolutely supernatural, and the presence of the Holy Spirit in souls."[36] Like Augustine before him, Aquinas turns to St. Paul to talk about sin and grace. But in spite of the obvious similarities between Augustine and Aquinas on grace, one is also aware of a different thrust in Thomas. It is true that his voice from the thirteenth century does not completely satisfy the probing questions we might have about how he ultimately harmonizes the traditional Augustinian tradition with the worldview of Aristotle—even granting his "christianization" of Aristotle. Nevertheless, Aquinas manages to point to a synthesis that struggles to maintain the transcendence of God and the freedom and integrity of the human person. One senses in Aquinas that the glory and potential of being human leads not to any diminishment of God, but rather to a mutual enhancement of both. As our understanding of human integrity and maturity develops, we can turn to Aquinas as one source in our tradition that upholds in a distinctive way the foundation for the possibility of human cooperation and participation in the redemptive process.

---

[35] *The Grace of Christ*, p. 223.
[36] Ibid., p. 244.

10

"And All Shall Be Well":
Julian of Norwich

Readers may register surprise at seeing Julian of Norwich
(c. 1342-c. 1416) included in an historical survey of the doctrine
of grace. Indeed, one's first question may be, "Who is Julian of
Norwich?" In brief, she was an "anchoress"—one who chose to
live a life of solitude and prayer—in fourteenth century
England. Being a recluse was a somewhat well known vocation
in fourteenth century England, and there were many solitary
dwellings, called hermitages, dotting the countryside or attached to local parish churches. Julian's cell adjoined the
parish church of St. Julian in Conisford at Norwich. She gave
herself to a life of prayer, but was always available to give
spiritual counsel to those in need through a window in her
dwelling.

At the age of thirty, on May 13, 1373, she received the gift
of sixteen visions or revelations of the crucified Jesus. She
recorded a brief account of the event some time after its
occurrence and then some twenty to thirty years later, wrote
an extended version, the fruit of many years of contemplation
on the meaning of the original event. The work is usually
referred to as *Showings* or *Revelations* and is her only extant
work.[1] The manuscript was soon eclipsed in the shuffle of

---

[1] Recent editions include: *Revelations of Divine Love*, trans. Clifton Wolters,
(Baltimore: Penguin Books, 1966); *A Book of Showings to the Anchoress Julian of
Norwich*, edited by Edmund Colledge and James Walsh (Toronto: Pontifical Institute
of Mediaeval Studies, 1978); *Showings*, trans. Edmund Colledge and James Walsh
(New York: Paulist Press, 1978).

history and has come to light again only in modern times. Serious scholarly analysis is now underway and *Showings* has experienced enormous popularity in the Christian community. She is perhaps the most frequently read mystic today except for Teresa of Avila. In her text, Julian protests that she is ignorant and unlearned in many ways, but such a disclaimer was a common literary device used to put the reader in a receptive mood. A study of her text reveals just the opposite— Julian is a sophisticated and subtle theologian, and as a woman of letters in the English language, has been compared to Geoffrey Chaucer.[2]

Julian's theology of grace, as it is revealed throughout *Showings*, is instructive for two reasons: (1) she is very much a child of the tradition inasmuch as she understands God to be the author and sole actor when it comes to grace; (2) her anthropology is quite a departure from the traditional under-standing of the human person as seriously depraved because of sin. (We have seen that Thomas also took exception to this position, though a bit differently from the way Julian does.) As we shall see, Julian is not at all naive about sin. She manages to take sin seriously, to take the sovereignty of God seriously and also to take seriously the exalted condition of the human person, created in God's image. In addition, Julian shows a deep appreciation for the natural as a vehicle that leads us, in grace, to the final consummation in God. There-fore, she is important in the context of a theology of grace because she offers a rare and distinctive way to look at a grace

---

[2]The secondary literature on Julian is growing rapidly. Suggested titles include: Robert Llewelyn, ed., *Julian: Woman of our Day* (Mystic, CT: Twenty-Third Pub-lications, 1987); and *All Shall Be Well: The Spirituality of Julian of Norwich for Today* (New York: Paulist, 1982); Grace Jantzen, *Julian of Norwich: Mystic and Theologian* (New York: Paulist Press, 1988); Brant Pelphrey, *Love Was His Meaning: The Theology and Mysticism of Julian of Norwich*. Salzburg Studies in English Literature (Atlantic Highlands, NJ: Humanities Press, 1982); Paul Molinari, *Julian of Norwich: The Teaching of a 14th Century English Mystic* (Darby, PA: Arden Library, 1978); Mary Paul, *All Shall Be Well: Julian of Norwich and the Compassion of God* (Oxford: SLG Press, 1975); Eric Colledge, *The Medieval Mystics of England* (London: John Murray, 1961); David Knowles, *The English Mystical Tradition* (New York: Harper Brothers, 1961).

that preserves God's role in the graced event without denigrating the human person.

Second, it is important to retrieve some female perspectives on grace, since our understanding of grace has been so dominated by male experience. Other potential candidates include Hildegard of Bingen (d. 1179), Hadewijch of Antwerp (mid-thirteenth century), Catherine of Siena (d. 1380), and Teresa of Avila (d. 1582), to name a few from the medieval period. However, it will become clear that Julian is an especially apt choice, given the topic of grace and the need to broaden the experiential base undergirding a contemporary theology.

Fourteenth Century England

It is astounding to discover such a profound flowering of spirituality in the midst of the social, political and ecclesiastical turmoil of the fourteenth century in Europe, a time of economic and demographic recession, a time characterized by frustration, disruption, dissolution and revolution. The Hundred Years' War was raging, and widespread peasant unrest led to a major revolt in 1381. The Great Schism divided the church, and there was an outcry against the possessions and financial claims of the papacy, the bishops and the religious orders. The Black Death or Plague ravaged Europe, by some estimates, wiping out one third of the population. In addition, there were roaming bands of mercenary soldiers, who when not engaged in battle, pillaged and raped at will throughout the countryside. One gets the sense that living in the fourteenth century was like living on the edge, without the prospect of stability or a secure life.

In the midst of this turmoil, there arose a number of mystical writers who shed a brilliant ray of light into the darkness. In addition to Julian's work, England produced the famous text by an unknown writer, *The Cloud of Unknowing*, composed some time between 1350 and 1400. Other well known English authors include Walter Hilton (d. 1395), Richard Rolle (d. 1349) and Margery Kempe (d.c. 1438). Because of the significant number of mystical treatises from this period, it is possible to speak of an "English school" of mysticism in the fourteenth century.

Several characteristics can be gleaned from these works: (1) There is a focus on the incarnate Christ, especially the suffering Christ. (2) One gets a glimpse in the various texts of the individual writer's personality—unlike the scholastic writings of the previous century that reveal little or nothing about the author's personality. (3) The role of the solitary life is central. (4) The use of the vernacular gives a distinctive flavor of charm and everydayness. For example, Margery Kempe refers to the dialogue of prayer as "homely dalliance," and both she and Richard Rolle call the beloved of God "Christ's own dear-worthy darling." Spiritual direction becomes "full merry counsel with one's ghostly father"; Julian sees other Christians as her equals, calling them her "even Christians," and English religion is described as "homely and full boisterous." (5) There is an emphasis on instruction. (6) The spiritual life is presented in a simple and direct way. (7) Finally, English mysticism of the fourteenth century is often described as affective, i.e., focussed on love, although one discerns a strong balance between the affective and intellective aspects of the spiritual life. Even though Julian's images function as vivid invitations to the heart, she is extremely concerned about understanding. She relies heavily on her reason to make sense out of her visions.

Julian's Theology

Julian's *Showings* reveal a number of distinctive themes for which she has become well-known. The theme most commonly associated with her is that of the motherhood of God. Julian repeatedly uses analogies to human motherhood when she speaks about God—giving life, feeding, being the object of implicit trust. Imagery for the female side of God has roots in the earliest cultures, and for the Judeo-Christian tradition goes back to the Hebrew scriptures. The Middle Ages witnessed a flowering of devotion to the motherhood of God, and Julian gives this devotion full expression.[3]

A second strength of her text is the sophisticated trinitarian theology that runs as a leitmotif throughout. Julian brings out in dramatic relief both the complexity and the intensity of the relationships within the Trinity. Mary is often brought into the intimate circle as well, with emphasis on her special relationship with Jesus. In Julian's understanding, the female aspect of God penetrates all the persons of the Trinity and is not limited to the Holy Spirit.

Her theology is also very christocentric and she pays special attention to the cross and passion of Christ. The visions themselves are of the crucified Christ, and while her initial description of the visions is graphic and bloody, there is no hint of morbidity. Rather, her description of Christ leads to a theology that is notable for its joy and optimism.

Let us look at those aspects of her theology that relate directly to her understanding of grace. These include: her image of God and the ways in which God functions in the event of grace; her anthropology, in which she portrays the human person in ways quite distinct from Augustine before her and Luther after her; her concept of sin and the struggles she experiences around this reality. We refer more frequently to the text itself than we have in previous chapters since readers may be less familiar with her work than with that of Augustine and Aquinas. The reader is encouraged to attend to Julian's texts carefully, as they reveal the heart and flavor of her theology, doing it justice in a way commentary simply cannot.

Image of God

1. God as Total Source of Grace

Julian's understanding of God's role in the grace event is closely consonant with the earlier tradition. She propounds a

---

[3]See Carolyn Walker Bynum, *Jesus as Mother*, (Berkeley: University of California Press, 1982).

strong doctrine of the complete efficacy and all-pervasiveness of God's activity. God does everything that is done, even what is done by creatures.

> And after this, I saw God in an instant of time, that is to say in my understanding, by which vision I saw that he is present in all things. I contemplated it carefully, seeing and recognizing through it that he does everything that is done. What is sin? For I saw truly that God does everything, however small it may be, and that nothing is done by chance, but all by God's prescient wisdom (Ch. 11)[4]

Julian says that she was not told about the work of creatures, but rather about the work of God in creatures, for God is at the center of everything and does everything.

> See, I am God. See, I am in all things. See, I do all things. See, I never remove my hands from my works, nor ever shall without end. See I guide all things to the end that I ordain them for, before time began, with the same power and wisdom and love with which I made them; how should anything be amiss (Ch. 11)?

God is also the initiator of the graced relationship. It is clear that Julian wants to emphasize God's initiative, since she places God's activity in the context of human blindness and foolishness—a negative description that appears rarely elsewhere in her work. Because humans are so blind and foolish, they never seek God until God, out of pure goodness chooses to be self-revealing. It is only after God's graced gesture that one is stirred by that grace to seek God with earnest longing (Ch. 10).

2. *God as Trinity*

Second, Julian's image of God is consistently and thoroughly trinitarian. In the very first vision, God is revealed as

---

[4]All references to Julian's text will indicate chapter numbers in the Long text as found in *Showings*, Trans. Edmund Colledge and James Walsh (New York: Paulist Press, 1978).

Trinity. "Suddenly the Trinity filled my heart full of the greatest joy, and I understood that it will be so in heaven.... For the Trinity is God and God is the Trinity" (Ch. 4). The Trinity is maker, protector, everlasting lover, endless joy and bliss. The vision itself, of course, is of the crucified Jesus and indeed, Jesus' suffering gives a distinctive cast to God's love. Julian is amazed by the wonder and marvel that God, who is to be so revered and feared would be so intimate with such a sinful creature. The Holy Spirit's task is to make it possible for humans to preserve the message of the revelations until the end of life, through faith (Ch. 7).

3. The Intimate God

Third, Julian's God is an intimate God. The intimacy with God that Julian experiences is evident in her language. When speaking about her relationship with God she uses terms such as "homely", "accessible" and "familiar". In chapter five, Julian uses a clothing metaphor to describe this intimacy.

> At the same time as I saw this sight of the head bleeding, our good Lord showed a spiritual sight of his familiar love, I saw that he is to us everything which is good and comforting for our help. He is our clothing, who wraps and enfolds us for love, embraces us and shelters us, surrounds us for his love, which is so tender that he may never desert us (Ch. 5).

And again in chapter six:

> For as the body is clad in the cloth, and the flesh in the skin, and the bones in the flesh, and the heart in the trunk, so are we, soul and body, clad and enclosed in the goodness of God. Yes, and more closely, for all these vanish and waste away; the goodness of God is always complete, and closer to us beyond any comparison (Ch. 6).

God is lover, mother, father, nurse. Julian's God is no distant, abstract figure. Her God desires to be in relationship with creatures; wishes to be seen, to be sought; desires to be expected and trusted because God is so "accessible, familiar and courteous" (Ch 10). God is present even in the most humble needs. Julian is famous for the passage in which she connects God even with the most basic, bodily purification processes.

> A man walks upright, and the food in his body is shut in as if in a well-made purse. When the time of necessity comes, the purse is opened and then shut again, in most seemly fashion. And it is God who does this, as it is shown when he says that he comes down to us in our humblest needs (Ch. 6).

4. God's View of Sin

Fourth, Julian further reveals God's reality in her presentation of the way God looks upon sin. Since God's view is quite different from that of humans, Julian explains it carefully. God sees sins that will be healed, not as wounds, but as honours.

> For every sinful soul must be healed by these medicines [contrition, compassion and longing]. Though he be healed, his wounds are not seen by God as wounds but as honours. And as we are punished here with sorrow and penance, in contrary fashion we shall be rewarded in heaven by the courteous love of our almighty God, who does not wish anyone who comes there to lose his labours in any degree. For he regards sin as sorrow and pains for his lovers, to whom for love he assigns no blame (Ch. 39).

Since Julian sees no anger in God (Ch. 13), when faced with sin, God chooses rather to protect and to reveal human faults lovingly. When one goes to God as sinner, God says, "My dear darling, I am glad that you have come to me in all your woe. I have always been with you, and now you see me loving, and we are made one in bliss" (Ch.40).

5. God Rejoices in Us

Julian's God is also one who rejoices greatly at the salvation and good fortune of creatures. It seems as though nothing delights God more than to love what God has made.

> And with this our good Lord said most joyfully: See how I love you, as if he had said, my darling, behold and see your Lord, your God, who is your Creator and your endless joy; see your own brother, your saviour; my child, behold and see what delight and bliss I have in your salvation, and for my love rejoice with me (Ch. 24).

God's delight is in human holiness and in the endless joy and bliss persons find in God (Ch. 24).

6. A God Without Blame

Finally, and most important, God doesn't blame the saved for sin. In chapter forty-five, Julian makes a distinction between the lower judgment of the church that does lay blame, and the higher judgment of God that does not. It is God's judgment that is revealed to her, but she says she cannot be fully comforted by this because the judgment of the church is always before her, a judgment by which she knows that she is a sinner. She struggles to reconcile the two positions. She goes on to say that it would be unkind to blame God or marvel at God on account of her sins, since God does not blame her for her sin (Ch. 27).

The most complete answer to the problem of sin as Julian sees it, is found in her famous parable of the lord and the servant (Ch. 51). In this story, the servant, eager to carry out the wishes of his beloved lord, runs at such a speed that he falls into a dell and is seriously wounded. The lord looks upon his beloved servant with great compassion and pity, and says,

> See my beloved servant, what harm and injuries he has had and accepted in my service for my love, yes, and for his good will. Is it not reasonable that I should reward him for his fright and his fear, his hurt and his injuries and all his woe? And furthermore, is it not proper for me to give him a gift, better for him and more honourable than his own health could have been? Otherwise, it seems to me that I should be ungracious (Ch. 51).

The lord in the story is God and the servant represents Adam. The meaning of the story emerged over the course of Julian's lifetime and reveals how God regards human beings in their failings. Only pain blames and punishes. Her courteous Lord only comforts and succors, kindly disposed to the soul at all times, loving and longing to bring the soul to bliss (Ch. 51).

The servant is also Christ. While God shows compassion and pity for creatures, joy and bliss are shown to Christ, who is the manifestation of God on earth. The parable is a graphic portrayal of how one should understand the grace of God. In Julian's theology, grace is the awesome gift of a tender, loving God, who views us in our sin, not as we might view ourselves or each other, but in a loving and non-judgmental way. This is a generous God who truly delights in the creature's well-being and happiness. "In this I saw him greatly rejoice over the honourable restoration to which he wants to bring and will bring his servant by his great and plentiful grace" (Ch. 51).

Anthropology

1. Imago Dei

Julian's extraordinary positive regard for God's creation is, in its rarity and in its presentation, a delightful discovery. She does point to the same foundation for this positive regard as her predecessors, namely that humans are made in the image and likeness of God—God as Trinity and God as revealed in Jesus Christ (Ch. 10). The soul is always like God in nature and substance, restored to God's image through grace, but often unlike God in condition because of sin (Ch. 43).

2. Humans are Weak and Passive

Julian is also very traditional in her view of the human person as small and in danger of falling into nothingness. In the first revelation, she sees a tiny hazelnut lying in the palm of her hand and realizes that it lasts and always will because God loves it (Ch. 5). We are like the little hazelnut. God made it; God loves it; and God preserves it.

In many ways, the human person has a passive role in the grace event, but for Julian, the grace of God is so effective that it allows her to speak more positively of human participation without in any way detracting from God. Julian's theology of grace focuses on both God's all encompassing gift and *also* on human goodness and cooperation. We do not have to turn aside from creation in order to meet God's love.

3. All Creation is Connected with God

But the efficaciousness of our being created in the image and likeness of God is broader and more certain in her view than in the view of those who went before her. Sin simply does not have the power to inflict irreparable damage on the goodness of creation. For Julian, this connection between God and creation is strong and intimate. "For God is everything that is good, as I see; and God has made everything that is made, and God loves everything that he has made" (Ch. 9). God's loving activity makes all things good.

There is also a connection between the human person and the rest of creation. Julian echoes the Pauline letters to the Ephesians and the Colossians in her cosmic view of God's grace.

> And he who has general love for all his fellow Christians in God has love towards everything that is. For in mankind which will be saved is comprehended all, that is to say all that is made and the maker of all. For God is in man and in God is all. And he who loves thus loves all (Ch 9).

God's love and mercy are powerful and affect every aspect of reality. One does not leave Julian's text with a sense of the "utter depravity" of the human person, nor does she reinforce the kinds of dualism to which we alluded in Part I. Rather, God's grace reaches out to every corner of reality.

4. Persons are Whole—Body and Soul

In the parable of the lord and servant, Julian differentiates among several different kinds of likenesses between the lord and the servant. The first level of likeness, revealed in her graphic mental image is bodily. "So for the first, I saw two persons in bodily likeness, that is to say a lord and a servant" (Ch. 51). One sits in state in rest and peace. The other stands before the lord respectfully, ready to do the lord's will. Since the servant represents both Adam and Christ, one senses that Julian is consciously including the body as one level of likeness between God and humans. Adam had a body, and God takes on a body in Christ. The tender regard of the lord for the servant is not simply intended for the servant's spiritual soul, but indeed for his entire being.

Julian also advocates a wholistic and healthy love of self and love of others. She speaks of God's wish that humans imitate God in undiminished, everlasting love toward themselves and others. Nor should one withdraw love of self and others because of sin (Ch. 40). Eschewing the harsh body/soul dualisms of the past, Julian regards the "self" as a total self, including both body and soul. We saw above how Julian's God, for love of the soul, is involved even in the most mundane bodily processes (Ch 6). We are enclosed, both body and soul, in the goodness of God.

5. Nature is Good

In chapter eleven, Julian states unequivocally that everything that God has made is totally good. Julian posits further that the function of natural will is to desire and to have God.

> And therefore we can with his grace and his help persevere in spiritual contemplation, with endless wonder at this high, surpassing, immeasurable love which our Lord in his goodness has for us; and therefore we may with reverence ask from our lover all that we will, for our natural will is to have God, and God's good will is to have us, and we can never stop willing or loving until we possess him in the fulness of joy (ch 6).

She also notes that humans tend to see some deeds as well done and others as evil, but that the Lord does not see them in this way. This is because "everything which exists in nature is of God's creation, so that everything which is done has the property of being of God's doing. God has ordered all things well and "no kind of things will fail in that respect, for he has made everything totally good" (Ch. 11). In this way the Trinity is always wholly pleased with all its works.

6. Humans are Seekers of God

As Julian describes the spiritual life in her *Showings*, she portrays the human person as a seeker, as one who desires to be "oned" with God. This trait of seeking/finding is not limited to her anthropology, since for Julian, God, too, is a seeker and discovers great delight in "finding" humans oned with Godself (Ch. 17, 31, 39, 40). She speaks movingly of the longing in God:

> For he still has that same thirst and longing which he had upon the Cross, which desire, longing, thirst, as I see it, were in him from without beginning; and he will have this until the time that the last soul which will be saved has come up into his bliss. For as truly as there is in God a quality of pity and compassion, so truly is there in God a quality of thirst and longing and the power of this longing in Christ enables us to respond to his longing, and without this no soul comes to heaven. And this quality of longing and thirst comes from God's everlasting goodness (Ch. 31).

But she also speaks with eloquence when she describes the pleasure God derives from a simple soul who comes naked to God, openly and familiarly.

> For this is the loving yearning of the soul through the touch of the Holy Spirit, from the understanding which I have in this revelation: God, of your goodness give me yourself, for you are enough for me, and I can ask for nothing which is less which can pay you full worship. And if I ask anything which is less, always I am in want; but only in you do I have everything (Ch. 5).

Julian discovers how much God is pleased by constant search. By the power of the Holy Spirit the soul cannot do more than seek, suffer and trust. The finding that is called illumination is a special grace of the Spirit. Seeking with faith, hope and love pleases the Lord and finding pleases the soul and fills it with joy.

> And so I was taught to understand that seeking is as good as contemplating.... It is God's will that we seek on until we see him, for it is through this that he will show himself to us, of his special grace, when it is his will (Ch. 10).

For Julian, the greatest honor one can pay to God is simply to surrender oneself to God with true confidence, whether in seeking or in contemplating. Seeking is common to everyone, and through grace, everyone can discern between good and evil and receive the teaching of the church (Ch.10).

God gifts us with the grace to seek diligently and willingly without laziness; joyfully and happily, without unreasonable depression and useless sorrow. Second, God allows us to *wait* for Godself steadfastly, out of love, without grumbling and contention until the end of our lives. Third, God gifts us with a great *trust* in God, out of a complete and true faith.

When Julian discusses prayer in Chapter forty-one, she states clearly that it is God who makes it possible to beseech God, to ask for mercy and grace. In fact, it is impossible to think that one would not receive what is requested since this is exactly what God wants. Because humans are ordained to the bliss of union with God, by nature they long for God. Longing and trusting are two primary activities for humans. If one asks for mercy and grace, one shall find in God everything that is lacking. This prayer is able to overcome all weakness and all doubting fears (Ch. 42).

7. Self-knowledge

Self-knowledge is important for Julian. Her focus is not primarily on knowing that we are sinners, but rather on knowing that we are beloved of God. In the parable, the servant suffers cruelly because he cannot see his lord, who is so meek and mild to him, but also because he cannot see himself in the sight of his loving lord. The tragedy of human life is not that we sin, but that we do not know how profoundly we are loved by God and how powerful and effective that love is on our behalf. We make the mistake of thinkng that God is snarling at us, when in truth God is always turning a tender, merciful and compassionate face towards us. God is one who succors and protects us, longing to bring us into eternal bliss (Ch. 51).

8. *Humans are God's Crown*

In God's perspective, as it was revealed to Julian, humans are so loved that acting on their behalf becomes a great joy to God. In the ninth revelation, Julian and the Lord have a short conversation:

> The Lord: Are you well satisfied that I suffered for you?
> Julian: Yes, good Lord, all my thanks to you; yes, good Lord, blessed may you be.
> The Lord: If you are satisfied, I am satisfied. It is a joy, a bliss, an endless delight to me that ever I suffered my Passion for you; and if I could suffer more, I should suffer more (Ch. 22).

Incredulity is a common response to an initial reading of this passage in the *Showings*. It is hard to imagine that God would be asking whether one is completely satisfied with the grace earned through the passion. One may also be taken aback by Julian's simple, straightforward response of thanks and praise. She is not struck dumb, nor does she fumble over herself or reject the question. Her response enables the conversation to move forward with another startling response in which the Lord suggests that his satisfaction is somehow dependent on hers. This dialogue adds a whole new dimension to understanding grace and the God who freely bestows it.

Not only Jesus, but the entire Trinity rejoices in our salvation.

> For he is well pleased with all the deeds that Jesus has done for our salvation; and therefore we are his, not only through our redemption but also by his Father's courteous gift. *We*

> *are his bliss, we are his reward, we are his honour, we are his crown. And this was a singular wonder and a most delectable contemplation, that we are his crown* (Ch. 22. Italics mine).

Julian returns to this motif in chapter thirty-one and in the parable of the lord and the servant in chapter fifty-one. At the end of the parable, she describes how the lord and the Son look in final, heavenly glory. The lord now sits on a rich and noble seat and the Son stands richly clothed in joyful amplitude, with a rich and precious crown upon his head. Then Julian says, "For it was revealed that we are his crown, which crown is the Father's joy, the Son's honour, the Holy Spirit's delight, and endless marvellous bliss to all who are in heaven" (Ch. 51).

Julian is not naive about the human condition, but her message is clear. God delights endlessly in our graced existence, and who are we to say we have no glory when God says that we are God's glory? Can we gainsay God? In chapter fifty-two, Julian says,

> During our lifetime here we have in us a marvellous mixture of both well-being and woe. We have in us our risen Lord Jesus Christ, and we have in us the wretchedness and the harm of Adam's falling. Dying we are constantly protected by Christ, and by the touching of his grace we are raised to true trust in salvation. And we are so afflicted in our feelings by Adam's falling in various ways, by sin and by different pains, and in this we are made dark and so blind that we can scarcely accept any comfort. But in our intention we wait for God, and trust faithfully to have mercy and grace (Ch. 52).

In our relationship with the Trinity, we are asked to accuse ourselves (God's act is to excuse us) to trust, to wait, to give our assent, and to cling to God (Ch. 52).

9. Sin

In Julian's treatment of sin, one encounters a creative tension. On the one hand, she is fully aware of the gravity of sin. The Lord reveals to her that sin is everything that is not good—the shameful contempt and the direst tribulation the Lord endured in this life, his death and all his pain, and finally the evil passions of God's creatures (Ch 27). Adam's sin, says Julian, was the greatest harm ever done (Ch. 29); sin is the cruellest hell (Ch. 40). In fact, she says that sin is all human beings do.

> And this is the highest joy that the soul understood, that God himself will do it [bring to righteousness], and I shall do nothing at all but sin; and my sin will not impede the operation of his goodness (Ch. 36).

On the other hand, as one can see from the final clause in the passage just quoted, the God who was revealed to her is so powerful that it is hard for her to imagine that sin could have the final word over against God's goodness. In the face of this goodness, even the devil is rendered impotent (Ch. 13).

It is also very clear to Julian that human frailty and weakness can never hinder God's love. "For our courteous Lord does not want his servants to despair because they fall often and grievously; for our falling does not hinder him in loving us" (Ch. 39).

She is aware that the church teaches that some souls will be condemned, but this seems to contradict one of the basic truths revealed in her visions. Her way out of the dilemma is to say that all things are possible with God.

> For just as the blessed Trinity created all things from nothing, just so will the same blessed Trinity make everything well which is not well.... And to this [the apparent contradiction] I had no other answer as a revelation from our Lord except this: What is impossible to you is not impossible to me. I shall preserve my word in everything, and I shall make everything well (Ch. 32).

There are two other aspects to Julian's response to the conundrum she experiences with regard to sin. First, she points to the utter mystery of God's ways. One cannot fully understand the answer here in this life, but it will be made clear in heaven

(Ch. 27). Second, Julian says that sin was simply not part of what was revealed to her, and that this is appropriate, since sin, according to the common medieval understanding, was nothing, the absence of substance (Ch. 11). In spite of the existence of a clear, contrary ecclesial position that Julian reveres, she remains faithful to her experience and reports her revelations as she experienced them, even when what was revealed clashed in significant ways with the inherited tradition. This is an extraordinary example of her freedom, her trust in her own experience, and her respect for the integrity of what she knew to be God's message.

Julian laughs at herself for her early naïveté about sin. Part of her wonders in all simplicity why God didn't simply rule out the existence of sin from the beginning.

> And after this our Lord brought to my mind the longing that I had for him before, and I saw that nothing hindered me but sin, and I saw that this is true of us all in general, and it seemed to me that if there had been no sin, we should all have been pure and as like our Lord as he created us. And so in my folly before this time I often wondered why, through the great prescient wisdom of God, the beginning of sin was not prevented. For then it seemed to me that all would have been well (Ch. 27).

God then revealed to her that sin was necessary, not as one might expect in order to preserve human freedom, but for a variety of other functions. First, sin has a purgative function. It can make persons more ready to be "oned" with God. Second, sin causes one to be humble (Ch. 36). It also leads humans to know themselves, to realize their need for God, and to cry out for God's mercy (Ch 27). In mercy, God allows sin to be seen, but God also protects the sinner from it.

> And this is a supreme friendship of our courteous Lord, that he protects us so tenderly whilst we are in our sins; and furthermore he touches us most secretly, and shows us our sins by the sweet light of mercy and grace (Ch. 40).

When we see ourselves so foul, we fear that God will be angry at us, so we are moved by the Spirit to contrition and prayer, desiring to amend our lives and to move toward peace and a good conscience. We hope with good reason that God will forgive us because this is true (Ch. 40).

> And then our courteous Lord shows himself to the soul, happily and with the gladdest countenance, welcoming it as a friend, as if it had been in pain and in prison, saying: My dear darling, I am glad that you have come to me in all your woe. I have always been with you, and now you see me loving, and we are made one in bliss (Ch. 40).

For Julian, sin is indeed painful, but the pain is for a good reason and lasts for only a short time, because sin is no stronghold against the tender, loving, mercy of God (Ch 27). Because of God's goodness, sin is not *merely* pain, but it also is the occasion for honor. Because of sin, one experiences God's compassion, and those who have sinned greatly experience the utter boundlessness of God's forgiving love. Julian points to David and Magdalen as outstanding examples of great sinners who were open to grace.

As one can see from Julian's texts, she is always ready to see sin in its most positive light. In her revelations, she experienced the extraordinary power of God's goodness, made manifest in Christ's blood—knowledge that leads her to see sin as real, but ultimately as defeated. It is because of love that we must hate sin (Ch. 40). She says, "For the soul which will come to heaven is so precious to God, and its place there so honourable, that God's goodness never suffers the soul to sin finally which will come there" (Ch.38).

But perhaps her most important insights about sin are that 1) it prevents us from seeing ourselves and God with God's vision; 2) it does not cause the withdrawal of God's love, nor should it cause us to withdraw our love.

Sin causes blindness in persons—a blindness that permits us only to see ourselves in a negative, limited way. In the parable of the lord and the servant, Julian says of the fallen servant:

> And this is a great sorrow and a cruel suffering to him, for he neither sees clearly his loving lord, who is so meek and

mild to him, nor does he truly see what he himself is in the sight of his loving lord. And I know well that when these two things are wisely and truly seen, we shall gain rest and peace, here in part and the fulness in the bliss of heaven, by God's plentiful grace (Ch. 51).

For Julian, one of the greatest effects of grace is enlightenment or vision by which we see our true condition, that is, we see ourselves as God sees us. By the power of grace, we are not condemned—in this life or in the next—to a miserly, mean, grudging image of ourselves. Further, our image or view of God is intimately linked with our self-image. Through grace, we are able to see as God sees, to know the truth about God, and to appropriate for ourselves God's view of things.

Second, Julian impresses on us that no sin, however horrific, has the power to force God to withdraw love.

> Here we may see that he is himself this love, and does to us as he teaches us to do; for he wishes us to be like him in undiminished, everlasting love towards ourselves and our fellow Christians. No more than his love towards us is withdrawn because of sin does he wish our love to be withdrawn from ourselves or from our fellow Christians; but we must unreservedly hate sin and endlessly love the soul as God loves it (Ch. 40).

These truths are the foundation for Julian's confidence, hope and optimism. She invites believers to be confident with her, to cooperate with God's plan and to know that nothing can stand in the way of or finally thwart the graceful love of God.

Conclusion

The story of Julian's relationship with God invites the reader to cross over into the psychological dynamics of this relationship in order to understand the ramifications they might have for one's understanding of God, of grace, and for one's own life with God. We have benefitted and will continue to benefit from the stories of persons like Augustine and Luther, but

Julian's story adds a crucial dimension to our understanding of the God-human relationship—one that has been obscured and neglected in the past.

Julian's theology of grace is profoundly communitarian and universal. Her message is not for the wise, who already know what she will say, but for the simple, that they may have comfort and strength. For Julian, we are all one in love. She says, "If I pay special attention to myself, I am nothing at all; but in general I am, I hope, in the unity of love with all my even-Christians" (Ch. 9). It is in this unity that the life of all persons who will be saved consists.

During the revelations, Julian recounts how she was greatly moved in love towards her even-Christians, wishing that they all might see and understand what she saw. Her visions were given her for all persons, that they might be comforted (Ch. 8). In the tenth revelation, Julian sees the wound in Christ's side, a wound that was large enough for all humankind. "Our Lord looked into his side, and he gazed with joy . . . and revealed a fair and delectable place, large enough for all mankind that will be saved and will rest in peace and in love" (Ch. 24). All the teaching and all the strengthening of this experience apply generally to all her even-Christians (Ch. 68).

Julian's theology of grace is one of boundless optimism. In her account of the final revelation, she repeats the refrain, "You will not be overcome. You will not be overcome" (Ch. 68). Julian states clearly and unequivocally that God is the sole source of grace, and yet this God is gracious in a way that calls us to ever fuller participation. God is gracious and courteous, and beholden to us (Ch. 43), yet powerful and reliable, one who will not fail us. God is a God of desire and the object of that desire is that we should know God, and that we be content, glad and joyful. God is presented as one who has a serious vested interest in our well-being and the power to effect it.

This God is a God whose fullest and most profound joy is celebrating the goodness shared with creatures. The human person, while a sinner, is not hopelessly depraved, nor condemned to immersion in guilt. Julian presents us with an anthropology that focusses on human goodness, on human desire for God. Readers of Julian's *Showings* cannot help but feel terrific about being children of God because God has such tender, unqualified, positive regard for us. The focus is always kept on God's grace and God's mercy rather than on sin. Sin is both horrible and nothing, but in either case, no measure for God's love.

In Julian's theology of grace we can see ourselves as the glory of God—that which causes unending celebration in the Trinity. God's activities include preparing our way, easing our conscience, comforting our souls, illumining our hearts, giving us knowledge of the blessed divinity, quickly picking us up when we fall, raising us up with a loving embrace and a gracious touch (Ch. 61). In heaven we shall truly see that we have sinned grievously in this life; but we shall also see that, notwithstanding this, we were never hurt in God's love, nor were we ever of less value in God's sight. "For enduring and marvellous is that love which cannot and will not be broken because of offenses" (Ch. 61).

Thus, God's care for us cannot be thwarted. To all of Julian's questions and doubts, God responds, most comfortingly:

> I may make all things well, and I can make all things well, and I shall make all things well, and I will make all things well; and you will see yourself that every kind of thing will be well (Ch. 31).

We are truly, so to speak, the feather in God's cap.

11

The Glory of the Cross:
Martin Luther

Martin Luther (1483-1546),[1] the son of a Saxon miner, began his studies in 1496 at a school in Magdeburg which was run by the Brethren of the Common Life, a group that advocated an interior, meditative piety known as the *devotio moderna*. In 1501, he matriculated at the University of Erfurt, where he earned his Master of Arts. Legend has it that in the midst of a thunderstorm in the summer of 1505, Luther made a vow to St. Anne to become a friar. To his father's dismay, Luther entered an Augustinian monastery and was ordained in 1507. He became a student of scripture and began lecturing in 1508 at the newly founded University of Wittenberg. After a trip to Rome (end of 1510), Luther became disillusioned with the worldliness of prelates and ecclesiastical politics. In his personal life, he was hounded with a sense of anxiety over sin and the threat of damnation.

He discovered his release from these fears in Paul's letter to the Romans—"the just are saved by faith." In 1517, at the age of thirty-four, Luther posted the famous Ninety-Five Theses attacking the practice of indulgences and of religious practices

---

[1]The Reformation produced several theologies of grace, each marked by distinctive characteristics. In choosing to discuss Luther's theology of grace, I do not intend to imply that this theology is representative of later developments, e.g., those found in the writings of Zwingli, Calvin or the more radical Anabaptist movements.

that involved seeking assurance of salvation by works.[2] The theses went to the heart of the late medieval hunger for reform. They provoked a widespread reaction (thirty reprints in 1518) that eventually led to what is now known as the Protestant Reformation.

Luther was a gifted writer and preacher, and took advantage of the printing press, (which he called "God's highest and ultimate gift of grace by which He would have his Gospel carried forward") to disseminate his reform ideas, especially those written in the vernacular. Studies of Luther's style reveal a humility about his writing, great imagination, a sense of humor, an ability to view himself with a grain of salt, and to attack his enemies without reservation.[3] Although his university lectures are carefully organized in a systematic way, most of his writings respond to specific, existential problems or situations. Therefore, there is an occasional nature to Luther's theology that must be taken into consideration by anyone attempting to uncover the systematic strains.

The disarray in the church—the Babylonian Captivity of the papacy (1309-1377) and the Great Schism (1378-1415), during which there were two popes, one in Rome and one in Avignon—was one factor that contributed to the success of the Reform. Other factors included the worldliness in the church, and the inability of current piety to satisfy a more and more educated and religiously interested laity. In contrast, Luther remained throughout his life an advocate of the common person. One of his central goals was to return religion to the people and wrest it from the hands of a clerical elite.

The Reformation is seen by scholars as both a culmination of and a going-beyond the tradition of the Middle Ages. The debate about the causes and reasons for the success of the Reform continue into our own day, and the issues are far too

[2]The posting of theses was a common practice at universities during this period. Such action served as an invitation to the scholarly community to discuss the issues posted. It was not an unusual occurrence nor one that suggested defiance or rebellion.

[3]See Heinrich Bornkamm, "Luther als Schriftsteller" in *Luther: Gestalt und Wirkungen* (Gutersloh: Bertelsmann, 1975), pp. 39-64.

complex to treat thoroughly here.[4] Scholars suggest that Luther's theology should not be seen as a radical break with late medieval thought, but rather viewed as a development within it.[5] Marked divergence did occur as the movement developed, but was not prominent in its inception.

We focus our attention on several important influences in Luther's milieu and on salient features of Luther's understanding of grace, with an eye to the ways in which his theology of grace might contribute to our understanding of grace. We draw on a variety of Luther's writings from different stages in his life.

Luther's Milieu

Luther cannot be properly understood outside of the context of late medieval scholasticism. He was trained at the University of Erfurt in the nominalist tradition that had begun with William of Ockham (d. 1349). In the nominalist view, God's power was seen as total, supreme and absolute. There was nothing that God's will could not command. God had indeed chosen to act in a certain manner, but God remained free to change that will in any way—even if that meant a reversal of previous decisions.[6] Cornelius Ernst suggests that the theological concerns of this period can be seen as "a resolute attempt to insist on the transcendence of God, perhaps as a counterbalance to a Christendom increasingly involved in

---

[4]The treatments of Luther and the Reform are legion. A small sampling might include: Francis Oakley, *The Western Church in the Later Middle Ages* (Ithaca: Cornell University Press, 1979); Steven Ozment, *The Age of Reform, 1250-1550: An Intellectual and Religious History of Late Medieval and Reformation Europe* (New Haven: Yale University Press, 1980); Alister McGrath, *The Intellectual Origins of the European Reformation* (Oxford: Basil Blackwell, 1987); Bernhard Lohse, *Martin Luther: An Introduction to His Life and His Work* (Philadelphia: Fortress Press, 1986).

[5]Alister McGrath, *The Intellectual Origins*, p. 199; see also Jaroslav Pelikan, *Obedient Rebel: Catholic Substance and Protestant Principle in Luther's Reformation* (New York:Harper & Row, 1964).

[6]The technical Latin terms used to distinguish God's absolute and actual will were *potentia absoluta* and *potentia ordinata*.

power politics and superstition.[7] Any sustained attention to the transcendence of God leads to the gradual dissociation of God from human experience. Late medieval theology lent support to the human disposition of awe and wonder at God's total power and otherness, but did not nurture the experience of an intimate connection with God in which one delights in the personal and social gifts offered by God to the world.

While in many respects Luther maintains a deep sense of the "otherness" of God, he reverses the trend of dissociating God from human experience. His own experience has a central role to play as he develops his theology of grace—a theology that places experience at the heart of the Christian life. He also confronts the trend he discerned in the late medieval church to remove this God experience from the realm of the simple, ordinary person. In his view, the scholastic method of doing theology involved language, categories and viewpoints that made it impossible for the ordinary person to be an active participant in the Christian life. As correctives, Luther translated the Bible into German, wrote simple *Catechisms* and hymns for worship services, and in his letters and some of his treatises, responded to the needs of ordinary persons, e.g., *A Simple Way to Pray*, written for his barber.[8]

The fifteenth and sixteenth centuries witnessed a number of upheavals—intellectual diversity, cultural renewal (the rise of humanism in several diverse forms); political shifts (a growing nationalism, conflict between papacy and monarchy); and spiritual ferment (the rise of diverse forms of piety). There was no lack of interest in religious affairs. If anything, there was an abundance of pious activity in Germany at this time. Lay groups such as the Brethren of the Common Life and the Beguines and Beghards continued to flourish throughout the Low Countries. Their religious practices took the form of what came to be called the *devotio moderna*, a movement that

---

[7]Cornelius Ernst, *The Theology of Grace*, (Notre Dame, IN: Fides Publishers, Inc. 1974), p. 58.

[8]*Luther's Works*, (Philadelphia and St. Louis: Fortress, 1955—), 43:187-211. Hereafter *LW*.

rejected the high speculation of the schools in favor of a simpler, more accessible form of piety. Monasticism alone was not adequate to satisfy growing and diverse religious and intellectual hungers.

Since there were few structures of doctrinal validation in place in the fifteenth century, divergent ideas developed and prospered. There was great debate about who did have the authority to validate theological opinions and pious practices. With two popes working at cross purposes, confusion reigned. To whom should one turn? Many turned to councils as the definitive arbiter in doctrinal matters. Others turned to theologians, but found not one, but a variety of schools of thought on any given issue. In the midst of this pluralism, Luther came forth with a powerful voice and an intense commitment to reform the church to which he was dedicated.

In the cultural sphere, a movement known as "humanism" exerted a great influence on church and society. Most humanists were Christian and did not see themselves as anti-church or secular in the way we sometimes hear the term used today. Erasmus of Rotterdam is perhaps the most well known humanist of this period. Humanism was characterized by a new found interest in ancient philosophies and letters. Rhetoric, eloquence of the written and spoken word, was valued above all. The humanists were focussed on human persons, their distinctive stories and their capabilities. Interest in philology led to the scholarly examination of texts, including the Bible. Humanists were interested in a return to the sources of the tradition, including the Fathers of the Church as well as ancient authors.[9] While Luther would have substantive differences with Erasmus and with some of the directions humanism would take, he relied heavily on its pedagogy, emphasis on rhetoric, and scholarly apparatus, especially in the initial stages of his movement.[10]

[9]This movement in the late Middle Ages to discover, reappropriate and imitate the early church is not unlike post Vatican II concern to return to the early church as a source of renewal in the church.

[10]Ernst, *The Theology of Grace*, p. 65.

Luther's Theology of Grace

Cornelius Ernst renders a very positive assessment of Luther's theology of grace: "Luther was a genuine novelty in the Christian tradition. Looking back at him from a distance of four centuries of European history, it is clear that his was a voice of the future, while the rejoinder of the Council of Trent was undoubtedly a voice of the Christian past."[11] Other attempts to respond to the needs of the time included speculative mysticism which harmonized scholastic theology with the truth of Christian experience. Luther takes this effort a step further, constructing a new style of theology which would take human experience seriously. From a contemporary perspective, one sees that Luther was trying to create a personal theology by describing a biblical, *personal* relationship to God in Christ: a theology expressed in terms of 'I', the self, rather than of the 'soul'.[12]

Luther's theology of grace has a dramatic style: it expresses the emergence into history of a renewed self-awareness, without losing sight of the tradition, especially as that was expressed in the thought of Paul and Augustine. For Luther, grace becomes above all the experience of a God—both lover and judge— who permits an encounter in a face-to-face relationship with persons who experience themselves as sinners. Luther revived the Western theology of grace as conversion by making the personal experience of conversion the centerpiece in his theology of grace.[13] We may now respond to the question, What are some of the distinctive characteristics of Luther's understanding of grace?

Grace as a Personal Relationship Initiated by God

Luther couples an image of God who is very much "Other" with an emphasis on the intensely personal quality of one's

---

[11]Ibid., p. 55.
[12]Ibid., pp. 55-56.
[13]Ibid., pp. 56-58.

encounter with God. The nominalist emphasis on God's sovereign will made suspect any reference to "works" or pious practices as means toward salvation. For Luther, God's will is the absolute source of grace. God is "other," bestowing grace from a transcendent realm, exterior to human life (*extra nos*).

An example will illustrate how committed Luther was to preserving God's exclusive power in the grace relationship. During the late Middle Ages, the scriptural image of the covenant had become a commanding metaphor by which nominalist theologians understood grace. Luther rejected this understanding of the God-human relationship because it implied reciprocity or mutuality between God and humans. He preferred the image of "testament" over "covenant" because the former better protected the exclusive action of God's promise or testament toward humans in the grace event. Luther regarded the God-human relationship in personal, relational terms, but God alone was the initiator and sustainer.

Another aspect of Luther's image of God highlighted the personal nature of the God-human relationship. Luther viewed grace, no longer in terms of an ontological change, as we found in Aquinas, but rather as a result of God's will or disposition toward humans.

> This final dismantling of the ontological framework of the God-man relationship may be regarded as the necessary prelude to Luther's 'biblical realism', in that it permitted this relationship to be conceived *personally*, allowing the same realistic imagery of the Old and New Testaments to be employed in responsible theological discussion.[14]

Luther's realistic portrayal of biblical scenes has the effect of engaging the listener on a personal level. In a sermon he presents the following image of the nativity:

> Think, women, there was no one there to bathe the Baby. No warm water, nor even cold. No fire, no light. The mother

---

[14]Ibid., p. 82.

was herself midwife and the maid. The cold manger was the bed and the bathtub. Who showed the poor girl what to do? She never had a baby before. I am amazed that the little one did not freeze. Do not make of Mary a stone. For the higher people are in the favor of God, the more tender are they.[15]

In addition, conversion, for Luther, was a penetrating personal experience of one's sinfulness, of one's need for justification, and of God's saving action that makes one just.

Finally, Luther's understanding of the personal nature of grace is especially obvious in his *Small Catechism*, written for the laity. In commenting on the Lord's Prayer, he asks why one could possibly need to pray, since God needs us not:

> We pray in this petition that [God's name] may also be holy *for us* ... we pray in this petition that [God's kingdom] may also come *to us* ... we pray in this petition that [God's will] may also be done *by us* ... we pray in this petition that God may make us aware of his gifts and enable us to receive our daily bread with thanksgiving (Italics mine).[16]

We see then, that Luther's ideas about grace include two emphases that, for him, co-exist harmoniously. On the one hand, grace comes totally from outside the human person as a free, gratuitous and exclusive action of God. God remains utterly transcendent and the absolute source of grace. Topics such as human cooperation in grace or the inherent goodness of nature disappear. Humans remain sinners even after justification (*simul justus et peccator*). On the other hand, the experience of grace for Luther was intensely personal. He sought to re-vitalize the powerful presence of God in human life and to call people to respond in faith and trust. This twofold emphasis is revealed in the following statement:

---

[15]Sermon on the Nativity, *LW* 52:11.

[16]*Small Catechism*, *D. Martin Luthers Werke* (Weimar, 1883—), 30.1:239f. Hereafter *WA*.

> Nothing is so small but God is still smaller, nothing so large but God is still larger, nothing is so short but God is still shorter, nothing is so long but God is still longer, nothing is so broad but God is still broader, nothing so narrow but God is still narrower, and so on. He is an inexpressible being, above and beyond all that can be described or imagined.[17]

For Luther, the grace of God in Christ was totally transcendent and yet was to be felt and personally appropriated in every aspect of one's life.

Grace: Justified by Faith Alone

A second major characteristic of Luther's concept of grace is reflected in the important role he gives to faith. In 1545, Luther articulates the new way in which he had come to understand justification:

> At last, by the mercy of God, meditating day and night, I gave heed to the context of the words, namely, "In it the righteousness of God is revealed, as it is written, '"He who through faith is righteous shall live.'" There I began to understand that the righteousness of God is revealed by the gospel, namely, the passive righteousness with which merciful God justifies us by faith, as it is written, "He who through faith is righteous shall live." Here I felt that I was altogether born again and had entered paradise itself through open gates.[18]

Faith was the universal element available to the entire believing community.

Faith, as the response to God's gift of justifying grace, was at the heart of all aspects of the Christian life. Faith involved

---

[17] *This Is My Body, WA* 26:339.

[18] Martin Luther, Preface to the Complete Edition of his Latin Writings, 1545. *LW* 34:337.

forgiveness of sin, friendship with God, the desire to serve the neighbor, and a universal priesthood.

> For faith must do everything. Faith alone is the true priestly office. It permits no one else to take its place. Therefore all Christian men are priests, all women priestesses, be they young or old, master or servant, mistress or maid, learned or unlearned. Here there is no difference, unless faith be unequal.[19]

Meditation on the gentle goodness of God allures the sinner to repentance, and faith produces and maintains it. When we hear that Christ suffered for us, faith and love arise.[20]

Through faith, we are able to apprehend the nature of God which is characterized by an eternal and almighty loving will. God's nature is merciful, pure benevolence, nothing but love.[21] God begets faith in the human person when the Good News is received and accepted. For Luther, faith is understood as confidence in God's goodness and mercy. Luther sees grace and faith connected inasmuch as they reflect the gift of assurance that God will make it well with us and that our lives and activities are pleasing in God's sight.

Faith also effects something new in the human person. This regeneration allows one to direct one's entire life toward God. One is totally converted, one's dispositions are transformed. In faith, the Holy Spirit successfully effects this new birth in persons, a birth that is deeply *felt* and that leads one especially to the performance of good works.

Grace Through the Cross

In a letter to Lazarus Spengler, the secretary to the city of Nuremberg, Luther described a seal he had designed for himself. The seal symbolized his theology:

---

[19]*Treatise on the New Testament, that is the Holy Mass*, 1520, *LW*, 35:100.

[20]*WA* 2:362-370 and 1:399.

[21]*WA*. 14:49.

> There is first to be a cross, black and placed in a heart,
> which should be of its natural color, so that I myself would
> be reminded that faith in the Crucified saves us. . . . For the
> just man lives by faith, but by faith in the Crucified One.[22]

Luther opposed what he called a "theology of glory" that was
characterized by speculation and a too high regard for reason
and human capabilities.[23] In Luther's eyes, such a theology
was susceptible to arrogance and was a falsification of the
truth of the gospel. At the Heidelberg Disputation in May of
1518, he states in Thesis 21: "A theology of glory calls evil
good and good evil. A theology of the cross calls the thing
what it actually is." Luther places the cross at the very heart of
the redemptive mystery. His theology is radically Christocentric and his Christology is a Christology of suffering and
humiliation. To stray from this central event of the Christian
myth is to abandon the truth.

> He who does not know Christ does not know God hidden
> in suffering. Therefore he prefers works to suffering, glory
> to the cross, strength to weakness, wisdom to folly, and, in
> general, good to evil. . . . God can be found only in suffering
> and the cross. . . . It is impossible for a person not to be
> puffed up by his good works unless he has first been deflated
> and destroyed by suffering and evil until he knows that he is
> worthless and that his works are not his but God's.[24]

The source and meaning of grace, then, for Luther, are to be
found in the cross of Christ. The suffering Christ reveals the
true love of God and it is in staying close to the cross that we
will participate most fully in the life of grace.

Luther's understanding of the cross as the primary means of

---

[22]"To Lazarus Spengler, Coburg, July 8, 1530," Letter 221, *LW*, 49:356-359.

[23]For a contemporary expression of Luther's theology of the cross, see Dietrich
Bonhoeffer's *The Cost of Discipleship*, Trans. R.H. Fuller, (New York:
Macmillan, 1959).

[24]Heidelberg Disputation, Thesis 21. *LW* 31:53.

grace involves him in assertions of paradox. The cross is the paradigm of the paradoxical nature of Christianity. In his commentary on the Psalms, he juxtaposes light and darkness, grace and humility:

> Light does not arise except with those who are in darkness.... "Therefore, we read that it is to the humble that God gives his grace [1 Peter 5:5]. And from this it follows that before all things we should be humiliated, so that we may receive light and grace, and indeed, that we may preserve light and grace. Humility and grace simply will not be separated.[25]

Luther's theology of grace is thus characterized by the simultaneity of opposites. His use of paradox opposes Aristotle's principle that two forms cannot coexist simultaneously and it also seems to reflect more accurately the way in which Luther experienced grace existentially. The cross and grace, sinful and justified, *Deus absconditus et revelatus*, God's mercy and judgment, are for Luther, inseparable.

Grace and the Human Person

Following in the footsteps of Augustine, Luther espouses an anthropology that sounds extremely negative to modern ears. With Julian of Norwich, he sees God as the sole actor in the redemptive process, bestowing grace on passive human beings, and yet his estimation of the human person is diametrically opposed to hers. Julian has a hard time figuring out how sin can possibly exist; Luther sees sin as the commanding, constitutive quality of human nature. Luther describes the proper subject of theology as "man guilty of sin and condemned, and God the Justifier and Savior of man the sinner."[26] The human race is mired in the dregs of sin.[27] In Luther's view, one never

---

[25]*Commentary on the Psalms*, Scholia on psalm 95. *LW* 11:252.

[26]*WA* 40.2:328.

[27]Luther often used graphic imagery to dramatize the utter fallenness of humanity. The often quoted example is "auf dies cloaca" —"in the toilet."

leaves sin behind, even with the power of grace. Grace prevents sin from being imputed, but the sin remains.

Luther wants to disabuse the church of the idea that good works *earn* salvation in any way. He wants to stress rather, that justification results in a passionate desire to love and serve the neighbor. Therefore, the human person becomes totally passive in the event of grace except for depending and trusting that God will offer the gift of grace. The only thing the human person has to do is to *realize* the truth that s/he is utterly sinful and thus, seek God's grace in Christ. Forgiveness is the primary experience of grace.

Luther's negative estimate of human capability is thoroughgoing. By nature, humans possess neither a right conscience, nor a good will.[28] By nature, humans possess only a concupiscent love which in every activity is evil.[29] In their natural state, humans are dominated by concupiscence, turned in on themselves (*incurvatus in se*), and acquiesce in their fallen condition. This sinful state involves a lack of belief and trust in God, a state of complete alienation. Any good that is accomplished by humans is done not by them but by God acting within them. Righteousness belongs to Christ; it is Christ. It does not belong to us, yet it becomes ours through faith.

> We do not live, speak and act, but Christ lives, acts and speaks in us; because what we do and say is accomplished by his acting within us and impelling us.[30]

Luther rejects both the nominalist position that the human will has the power to choose the good and the still more optimistic anthropology of the humanists, opting instead for a radical theocentrism.

In such a theology, grace becomes, above all, a curative reality. Since the utter fallenness of human nature perdures throughout one's life, grace functions continually and primarily

---

[28] *Disputation Against the Scholastics*, Thesis 34. *LW* 31:11.

[29] Ibid., Thesis 21 and 22. *LW* 31:10.

[30] *WA* 4:646.

as a medicinal power. The primary experience of this cure is the forgiveness of sin, and Luther makes a clear distinction between sin in one who rejects grace and in one who accepts it. But in spite of the utter depravity of human nature, grace is successful. "Yet grace does so much, that we are accounted altogether and fully righteous before God."[31] Even though one remains forever a sinner in this life, grace does really effect a new creation. The grace-filled person is the healthy person, empowered by the gift of love.

Grace in Word and Sacrament

Finally, we need to mention briefly the importance of the ecclesial, liturgical, sacramental aspects of Luther's theology of grace—all of which reflect his emphasis on the incarnation. Only through Word and sacrament does the Spirit, operating within the heart, come.[32] Luther's regard for the Word of God is universally acknowledged as a centerpiece of his theology. "The word alone is the vehicle of grace." Therefore one should hear the word and meditate upon it.[33]

Since faith comes through hearing the Word, preaching for Luther was an indispensable avenue of grace. We have 2,300 extant sermons from Luther.

> Again, I preach the gospel of Christ, and with my bodily voice I bring Christ into your heart, so that you may form him within yourself.[34]

Throughout his life, Luther taught that the presence of the Word means the presence of Christ and the Spirit. The Spirit "speaks to the heart," "impressess" the word upon the heart,

---

[31]Erlangen, 63:124.

[32]*WA* 1:632 and 2:112

[33]*WA* 2:509

[34]*The Sacrament of the Body and Blood of Christ—Against the Fanatics,* LW 36:340

"touches and moves the heart" of those who listen.[35]

We have seen the close connection that Luther makes between grace and faith. Luther makes a similar connection between faith and the sacraments.[36] The efficacy of the sacraments depends entirely on faith. The sacraments are signs which incite one to faith and without faith they are of no benefit.[37] The sacraments effect what they signify because of faith. They are symbols which awaken faith, and thus promise grace to all, but actually confer it only on believers.[38]

Eucharist

Luther insisted on the real presence of Christ in the bread and wine. For Luther, the Lord's Supper established a community with Christ and with all the saints in heaven and on earth. The believer becomes intimately connected, not only with Christ but also with all other believers. Further, community involves mutual love, and the body of Christ, really present in the signs of bread and wine, instills in the believer the desire to serve others in love. The Supper is the sign that effects in us the power of self-sacrificing love.

Finally, for Luther, the presence of the body of Christ is the greatest testimony to the grace of God. For it was in the very offering of his body that Christ obtained grace for those who believe. The gracious love of God remains in some sense always veiled, but in the Lord's Supper it is most clearly revealed.[39]

---

[35]Erlangen, 9:232.

[36]In the Bible, Luther finds evidence for only three sacraments—baptism, the Lord's supper, and repentance. Since repentance should not be considered a sacrament in the strict sense, one usually speaks of only two sacraments in the Lutheran tradition.

[37]*WA* 2:686.

[38]*WA* 6:86.

[39]After 1522, in response to certain interpretations of the Lord's Supper as merely a symbol, Luther is led to put more and more emphasis on the real presence in the bread and wine. Originally, he saw the body as a means of realizing the sacramental gift, but later regarded it as the gift itself.

Baptism

The other sacrament especially worthy of note with regard to grace is baptism.[40] For Luther, baptism is a key element in his efforts to democratize grace. He inveighed against a two-tiered Christianity in which monastic vows constituted a "higher" way of life. Luther switches the focus almost entirely to baptism, by which we become new persons by the power of the Holy Spirit; are washed clean; have our entire nature transformed; and are infused with grace. The work of baptism continues throughout life as one continues the struggle to remain renewed. Baptism enables us to *trust* that God remains ever ready to forgive us.

Luther's doctrine of baptism is a complement to his doctrine of grace operative in the Word. Baptism imbues the believer with an open disposition to receive the Word and it is present throughout one's life to nurture the continued effects of the Spirit's power within us.

Conclusion

In summary, Luther's rather pessimistic view of the human person does not lead him to deny the presence of the positive effects of grace, but one does not go to Augustine or to Luther for a detailed description of the human person fully alive. Their experience and awareness of sin precludes emphasis on human capabilities and cooperation with God in grace. Today, we are more aware of the breadth of God's gracious activity. We welcome a theology of grace in which grace is not exhausted by the forgiveness of sin. God is gracious to us as persons in our totality, not just to us as sinners in need of forgiveness.

For Luther, grace is primarily the favor of God, expressed in God's merciful will as it is revealed and proclaimed by

---

[40]Luther treats the subject of baptism extensively in *The Babylonian Capitivity of the Church, LW* 6: 381-469.

Christ.[41] This favor results in a unilateral relationship whose characteristics in humans are forgiveness and salvation. Luther's grace is an active force:

> It is a very great, strong, powerful, and active thing—this grace of God. It does not lie, as the dream-preachers falsely teach, in the souls of men and sleep and allow itself to be carried by them as a painted board carries its color. Nay, not so! It carries, it leads, it drives, it begets, it transforms, it works all things in man, and makes itself felt and experienced.[42]

In harmony with both scripture and the tradition, Luther sees grace as gift, as the personal, loving will of God which works within the hearts of believers. The fruit of this transformation is an altruistic passion to serve the neighbor. Luther's experience of grace is preeminently passive and yet it leads to unstinting and self-sacrificing activity on behalf of the "other."

There are many aspects of Luther's theology of grace that remain useful. The personal, existential, and affective characteristics of his portrayal of grace reverberate with much of contemporary experience, and his theology of the cross is a rich resource for us as we search for the meaning of grace in the midst of personal and global suffering. In addition, Luther had an incredible ability to make grace real, concrete, practical, and "everyday." Luther was a scholar and a religious genius, but he was also a simple, holy man. One also connects Luther's desire to recover the bible for the whole people with present widespread interest in bible study.

However, his theology of grace does not reflect in any significant way that aspect of human life in which we become co-workers with God, invited by God to participate truly in God's life and in the on-going process of redemption. We repeat the principle mentioned earlier that a real and authentically human role in the grace event need not imply any lessening of God. Nor does participation in grace demand

---

41 *WA* 6:209.
42 *WA* 7:170.

denial of the inherent goodness of the creature, made in God's image and likeness. Indeed, in this context, one could employ Luther's penchant for paradox. We are striving for a theology of grace that attributes the gift of grace totally to God and yet allows for the full, responsible and real participation of the human community.

12

A Tug of War:
Trent, Molinism and Jansenism

While this survey of significant moments in the history of grace is not intended to be comprehensive, it seems necessary to mention briefly three theological positions that together formed a response to the Reformation—the Council of Trent, the response of the Jesuits spearheaded by the Spanish Jesuit Luis Molina (d. 1600), and a seventeenth century movement in France named after one of its founders, Cornelius Jansen (d. 1638). We will focus on the ways these various understandings of grace continue to influence Christian theology and practice.

The Council of Trent

The Council of Trent opened December 13, 1545 and met intermittently for 18 years, holding thirty-five sessions in Trent and Bologna, closing in December of 1563. The Council dealt with both doctrinal issues and those more practical concerns related to the reformation of the church. As we have seen, there were a variety of theological positions within the church at this time. But rather than attempt to sort out internal differences, the Council struggled to keep its eye on clarifying its own doctrine and practice over against those of the Protestants. The Protestant Reform caused the church to define more carefully positions that had been fluid before Luther's challenge.

In the process of defining Catholic particularity, doctrinal emphases that had previously been able to coexist as parts of a comprehensive (or undifferentiated) Catholic tradition now became the themes of opposing and mutually exclusive systems, only one of which eventually took the name "Catholic" as its own.[1]

Heresy and schism were not new to the church, but it soon became clear that the Protestant Reformation represented an unprecedented threat to the church, demanding a concerted response.[2] We have seen throughout this survey how important a role socio-historical events play in the theology of any period. This was no less true of the Council of Trent. Its goals were directly related to the events of the sixteenth century, and while Trent's treatment of grace remains in place as the church's official written account of its understanding of grace, we are now aware of its limitations as well as its strengths. The goals of the Council included (1) consolidation against Protestant positions; (2) reform of the church, both in its structure and members; (3) clarification and sharpening of doctrinal understandings and statements.

The Council addressed many issues, including the sacraments, free will, predestination, the certitude of salvation, the authority of the church, the cult of the saints, Mary, original sin and justification. While it is accurate to say that the entire council was concerned with the doctrine of grace, the most direct treatment is found in the *Decree on Justification*, a document that was discussed and revised during a seven-month period, being finally approved on January 13, 1547. In its documents, the Council intentionally avoided scholastic terminology in favor of biblical language and images, but its understanding of doctrine was steeped in scholastic categories. This accounts for some of the differences between the theology of Trent and that of Luther.[3]

[1]Jaroslav Pelikan, *The Christian Tradition: A History of the Development of Doctrine*, v. 4, *Reformation of Church and Dogma (1300-1700)*, (Chicago: University of Chicago Press, 1984), p. 245.

[2]Ibid., p. 246

[3]In *The Experience and Language of Grace*, Roger Haight focusses specifically on the language issue. See pp. 105-118.

As the church struggled to define itself against the reformers, its understanding of grace took on a more definitive shape. I sense two clear emphases. First, the Council wanted to safeguard the real role of the human person in the grace event over against Luther's extreme theocentrism. Second, the church wanted to broaden the horizon of grace against Luther's "grace alone," "faith alone," "God alone" position.

The Role of the Person in Grace

Even as Trent reaffirmed the totally free and gratuitous nature of grace, the Council also wanted to preserve the *real* role that the human person had in the experience of grace. Although the Council fathers chose not to use Aquinas' term, "created grace" they sought to uphold the reality behind the term. They disagreed with Luther's use of forensic, juridical categories, i.e., that through grace sin was not imputed to us, and opted rather for the position that grace effected a *real* change in the human person. The person truly became a "new creation" in grace. Grace effected an ontological change, a genuine transformation in the person and was not merely the extrinsic imputation of God's righteousness. The justice that grace effects in the human person *really* belongs to the person and is not simply God's justice existing in us.

A second concern of the Council was the preservation of free will. Persons are not coerced to accept grace by some inner force, but are genuinely free to reject it or accept it. In order to preserve both the gratuitous character of grace and free will, the Council stated that grace and free will operate in such a way that all works are completely divine and completely human. Works did not earn salvation independently of God, but the Christian was free to choose to cooperate with the gift of grace, a cooperation that was real and that became concrete in good works and a virtuous life. Grace was the leader and human will was the partner in grace. The *Decree on Justification* states:

> ...while God touches the heart of man through the illumination of the Holy Spirit, man himself neither does

absolutely nothing while receiving that inspiration, since he can also reject it, nor yet is he able by his own free will and without the grace of God to move himself to justice in His sight.[4]

The human role in the grace event is not a purely passive one, but rather one of active, cooperative choice.

Also, since the Bible often spoke of merit, the Council wanted to be clear about how that was to be understood. They modified the meaning of the term to insure God's role, calling it "gratuitous merit" since merit was both bestowed as a gift and earned as a reward.

The tridentine doctrine of grace is faithful to Augustine inasmuch as it enters into and respects the existential, psychological process of graced existence—moments of preparation, effort, struggle, growth and fulfillment. It also modifies Augustine and Luther, advocating, as did Aquinas, a more positive view of human nature. Original sin does not cast one irrevocably into evil. The power of grace is seen as an effective antidote to sin, not by eliminating it but by mitigating its power to "incline to evil." Its anthropology strikes a more optimistic tone and rejects the thesis that says all human efforts and hope for reward involve disorder and sin.[5]

Broadening the Horizon of Grace

Trent also sought to broaden the horizons in which grace functioned and was understood. The Council fathers wished to counter Luther's emphasis on grace as forgiveness of sin by emphasizing other effects of grace. Primary among these was

---

[4]*Decree on Justification*, Ch. 5; in *Canons and Decrees of the Council of Trent*, trans. H.J. Schroeder, (St. Louis: B. Herder Book Co., 1941), p. 32

[5]*Decree on Justification*, Ch. 11. See Rondet, *The Grace of Christ*, p. 306. Trent's optimistic anthropology (responding to Luther's *sola gratia*) may be profitably contrasted with the negative anthropology of the Council of Orange (529) which was responding to semi-Pelagianism's weakening of grace. Here the will was described as "depraved" and "weakened" in order to counteract what was conceived as a too positive valuation of the powers of human nature and free will.

true participation in the divine nature. The theme of salvation as deification, although never a major theme, would be sounded several times at the Council.[6] The *Decree on Justification* states that justification

> is not only a remission of sins but also the sanctification and renewal of the inward person through the voluntary reception of the grace and gifts whereby an unjust person becomes just and from being an enemy becomes a friend, that he may be "an heir according to hope of life everlasting" (Titus 3:7).[7]

This doctrinal emphasis on the life-long activity of divine-human cooperation in the growth and development of the spiritual life is a superb foundation upon which to build a theology of grace of everyday existence. Grace has the potential to be discovered and named in any experience that enhances one's friendship with God and effects renewal in any aspect of one's total self.

A second arena in which the Council sought a broadening of the understanding of grace focussed on the sacraments. The Council reaffirmed the validity of all seven sacraments in response to the Protestant protest that some of the sacraments had no foundation in scripture. Further, the Council fathers established a close connection between grace and the sacraments—a counter position to Luther's stance of "faith alone."

Finally, also in response to Luther's emphasis on "faith alone," the Council pointed to the importance of all the theological virtues, in particular to the primacy of charity as found in John's gospel and Paul's letters. Both Augustine and Aquinas provided touchstones in the tradition for a more wholistic understanding of the interaction of all the virtues and gifts in the life of grace. Luther preached "faith alone" to confront the growing tendency in the medieval church to "earn" or "buy" salvation. Trent countered by contrasting a faith

---

[6] Pelikan, Ibid., p. 255

[7] *Decree on Justification*, Ch. 7.

infused with love to what they perceived as a barren "faith alone." The Council of Trent was the church's response to the Reformation, as well as an act of self-reflection and self-renewal.[8] Its primary aim was to establish clearly the church's teaching against that of the reformers. Hubert Jedin calls the doctrinal statements "boundary stones" that helped establish the identity of the Roman Catholic church in the face of Protestantism. In the period that followed the Council, the decrees of Trent were regarded by Catholics and Protestants alike, no longer as "boundary stones" but as "barbed wire." "Both sides withdrew to hedgehog positions of defence."[9]

Molinism

The Society of Jesus was founded by Ignatius Loyola in 1540, and entrusted with the task of helping the papacy to counteract the Protestant movement in Europe. Alarmed at the doctrine of predestination by which God chooses to bestow efficacious grace on some who are then saved, and to withhold it from others, who are then destined for eternal damnation, the Jesuits proposed a less harsh understanding of grace that also sought to protect free will and to present the human person in a more positive light. In 1588, the Jesuit, Luis Molina, issued a document (*Concordia liberi arbitrii cum gratiae donis*) that sought to harmonize the gift of grace with human freedom—thus the name of this position, Molinism.

The Jesuits were sympathetic to the ideas of humanism and the Renaissance, seeing them as a way to articulate a theology, in the words of their General, Lainez, "better accommodated to the needs of the times."[10] They strove to minimize the idea of the natural depravity of the human person and the effects of original sin. Instead, building on the humanist positive valuing

---

[8]Hubert Jedin, *Crisis and Closure of the Council of Trent*, trans. N. D. Smith, (London: Sheed & Ward, 1967), p. 160

[9]Ibid., p. 164.

[10]Cited in *The Jansenists and the Expulsion of the Jesuits from France, 1757-1765* by Dale Van Kley (New Haven, CT: Yale University Press, 1975), p. 7.

of the person, they emphasized the natural goodness of persons and the freedom of the will in matters pertaining to salvation. Molina did not contest the doctrine of Adam's fall, but did contest its results. Instead of utter and total depravity, the fall brought about the loss of God's supernatural gifts such as eternal life. Human nature, and especially the human freedom to choose between good and evil, remained essentially intact.[11]

For Molina, nature and grace worked together harmoniously. The radical conversion made necessary by the radical depravity of the human person in Protestant anthropology was no longer necessary. In addition to a positive stance toward the human person in her or his present condition, Molina upheld the freedom of the will, the possibility that one could grow and improve in the life of grace, and the value of this earthly life. This latter position led to a certain optimism about society with the concomitant motivation to become involved in political thought and activity.[12] This understanding of grace is reminiscent of the Jesuit maxim that challenges the Christian "to find God in all things" and offers yet another important resource for a contemporary understanding of grace.

Jansenism

Cornelius Jansen, a professor of theology at the University of Louvain and later bishop of Ypres (1626-38), became the figurehead for a diverse movement that is generally known as Jansenism. Its proximate origins are usually traced to the immediate aftermath of the Council of Trent, and to an Augustinian at Louvain, Michel de Bay, known as Baius (d. 1589).

Baius eschewed Aquinas and scholasticism in favor of a narrowly interpreted Augustinianism. He made a sharp distinction between the original state of innocence in which the human person was by nature immortal and capable of participating freely in the divine nature, and the state of fallen nature

---

[11] Ibid.
[12] Ibid., p. 8.

in which persons are incapable of any free acts—where in fact even good desires are sinful. For Baius, every sin is worthy of eternal damnation and all acts of "infidels and philosophers" are sinful. He espoused a doctrine of the radical impotence of the fallen will and of persons' incapacity to share in God's life. Natural good did not exist.

The ongoing debate in the theology of grace between the gratuity of grace and the freedom of the human will takes on a sharply delimited shape in this period of the sixteenth to the seventeenth centuries. On the one side were the Renaissance, humanism, the rise of science with its interest in the empirical study of the physical world, and the Jesuits under the banner of Molinism. Arrayed against this more positive sense of the human person were the strict Augustinians who feared the neo-Pelagian tendencies of the above positions and opted for a more pessimistic appraisal of human capabilities resulting from the fall. In this group we find Luther, Calvin, Baius, and the many adherents to the movement known as Jansenism.

Even though Baianism was condemned in 1567 by Pius V and again in 1580, its ideas perdured. In 1640, two years after his death, a treatise by Jansen was published entitled *Augustinus*. This was a systematic rebuttal of the Jesuit position that became the catalyst for a popular movement in the Netherlands and especially in France. It attracted influential persons such as Saint-Cyran, important Parisian families such as the Arnaulds, politicians in the parlement of Paris, several bishops, and leading intellectuals such as Pascal. The Abbey of Port Royal in France became a center for Jansenist ideas and practices.

Like Baius, Jansen insisted on the full gravity of the fall, resulting in the utter depravity of human nature, and a will that was invincibly prone toward all manner of evil and incapable of loving God or keeping the commandments.[13] Van Kley states the case dramatically:

> Against, then, Molinism's rather optimistic and complacent vision of human nature and somewhat terrestrial interpre-

[13] Ibid.

tation of Christianity as a whole, Jansenius pitted the most
tragic and pessimistic vision of man and an interpretation
of both human nature and Christianity full of the sharpest,
almost lunar contrasts.[14]

Good works related to salvation could be accomplished if they
were done in charity, and charity was available only to those
few to whom God chose to give efficacious grace. For
Jansenists, the world was a place of evil, full of temptations
that might lure one away from the narrow way. Jansenist
conversions resulted typically in the cessation of all secular
activity and in an ascetic retreat from the world. Seventeenth
century Jansenism was more pessimistic, ascetic, and other-
worldly than either Calvinism or Molinism.[15]

However, some adherents to Jansenism took more moderate
positions. Not all were rabidly anti-worldly and pessimistic.
But it is still accurate to say that this religious vision is anti-
thetical in the extreme to one that is open to the possibility
that the grace of God can be revealed in any and every aspect
of human life. In 1653, Innocent X condemned several of the
Jansenist positions that involved a narrow doctrine of predestination for the few, the denial of one's ability to choose
between good and evil, and the inability of just persons to
keep the commandments. In 1713 the bull *Unigenitus* again
condemned Jansenist positions, articulated by Pasquier
Quesnel, that denied the universality of redemption and upheld
the irresistibility of grace. But in spite of these attempts to
protect a more balanced theology of grace, some of the narrow
and pessimistic aspects of Jansenism, although no longer an
influence in most Catholic theology, remain an unwelcome
influence in Christian life.

Some of the tenets of Jansenism (and at times their mis-
interpretation) have led to unhelpful understandings of grace.
These include cynicism or skepticism about the possibility and

---

[14] Ibid.

[15] Ibid., p. 10. Blaise Pascal was a prime example of one converted to Jansenism
who then retreated from a promising scientific career to the secluded, meditative
atmosphere of Port-Royal. One can with profit read his *Provincial Letters* (1657) to
get a flavor of the debate with Molinism and the Jesuits.

efficacy of God's gift of grace to all; the denial of human freedom or the refusal to use that freedom to cooperate with God in making this world a better place in which to live; the refusal to see the world as the locus of God's revelation and the failure, therefore, to be on the lookout for the presence of God in that world. Finally, the ethos of Jansenism has influenced our image of God. The God that is implicit in a system like Jansenism is not the God of the Judeo-Christian story, but rather a harsh and demanding God who chooses arbitrarily to grace some and not others. This God is a dour God, not one who is joyful, who celebrates the gifts of grace, or who wishes happiness for creatures.

Modern Theologians of Grace

In the nineteenth and twentieth centuries, theologians such as Matthias Scheeben, Garrigou-Lagrange, Robert Gleason, Piet Fransen, Henri de Lubac and Henri Rondet have struck out in new directions. We continue to appreciate the incomparable legacy of Augustine and also to realize that his theology of grace was conditioned by the circumstances of his time and needs to be modified in light of our times. While the mystery of grace will never receive its definitive expression, we do know that we need not oppose grace to freedom and human goodness. It is possible for grace and freedom to increase proportionately. God and human persons can work as real, cooperative partners—each to full capacity.

> Grace frees man and creates in him an ever greater freedom. Sin in itself is not an obstacle to grace, since our Lord came precisely to save what was lost. The most radical Augustinian pessimism can be accepted, as long as it is corrected with an optimism of grace which stresses the salvific will and man's free cooperation, and thus ultimately glorifies nature itself.[16]

[16]Rondet, *The Grace of Christ*, p. 335.

Most influential at the present time in Catholic theology is the work of the German Jesuit, Karl Rahner (d. 1985). In his theology of grace, Rahner posits an extremely positive anthropology, defining the human person as one who by nature, is open to, and reaches out to, the transcendent.[17] Rahner also restores the scholastic notion of uncreated grace to a central position. Grace, for Rahner, is above all God's free, personal self-communication to creatures. Finally, Rahner stresses the continuity between the experience of grace on earth and the beatific vision. Even though our present, earthly experience of grace is partial and often hidden, it is nonetheless the same basic reality as the face-to-face vision of God in life beyond death.

The place to look for grace is in nature and in history—both one's personal history and the history of the world.[18] For the believer, the story of grace, even though transcendent, is found precisely within the history of the world. Rahner is critical of the view that sees nature and grace as two layers of reality that have little to do with each other. Unless we discover compelling ways to talk about the interrelationship of nature and grace, our daily activities will neveɪ become the primary locus of the revelation of God in grace.

There are many sources in the tradition that can assist in this task. In addition to the Augustinian and Lutheran orientations, theologians look to the Greek Fathers such as Cyril of Alexandria, Origen and Irenaeus. The traditional emphasis of Eastern Orthodox doctrines on the Holy Spirit and on deification as the primary effect and goal of grace are also valuable resources for a contemporary understanding of grace. Theologians are also beginning to reclaim the mystics and spiritual writers as primary sources for a theology of grace—

---

[17]For a fuller treatment of Rahner's theology of grace see Leo J. O'Donovan, ed. *A World of Grace: An Introduction to the Themes and Foundations of Karl Rahner's Theology* (New York: Seabury Press, 1980). A brief analysis may be found in Roger Haight, *The Experience and Language of Grace* pp. 119-142.

[18]One may recall here the aphorism, "The Christian is the one with the Bible in one hand and *The New York Times* in the other."

Julian of Norwich, Teresa of Avila, John of the Cross, Ignatius of Loyola, and Francis de Sales, to name a few.[19] This work has begun, but there remains an enormous amount of research to be done.

[19]Examples of the use of the saints as a source for theology include: William M. Thompson, *Fire & Light: The Saints and Theology* (New York: Paulist Press, 1987); Ewert Cousins, "Spirituality: A Resource for Theology," *Proceedings of the Catholic Theology Society of America* 35 (1980): 124-137; Karl Rahner, "Mystical Experience and Mystical Theology", in *Theological Investigations*, 17, (New York: Crossroad, 1981). pp. 90-99.

Part III

Grace Today

Without a doubt, it's a great grace to receive the sacraments; but when God doesn't allow it, it's good just the same; everything is a grace.

Thérèse of Lisieux
Her Last Conversations

Introduction

This brief look at past theologies of grace shows clearly that the experience and understanding of grace are influenced by a variety of factors, including theological debates, changing situations in the church, historical exigencies, socio-cultural events, and personality.[1] A knowledge of history can help us to understand this process, to know and appreciate past efforts, and on that basis to create a theology of grace for our own times—one that both builds on the tradition and takes our present situation into account. The task in any period is to remain faithful to the inheritance of faith and at the same time faithful to our experience. Any theology of grace is truncated if one or the other of these poles is neglected.

Cornelius Ernst laments in rather strong terms the framework of much of our past theology of grace:

---

[1]See Roger Haight, *The Experience and Language of Grace,* for a discussion of the various models that have been used throughout history to talk about grace, p. 25.

It is unfortunate that just because of the pressures of controversy, the official teaching of the Church on grace has found expression in definitions which exclude Pelagianism and later, 'semi-Pelagianism', since all these controversies have tended to concentrate on limited aspects of God's gracious self-communication. The accumulated weight of these definitions has tended to make the theology of grace, quite inappropriately, into a singularly cumbersome and even repellent affair.[2]

The important term in Ernst's statement is "limited". The emphases and horizons of past theologies of grace—while true and helpful and often brilliantly stated—have limitations when examined in the light of present experience. One can also be assured that our understanding of grace will prove limited to those who come after us. In addition, hidden fears, apprehensions, and other psychological factors beyond reach, have a part in limiting our understanding of grace.

In his book, *Essays on Nature and Grace*, Joseph Sittler calls attention to the need to take seriously the experience of the modern world in our theology of grace. "The old theological rubrics of 'Nature and Grace' did not have to attend to Copernicus, Newton, Darwin, Marx, Freud...."[3] If a theology of grace is to address us in a meaningful way, these factors must be considered. Our formulations of grace must follow the energies of reality. We must attend to the diverse contours of the energies we do experience.

Also in the past, doctrines of grace have been extremely preoccupied with the human person as sinner and the need for redemption from sin. I don't think anyone would quarrel with the importance of this position. What is open to criticism is the almost exclusive concern with sin. It is both possible and desirable to recover and celebrate the power, presence and hope of grace, *within* the goodness of human life in the world-as-creation as well as in hearing and receiving the word of

---

[2] *The Theology of Grace*, p. 30-31

[3] Joseph Sittler, *Essays on Nature and Grace*, (Philadelphia: Fortress Press, 1972), p. 1.

forgiveness for sin.[4] The tradition itself has the potential to assist us in this task. There are strains less well known, less developed that can be drawn forth as we attempt to speak of grace in a way that will resonate clearly and powerfully with present experience. As we saw above, Julian of Norwich provides one such strain.

We know that the concept of grace raises basic questions about God, about the human person and the cosmos in which we live, and about their interrelations. In some ways, past theologies have put these two realities over against each other. The truth, "God does all" has been well served by the tradition. We have been less successful at figuring out how to talk about the contribution humans make in this process we call salvation. From one perspective, credit given to humans is seen to detract from God. In this view, the question is set in the context of two scales—if one posits a real and active role for humans, somehow the grandeur of God is lessened. From another perspective, one answers the question by saying that God does 99% and humans do 1%. But that 1% is seen as enormously important because all our attention is focussed on that one part about which we know something and over which we have some control.

I agree with Roger Haight's statement that "A way must be found in which the total gratuity of grace and the dependency of humanity on God are affirmed in a way that also preserves human autonomy or self-determination and our ability to freely respond to God as persons."[5] Such a way will need to embrace more fully the inexhaustibility, the boundlessness of God's love that cuts through the kind of thinking that sees grace as the activity of *either* God *or* humans. Why can't our ideas about grace encompass our experience of *both* the fullness of God *and* the fullness of the human person, created in God's image?

---

[4] Ibid., p. 17.

[5] *The Experience and Language of Grace*, p. 44. Haight's chapter on Karl Rahner is recommended (pp. 119-142). Rahner's theology of grace is an excellent example of a theology that returns to an emphasis on grace as God's gracious self-gift but also does justice to the human who is seen as created with an openness, a capacity for God.

In her *Life*, Teresa of Avila speaks about the role of God and of humans in grace through her well-known image of watering the garden. For Teresa, human activity is more prominent at the beginning stages of the spiritual life. Effort is required as we pull the water up out of the well in a bucket. At a later stage, the garden is watered by an irrigation system that requires less effort. At the final stages one experiences God's grace like the rain, flowing down abundantly and freely—an experience requiring no effort at all.

This metaphor need not suggest that human activity ceases as one progresses in the life of grace, but that it becomes easier, more grace-full both as one acquires the habit of cooperating with grace and as one is able to relax, trusting in the God who is the faithful and generous giver. Contemplatives speak of this willingness to trust God as "surrender", as "letting-go", as relinquishing a false kind of control over life.[6] But the process of deepening surrender should not result in total passivity. We always have a part to play, and grace calls us to be responsible and accountable in the ways in which we cooperate with it. In fact, one's ability to cooperate with and act on the gifts of grace should increase as one advances on the journey toward fullness of life in God.

The way in which we talk about grace must also reflect specific historical, cultural and geographic differences in the various human communities. We need to ask, What are some of the important factors in twentieth-century American life that must be taken into consideration in any relevant theology of grace, knowing that these factors will be different for Europeans, Central Americans, Japanese or Africans. At the same time, all nations are experiencing themselves more and more as a global community in which ripples in one part of the globe turn into tidal waves somewhere else.

As the early Christian community, Augustine, Aquinas, Julian and Luther took up the challenge of speaking about grace in ways that made sense in their times, so must we. If grace is real, it is experienced and if grace is a reality in the

---

[6]Gerald May discusses grace in this context in *Will and Spirit: A Contemplative Psychology*, (San Francisco: Harper & Row, 1982), pp. 208-209.

world, it must become manifest, in visible activity and tangible presence that confront oppressive, alienating, freedom-denying and dehumanizing forces in our world.[7]

The task of speaking in a meaningful way about grace is difficult and we can do no more than point to a few fresh directions. We can't presume to be exhaustive, but we hope to provoke a faithful, creative, and imaginative response to the call to speak about the ways in which God's presence is felt in our lives. We want to keep in mind 1) those familiar aspects of ordinary life that are available to everyone and that have the potential to reveal and enhance God's graceful presence; 2) those ways of understanding grace that speak to some of the pressing needs of people today.

Language about grace that is faithful to the tradition and to our experience can clarify, affirm, correct and enhance one's love affair with God. It will lead to an affirmation of the human person "fully alive" and to the greater glory and praise of God.

[7]Ibid., p. 50.

13

The Passion of God:
Grace as Self-Gift

Contemporary theology has successfully called into question that understanding of grace in which the natural and supernatural spheres are seen as separate, self-contained realities—an approach that led to the depersonalization of grace. Grace was seen as "something" that God gave and that we received or earned, or even bought. We have noted that in this century, theologians such as Piet Fransen, Henri Rondet, Paul Tillich and Karl Rahner fought against this reifying tendency. Karl Rahner underlines the importance of the personal nature of grace:

> Grace is God himself, the communication in which he gives himself to man as the divinizing favour which he is himself. Here his work is really *himself*, since it is he who is imparted. Such grace, from the very start, cannot be thought of independently of the personal love of God and its answer in man.[8]

We have also returned to scriptural images of God, some of which were discussed in Part II. The God of the Judeo-Christian tradition is one who desires to give God's very self to the human community in freedom and love. This God is one whose loving generosity knows no bounds. The very being of

---

[8]"Nature and Grace," *Theological Investigations* IV, (Baltimore, MD: Helicon Press, 1966), p. 177.

God is extended in endless gestures of care. When we ask the question, Who is God?, the answer is that God is the incredibly generous and compassionate one. Grace is not a "thing", but rather has to do with the very nature of God; grace is God in God's graciousness. Two paradigmatic gestures of this graciousness are creation and incarnation.

Creation

Creation is the result of God's desire to extend the sphere of love beyond Godself. If grace is primarily the gift of Godself, creation is the resulting embodiment of that gift. The lovely poetry of the Genesis story provides a crucial foundation for any theology of grace. For the Israelites, the power and reliability of God as they are expressed in the created world are reasons for trusting God. Creation is one reason for dependence on God, for trust, thankfulness and obedience (Isa 17:7; 22:11; 40:26f). As a product of God's creative activity, all of creation shares in its very existence in the goodness of God. The refrain in the story reminds us of this: "And God saw that it was good." "And God saw that it was good." "And God saw that it was good" (Gen. 1:1-31). Genesis 1 implies that there is no ontological distinction among created beings between the sacred and the profane, the holy and the secular.

By regarding creation as a caring gesture of a personal God, we avoid seeing the relationship of God and the world as one-sided and dominating, or as distant and indifferent. Theologically speaking, creation is a living expression of God's loving decision and ultimate design. We are freed then, to see the connections between the divine and the human as part of an intimate yet complex relationship. The God of the cosmos has chosen to initiate, to reach out in creative and creating love.

A theology of grace that takes God's loving being and activity as its starting point has several commitments. First, since creation is a divine gesture, it reflects divinity in its very being. Since creation comes forth from God, it follows that in some way it must be "of God." Creation is full of grace because God is its source and sustainer. Second, as we become aware of, and reflect on this gift, we are moved to awe, to praise and to thanksgiving. Our very existence is the result of divine generosity that desires us, loves us, and holds us in being.

In the biblical tradition, creation was central, but often more as part of the scenery than as an overt topic of discussion. The entire drama of redemption is built on the presupposition of creation, yet in some ways it is taken for granted. The New Testament says little about the inner nature of creation. But it is appropriate in our time to bring to light the complex anatomy of creation. This is happening spontaneously in our growing concern for the ecological well-being of our universe.[9] "It is even possible that in his protest against pollution modern man finds his way back to natural experiences as a kind of preamble to faith, an openness for deeper experiences of the senses."[10] For believers, this knowledge can provide a cornerstone for a new awareness of grace, for a recovery of the sense of being gifted in astounding ways in the natural world around us, for an awakened responsibility to protect and nurture that world, and for coming to know the generous God behind the gift.

Incarnation

For the New Testament community, creation and salvation come together in Jesus. In the Christian *mythos*, the gift of Godself takes on a further, more intimate expression. Not only does God enter into community with us through creation, but God becomes one of us, enters history, and experiences the joys and sufferings of human living and dying. For Christians, Jesus becomes further, personal *manifestation* of God. Theologians debate whether the incarnation would have taken place had sin not entered the world. Unfortunately, we cannot speak from the experience of a sinless world, but we can imagine that a loving God would place no limits on

[9]The evening news' vivid footage of syringes and hypodermic needles littering the beaches becomes more alarming each summer.

[10]Edward Schillebeeckx, *Christ,* (New York: Seabury Press, 1980), p. 529.

creative ways to express love. We see Jesus as the one who
maintains and deepens the possibilities for a graceful relationship between God and ourselves in spite of sin.

God's message to us in Christ calls into question the exclusive distinction between sacred and secular spheres inasmuch as now everything and everyone and every aspect of life
is in principle holy. This view does not preclude the choice to
endow certain places or times as especially sacred. It *does* call
into question positions that arbitrarily secularize parts of
creation or that deny the possibility of the numinous in any
and all spheres of life.

Relationship

There have been many terms used to describe the result of
God's self-communication to the world—we enter into covenant; we are children of God; we are God's heirs; we share or
participate in the divine nature; we see and love as God sees
and loves; our wills are joined with God's will. Edward
Schillebeeckx reminds us that communion with God through
the Son in the Spirit is in fact a living communion that *can be
experienced.*[11] We have seen the evidence of how the nature of
that experience and the ways in which it is expressed change
from age to age. One can concentrate on the distance between
the divine and the human, or one can attend primarily to their
closeness. The truth of God's utter transcendence has been the
bedrock of past doctrines of grace. The truth of the utter
immanence of God has been highlighted in the writings of the
mystics who speak of "union with God."[12]

The challenge, as I see it, is to extend and maintain both

---

[11] *Christ*, p. 473.

[12] Cornelius Ernst makes a perceptive observation in this regard: "... in our review
of the New Testament, union with God is by no means the primary sense of the word
charis. The primary sense is that of free giving, the mystery of God's incomprehensible
generosity.... From the New Testament and St. Augustine we may gradually learn
to appreciate the texture of our entire experience as a disclosure of God's free
generosity in our free response to that generosity." *Theology of Grace*, p. 48.

ends of the paradox. Is there a way to uphold the total otherness of God that is not at the expense of the world and the human person, God's creation? One frequently runs across theological statements that underscore the truth of the vast chasm between the Creator and the creature:

> Between our human nature and our destiny, there lies an infinite disproportion.

> The Kingdom of God is not a world, is not to be classed with this world. Its relationship is one of radical heterogeneity.

> One cannot, whether for oneself or for the world, plan for it (salvation), organize it, build it, construct it; one cannot even imagine it or get any idea of it; for it is something given, a bequest; we can only inherit it.[13]

Such statements need to be explained and balanced with expressions that reflect the intimate divine/human connection, both in the incarnation and in persons' experiences. The former statements, taken in isolation, have often led to disvaluing the world and the human.

At times, such exclusive statements on the otherness of God arise out of the utter truth of human experience. But in other instances, one senses a fear that talk about the closeness of God will strip faith of its mystery, reduce it to a social datum that is totally secularized. "Thus losing her own soul, she (the church) would be reduced to a *mere* human organization, and a totally ineffective one at that (emphasis mine)."[14]

Of course one is right to guard against what appear to be dangers to faith. But from another vantage point, one wonders if the transcendent is truly being eclipsed, especially in the United States. An argument can be made that indeed the opposite is the case—that the transcendent is very much alive

---

[13]Henri de Lubac, *A Brief Catechism on Nature and Grace*, Trans. Richard Arnandez, (San Francisco: Ignatius Press, 1984), pp. 32, 37, 106-107.

[14]Ibid., p. 112.

and well in this country, but often at the expense of "the world."[15] Is it possible that the chasm set up between the sacred and the secular blocks our ability to see God in the everyday, or leads us to see the latter as a diminishment of God? Indeed, for the Christian believer, do not creation and incarnation destroy forever the possibility of the existence of the purely secular? Can we ever again legitimately talk about the *merely* human?

One wonders whether abrupt distinctions between sacred and secular are necessary accompaniments of the quest for God, or whether they are a defense mechanism, rooted in false fear of, rather than in love for, divinity. If we have a sense that God is dangerous in a destructive sense, the division of life into sacred and secular may be as much a protection against God as against evil.[16] Is it not preferable to acknowledge humbly the gift of a "holy cosmos" and to look to our lives, limited though they be, for hints of God and for the means by which we can enhance appreciation for, and growth in, grace? Let us turn now to a specific dimension of our experience—relationships.

Relationships Among Humans

It is a commonplace to say that relationship with God is not the same as relationship among human beings. However, it is true that our experience of human relationships becomes a valuable resource to enhance our relationship with God. This statement is not intended to reduce love among humans to a purely utilitarian function in which we *use* people in order to become "holy". In fact, as will be shown in the next chapter, relationships among humans are a most treasured arena of grace. But the dynamics of mutual human love are tangible

[15]Recent surveys have produced statistics that indicate that between 80-90% of Americans believe in God, have significant religious experience and are active in faith communities. One such survey was presented in *Better Homes and Gardens*, (January, 1988).

[16]Edmund Hill, *Being Human: A Biblical Perspective,* (London: Geoffrey Chapman, 1984), p. 247-248.

and accessible in a way that one's relationship with God is not—and vice versa. Love among humans and divine/human love are ordained to be mutually enriching. Let us look at several key dynamics.

To begin, if someone approaches us or manifests an interest in us, we become curious. If we think highly of this person, we feel flattered. We may wonder what the person sees in us. But almost always we want to know more and more about who this person is. In a relationship with God, it may never occur to us that God is making overtures to us. We may not be conscious that the God of Christianity is a God who desires to be self-revealing. And even if we do believe this, it doesn't necessarily follow that we allow ourselves to become curious about just who this God is.

We are familiar with the ways in which we satisfy our curiosity about someone. We pay attention to the person; we spend time with and listen to the person; we ask questions; we find out about the person's history, likes and dislikes, talents, shortcomings. We may even consult other persons who know her well to get other insights and perspectives. There are some difficulties, of course, when the partner is God. It is not possible *literally* to go for a walk, to find out about likes and dislikes. But it is possible to do all of these things *really*, and discovering this God is at the heart of any experience of grace. God is the person who wishes us well in all things, who *wants* to tell us who God is, who *desires* to know us and be known by us.

The tradition also speaks about the graced relationship in terms of union, of divinization, of sharing in God's life. God's offer of self makes it possible for us to participate in the inner relationships of the Trinity. Here again, we may ask in what ways we experience participation with others in human relationships. Persons who love each other share in each other's gifts. These may include artistic talents, a sense of humor, intellectual or physical prowess, fidelity, simplicity—material and spiritual gifts of all kinds. We feel enriched when the gifts of another are offered as an enrichment to our own gifts. We may experience pleasure at inviting the other to share our gifts and talents.

After many years in relationship, we may begin to see things as the other sees them, to love as the other loves. In theological terms, this experience of grace is spoken of in terms of a union of wills. As one's relationship with God grows in intimacy, one begins to see things from God's perspective, to love as God loves. This does not mean that I give up my will, but that my will becomes ever more conditioned to desire the good. It is in this context that Augustine says, "Love God and do what you will." God's self-gift enables us to discover who God is and to become like God. The incarnation assists us in making manifest in the life of Jesus what it means to become like God. The gospel stories offer us in broad strokes the shape of a life lived in union with God's will. We can look to Jesus for guidelines about inner attitudes and dispositions, about ways to live and act toward others.

God as Mystery

Before concluding our discussion on grace as God's self-revelation, we want to call attention to one of the more popular names for God today—God as Mystery.[17] God's self-revelation creates a tension between knowing and not-knowing God. On the one hand, there are myriad concrete ways in which the human community experiences grace as the presence of God. These are real and true and crucial to a theology of grace. But we also have the experience of the utter unknowability of God. How can we even begin to know this God who is the fullness, the totality of everything we know to be good?

In the tradition, some theologian/mystics emphasize the positive ways in which they experience God. Others find God predominantly through what God is not, since our notions about who God truly is fall far short of the fullness of God's reality. The Greek terms used to describe these two different ways are "apophatic" (negative) and "kataphatic" (positive). But the best writers encompass both aspects, e.g., Irenaeus, Gregory of Nyssa, Bernard of Clairvaux, Julian of Norwich, John of the Cross, Teresa of Avila, to name a few. They

---

[17]Karl Rahner has built his entire theological system on the idea of God as Mystery.

include both the "otherness" of God, reflected in the Hebrew refusal to image God, and the "manifestation" of God in Jesus Christ and in their lives.

One consequence of the utter mysteriousness of God is the unending nature of our discovery of who God is. In a similar way, one never reaches the totality of knowledge of another person. Humans participate in God's mystery. That is why language like "I've got her number", or "I've figured him out" or "She handles him well" is so offensive. One notices the fruit of grace in persons who remain in awe and wonder at each other even after long association.

Part of what makes God God is that we will never completely fathom or contain God. No matter how curious we become, no matter how much we find out about God, and no matter to what extent we become like God, there will always be more. As Rahner says, even in heaven the quest to know and love God will remain endless for all eternity.

We have been looking at grace as God's self-revelation, and at the God who is revealed as one who wishes with full heart to shower us with gifts of every kind. This means that the joy of coming to know and love this generous God, and the joy of accepting gifts wonderful beyond our imagining, is an endless joy. The experience of grace is boundless because the God who is grace for us is and will remain infinite Mystery.

14

The Human Person Fully Alive[1]

Introduction

In addition to being the gift of God's self-revelation, grace is also God's wish to be present in every aspect of creation. This desire on God's part affects the ways in which we understand the human person. That is, the theology of grace raises the fundamental issue of Christian anthropology. How do we talk about the graced person? We have stated that past theologies have seen grace too exclusively as an antidote to sin. Without undercutting the universal experience of sin and the ensuing need for grace, let us examine ways in which grace suffuses human experience. The human person does not live in isolation, but as a distinctive actor in a wider, cosmic milieu. The graced person is an integral part of a graced cosmos and of the many communities that constitute it.

Imago Dei

As we have seen above, in the very act of creation God has caused the world to be graced. In Genesis 1, we read that the

---

[1]The meaning of this famous phrase (*gloria enim Dei vivens homo, vita autem hominis visio Dei*) from Irenaeus' *Against Heresies* (late second century) is analysed by Mary Ann Donovan, "Alive to the Glory of God: A Key Insight in St. Irenaeus," *Theological Studies* 49 (1988): 283-297. The use of the phrase is especially apt in the context of grace, since according to Donovan, Irenaeus understands the glory of the human person to be essentially connected with the vision of God, which vision is present in this life but complete only in the final resurrection. The vision of God is made possible through the love and kindness God offers, and the life of persons lies in participation in God—knowing God and enjoying God's goodness—graces all.

human person was created "in the image and likeness of God."
Imago Dei has been one of the foundations on which theologies of grace have been built. Because we have been created
in God's image, there is an intimate bond or affinity between
Creator and creature. We have been created *capax Dei*, i.e.,
receptive to God, by nature, created in God's image and
likeness. It is God's desire from the beginning that we be full of
grace, i.e., full of God, and therefore wondrous. The psalmist
sings:

> Truly you have formed my inmost being;
> You knit me in my mother's womb.
> I give thanks that I am fearfully, wonderfully made;
> Wonderful are your works (Ps 139:13-14).

Even the willful straining of that connection through sin is not
fatal. As was so clear to Julian of Norwich, the power of God's
love ultimately reigns over the ravages of sin and death.

In addition to the grace of creation, we have seen that
incarnation brings yet another dimension of sacrality to nature,
history, and especially to the human person, inasmuch as in
Jesus, God takes on the specific, concrete existence of humanity, experiencing both its struggles and rewards. Mindful
of these theological foundations supporting the graced nature
of creation, let us examine in greater depth the meaning of
grace—paying special attention to contemporary sensibilities.
After a look at the nature of the change effected by grace, we
will discuss two characteristics of this "graceful" person—
freedom and maturity.

Grace as Renewed Creation

The biblical record, as well as doctrinal and theological
statements, attests to grace as that which makes of us "new
creatures" (Gal. 6:15; 2 Cor. 5:17). In John's gospel, the grace
of this newness is spoken of primarily in terms of "life". In the
Hebrew scriptures, Ezekiel offers us both the powerful image
of the heart of flesh replacing the heart of stone (36:26), and
the unforgettable image (made famous in the familiar Negro

spiritual) of dry bones taking on sinews and flesh and skin and the breath of life (37:1-14). Whether in a sudden or in a gradual way, the experience of being profoundly fulfilled or altered is the experience of grace. The term "profound" is not meant to imply only earth-shattering experiences. The profundity of grace can be experienced just as well in the simple sense of gratitude and praise evoked by the sight of the first shoot coming out of the ground each spring.

Grace affects who we are as persons; it alters our consciousness; it influences and supports certain attitudes and flows outward into the way we live, into the choices we make and the actions we undertake.

In a book to which we have referred often in these pages, *The Theology of Grace*, Cornelius Ernst employs the theme of novelty as a leitmotif. More traditional terms include transfiguration or transformation, and it is to this that we are all called. Paul expresses this central meaning of grace: "Lo, I tell you a mystery. We shall not all sleep, but we shall all be changed, in a moment, in the twinkling of an eye, at the last trumpet" (1 Cor. 15:51). And again: "And we all, with unveiled face, beholding the glory of the Lord, are being changed into his likeness from one degree of glory to another" (2 Cor 3:18).

Ernst speaks about the "genetic moment", the universal experience of the new as constituting the meaning and reality of human life. For believers, this experience receives a uniquely new sense in the resurrection of Jesus Christ. This transcendent novelty is disclosed in our lives as the gift of God in Jesus Christ—a primary element in our understanding of grace.[2] The genetic moment is described as

> ...a mystery. It is dawn, discovery, spring, new birth, coming to the light, awakening, transcendence, liberation, ecstasy, bridal consent, gift, forgiveness, reconciliation, revolution, faith, hope, love. It could be said that Christianity is the consecration of the genetic moment, the living centre from which it reviews the indefinitely various and shifting perspectives of human experience in history. That,

[2]p. 75.

at least, is or ought to be its claim: that it is the power to transform and renew all things. "Behold, I make all things new" (Apoc 21:5).[3]

It should not be difficult to reflect on our own experiences, both individual and communal, that fit into some of these descriptive categories.

Such reflections on new life as grace can serve as a catalyst to probe even further the experience and understanding of newness in our lives. Undoubtedly our memories of newness will be tied to specific experiences that will lend particular nuances to our ideas about grace. An important part of such an exercise is to allow ourselves to "cross over" into those experiences of newness in order to get in touch again with what it feels like to be born anew, to be dead and to be alive again.

A problem with past deductive theologies is that the method itself was prone to lead to a disconnection between theology and life. One doesn't read about new life and then apply it willy nilly to one's life. Rather one looks to the actual, true, authentic experiences of new life that one has had, and in the light of faith, recognizes and calls those events "grace." In this latter approach there is no doubt about what grace means, or about what it feels like. The experience of grace is the experience of the *success* of God's universal and unlimited desire for us to be fully human, fully alive.

Some concrete examples that come to mind include: the miracle of childbirth, the participation in the generation of a new human being out of love; the sober existence of a recovering alcoholic, who through the graces of courage, determination and with or without community support has come to know what it means to be dead and then alive again; the adolescent's exhilarating experience of first love in which one discovers the joy of being loved and accepted, of loving and accepting another person; the quiet lifting of spirit and the steady signal of hope that is felt at the first blush of spring—the first robin, the shoots of new life emerging from the ground and tree branches, the smell of the thawing earth; the aftermath

[3]Ibid. pp. 74-75.

of successful by-pass surgery or chemo-therapy that signals the continuation of life; the small but significant events of liberation of a people struggling for dignity and freedom from oppression; the sense of control and accomplishment written all over the face of a one-year-old after her first independent step; and at the end of life, the peace-filled anticipation of the fullfillment of humanity and freedom that is promised to all.

These are the kinds of events that we experience as grace. They give us a sense of what God wants for us, of what grace looks like and feels like in daily life. The journey of the spiritual life under grace is a journey that involves wanting, being open to, discovering, nurturing and celebrating new life—the new life of persons, of the earth, of the cosmos.

> Cease to dwell on days gone by
> and to brood over past history.
> Here and now I will do a new thing;
>   this moment it will break from the bud.
> Can you not perceive it? (Is 43:18-19)

Grace as Liberation

Some theologians place liberation at the very heart of a theology of grace, seeing it as the most all-embracing effect of grace.[4] This is appropriate for many reasons. One does not have to ponder the human condition long to see the centrality of the struggle for freedom. The Israelites experienced the power of God in the Exodus—their journey out of bondage to an alien people. The early Christian community experienced Jesus as savior—freeing them from sin and death. History is strewn with peoples and nations struggling for any number of freedoms—life, a place to live, a chance to grow and develop, to speak, to believe. Minorities and oppressed groups denied basic freedoms are the authorities to whom we must turn.

In our own time we are reminded of Martin Luther King's famous speech, "Free at last, free at last, thank God almighty,

---

[4]See Roger Haight, *The Experience and Language of Grace,* p. 154ff; Bernard Häring, *Sin in the Secular Age* (Garden City, NY: Doubleday, 1974), pp. 135-168.

free at last", and the struggles of Africans, American Indians, Chileans, Nicaraguans, and the efforts of the poor and of women to liberate themselves from poverty and discrimination. In some ways, freedom is a distinctive hallmark of the United States. Our nation began with a struggle for freedom and it has become something in which we take great pride and go to great lengths to protect. Although we are all too aware of the abuses of it, freedom is a primary category by which we understand ourselves in "the land of the free and the home of the brave." This reservoir of experience can be used to help us make the experience of grace concrete and real.

But it would be a mistake to consider freedom as exclusively or even primarily "from" constraint. Equally important is freedom "for". One goes hand-in-hand with the other. The dynamic power of grace hinges on our God-given ability to say 'yes' to the loving purpose of God or to withdraw into isolation. "Human freedom is liberated into love" by God's grace, or it "contracts into a private prison, a solitude where love can only be experienced as an alien compulsion, as wrath."[5] The freedom of which we speak does not refer primarily to the many choices put before us in a day's time. Rather, we speak of the ultimate horizon in which all free acts take place. Our choices are assessed in the context of our ultimate destiny. To what extent do I freely choose to co-operate in the plan of God for the final happiness and fulfill-ment of the world?

In his discussion of grace in the New Testament, Edward Schillebeeckx summarizes his conclusions under the heading, "Free from what and for what?"[6] Below is a schematic listing of these conclusions. It is offered as a broad framework and touchstone for further reflection.

Freedom for	*Freedom from*
freedom	sin
righteousness	guilt

---

[5]Cornelius Ernst, *The Theology of Grace*, p. 81.
[6]Edward Schillebeeckx, *Christ*, pp. 512-514.

peace with God/others
confidence in life
new creation
restoration of all things
joy
happiness
living
life in eternal glory
love
hope
sanctification
ethical commitment to
    the good
all that is true, noble, just,
    pure, attractive, deserving
    of love
to be generous and warm to
    each other
to overcome evil with good
to share goods
for healing and making whole
to be imitators of God
to walk in love as Christ
    loved us

existential anxieties
    fear of demons
    grip of fate
    death
    everyday cares/concerns
    sorrow
    despair/hopelessness
dissatisfaction with God/
    others
no freedom
oppressive/alienating ties
lovelessness
arbitrariness
egotism
exploitation of credibility
merciless condemnation of
    others
concern about reputation
trying to impress others
panic
absence of pleasure

No doubt you, the reader, can put flesh and blood on many of these examples and even add your own specific nuances. But one point that Schillebeeckx wants to make is that this liberation is *both* a gift and a task to be done. It is "already" and "not yet". We have spoken well to the "not yet". It is not difficult to embrace that aspect of faith that tells us that the fullness of history is outside of history and time. What we find more challenging, and what, in serious ways, we have neglected is the "already" dimension of grace. Unless we see the events of daily, earthly existence as loci of God's self-gift, it is impossible to understand those moments of newness and liberation as a foretaste—though none the less real—of the fullness of grace to come. The Christian *mythos* tells us that the eschaton is realized now as well as in the future.

One can reflect on one's life in order to get a glimpse of moments when liberation was truly experienced. It *is* possible to understand in small but real ways what it is like to live in the freedom of a graced existence. It is a tragedy when we don't recognize these moments of freedom or when we are unaware of the many unfreedoms in our lives—a situation that prevents us from recognizing our need for liberation.

However, the freedom we do know, however partial, is exhilarating and alluring. To experience this exhilaration is to desire more. This desire calls for a willingness both to continue to receive the graces of liberation and to do what is necessary to cooperate with and nurture this gift.

Grace as Mature Responsibility for Life

Contemporary psychology has helped us to become familiar with the various stages of human development and of the characteristics by which we identify human maturity.[7] One is reminded of the questions raised in the chapter on Augustine and Pelagius and the images they used in their theologies. Augustine portrays the person under grace as an infant at his mother's breast. Pelagius, on the other hand, presents the person under grace as a mature, responsible adult. The image of the infant suggests dependence, helplessness, the need to rely totally on those around us. In terms of grace, no one denies that in real ways we depend totally on God's beneficence. But if we want to move away from an either/or stance to one that is both/and, is it not possible and imperative that we retrieve that part of Pelagius' message that calls us to adulthood and maturity under grace? It is crucial to understand that placing emphasis on a mature, responsible faith need not undercut the total gratuity of God's gift. Rather, we must search for a way to understand grace as all God's doing *and* all our doing as well.

---

[7]To a large extent our ideas about human maturity have been based exclusively on male experience. On the specific topic of women's maturity, see Joann Wolski Conn, *Women's Spirituality* (New York: Paulist Press, 1986).

In his provocative and extremely helpful book, *In Man We Trust*, Walter Brueggemann calls attention to a neglected part of the biblical tradition—the part that affirms the world, celebrates culture and affirms human responsibility and capability.[8] That neglected source is the wisdom literature.[9] Brueggemann suggests that the major features of wisdom theology stand in direct contradiction to, and therefore challenge many of the central tenets preached in the church. He says,

> The wise in Israel characteristically appreciate life, love life, value it, and enjoy it. They appropriate the best learning, newest knowledge, and most ingenious cultural achievements.[10]

Brueggeman, who speaks out of a neoorthodox, evangelical tradition, addresses Protestantism, which he sees by and large as a culture-fearing, culture-negating tradition. I suggest, that while there are significant differences between Protestantism and Roman Catholicism, the latter is also seriously guilty of these charges. One can also point to the fact that the Protestant ethos has been the dominant one in the United States, influencing all religious groups in a variety of ways.

Brueggemann posits five characteristics of wisdom literature:

> 1. Wisdom believes that the goal and meaning of human existence is *life*.[11] The instructions of Proverbs are designed to provide guidance on how to create and maintain life in all its fullness.

---

[8]Walter Brueggemann, *In Man We Trust*, (Atlanta: John Knox Press, 1972), p. 7. I will be relying frequently throughout this section on the insights of Dr. Brueggemann.

[9]Literature that deals with the quest for the meaning of life is often called "wisdom literature." Wisdom writings date back as far as the Egyptian Pyramid Age (c. 2600-2175 B.C.). In the post-exilic period, influenced by the wisdom literature of her neighbors, the Israelites composed most of her wisdom literature. The wisdom books in the Hebrew Scriptures include Proverbs, Ecclesiastes, The Song of Songs, Job, Ecclesiasticus, the Wisdom of Solomon, and parts of the Psalms.

[10]Ibid. p. 14.

[11]Roland Murphy, "The Kerygma of the Book of Proverbs," *Interpretation*, XX (January 1966), pp. 3-14.

2. Wisdom affirms that the *authority* for life is to be discerned in the common experience of humanity. What is right and good is not identified by some office or person, or institution, but only by patient, careful discernment of what we ought to be doing to be *us*.

3. Wisdom affirms that persons have primary responsibility for their destiny. The choices one makes and the fidelities one honors have an effect on destiny. Persons are capable of choosing wisely and deciding responsibly. Wisdom sees human beings in their strength; in their courage to function responsibly.

4. Wisdom believes that persons are meant for an orderly role in an orderly cosmos. Our rightful destiny is to discern that order and find our responsible share in it.

5. Wisdom is the celebration of the human person as lord of creation. Human capabilities and responsibilities are related to the natural and social environment. Creation is viewed as a good place to live, intended by God to be enjoyed [and in our day protected]. Wisdom's teachers reflected on the splendor, order, beauty, and goodness of creation.[12]

Brueggemann suggests that scripture has been interpreted primarily around the traditional theme of redemption which stresses the gracious, powerful role of God, the despair and helplessness of the human person, takes a dim view of the world and rejects cultural achievements.[13] The danger in such a view of the human person is that it tends to view humans as incompetent, ill-equipped, and lacking in confidence for the decisions and actions required by their power and knowledge.[14] While no one would deny that the scriptures present the human person before God as totally dependent on God's power, this is not their only viewpoint.

---

[12]Brueggemann, *In Man We Trust,* pp. 14-25.

[13]Matthew Fox makes the same point from the perspective of spirituality in *Original Blessing* (Santa Fe, NM: Bear & Co., 1983).

[14]Ibid., p. 25.

The wisdom tradition is often considered within the context of a theology of creation. In this theology of creation, according to Brueggemann, several things become clear. First, the human person is seen as a trusted, valued creature in God's assessment, and therefore to be trusted and valued by us. The goal and meaning of human existence is healthy human community which God values and for which God has ordered the cosmos. This view rejects the notion that the goal of life is extrinsic to the process and to be found in another world. Wisdom values human enterprise and eschews grace as an escape from the exigencies, joys and sorrows of earthly life.[15]

Second, wisdom escapes the trap of making special claims for the faith community *at the expense* of the human community. The temptation to imperialism is overcome in the stance that the fullness of new life is available to all who choose to cooperate with the call of God. Salvation is not the hegemony of any one group of people.[16] In this respect wisdom can open our eyes to the boundless presence of God's grace in the world. We begin to remove the blinders that limit us to recognizing grace only in church, or in prayers, or in ministers. Once again, it becomes possible to be surprised by grace—or surprised by joy, as the title of a famous book by C.S. Lewis has it. Our desires to be on the lookout for the Word of God in the world, become enkindled anew and we discover God in unexpected times and places.

To sum up, then, one can say that the goals of wisdom are intimately connected with the goals for human community—goals with which we are already familiar because we live as members of that community. The goals of faith, the goals of grace can never stand in contradiction to the goals of people for responsible human community. Loving ourselves and loving others means affirming, celebrating, enhancing our human existence as well as critiquing it. We need to call each other, in grace, to mature adulthood. Wisdom undermines both childish dependence on external authority and adolescent

[15]Ibid., p. 26.
[16]Ibid., p. 27.

rebellion against it. The grace of wisdom is the grace to respond to God's call to the fullness of humanity; to thoughtful, responsible decision and action; to be courageous and risk living in the freedom God's grace holds out to us. In significant ways, we *do know* what is good for humanity and for the cosmos. Will we commit ourselves to the grace empowering us to bring it about?

Likewise, in these pages, we have attempted to speak about grace in a way that upholds both the graciousness of God *and* the goodness and capabilities of persons and the world. This theology of grace takes into account a wider spectrum of human experience. It allows us to speak about grace both when we feel helpless and totally in need of God *and* when we feel alive, competent and fully cooperative with God's grace. Finally, this theology of grace does not set these human experiences over against one another. They do not cancel each other out, but rather reflect the great range of human dispositions experienced in our relationships with God, with each other and with the cosmos. God is not partial to one aspect of human existence, but is potentially present in all of them— even indirectly in sin out of which good is called forth and over which grace prevails.

This leads us to the topic of sin. We look at the ways in which sin is discussed today; examine some common images of sin; and explore sin and grace in more detail from a feminist perspective—a pressing issue for our time.

The Discussion of Sin Today

From one perspective, one can legitimately complain that theologies of grace in the past have been entirely too focussed on sin. These theologies take sin as their starting point, see sin as the sole reason for grace, and view the human person almost exclusively in terms of depravity, with little acknowledgment of the goodness of a creation made in God's image. Yet from another perspective, one can also legitimately complain about how little we talk about sin today, how rarely public figures own up to wrongdoing and how unrepentant we all seem to be. Why do both of these perspectives seem to be simultaneously true?

Though not always overtly stated, the tradition has been consistent in its acknowledgment that one manifestation of grace is our mature willingness to own our sin, reflect on it, repent, and be resolved to sin no more. It is imperative to deal honestly with sin in order to stand in the truth of who we are, to open ourselves to God's merciful love, and to come to an even fuller appreciation of the totality of our existence. The failure to deal with sin results in the commonplaces of history: we live in illusion, shut up within ourselves; we are prevented from experiencing the fullness of life; and finally, sin denied is then projected onto others who are then persecuted. How can we talk about sin (in the context of a theology of grace) in a way that does justice to both the gravity and pervasiveness of sin and also to the glorious capabilities of humanity?

In 1973, Karl Menninger, the well-known psychiatrist, called attention to the lack of discussion about sin in the wider social community in his book, *Whatever Became of Sin?*[17] In his practice, he saw firsthand the wages on the human psyche of *not* dealing with this important reality, and called the churches to task for the failure to make use of the positive resources of the Judeo-Christian tradition to address the issue of sin. Two of the reasons for this lack are: 1) We understand sin, in the context of a self-centered insecurity about ourselves, as something that is threatening, that drags us down and belittles us in our own eyes. To the extent that we see sin in this light, we are absolutely correct in not wanting to focus on it. 2) We have trivialized sin. In an age in which we struggle with the possibility of a nuclear war, a failing economy, world famine, war, imprisonment and torture all over the globe, we too often see sin as not keeping the house straightened up, or not going to church on Sunday, or expressing legitimate anger! Again we are correct in avoiding talk about this kind of sin, which can only be boring to God and to ourselves. The reality of sin belongs to the same *genre* as the reality of love, since sin is the

---

[17]Karl Menninger, *Whatever Became of Sin?* (New York: Hawthorn Books, 1973).

failure of love. Sin is huge, profound, and significant. It is a refusal of love and life, a refusal to become the person God intended us to become.

Some Images of Sin

According to the biblical account, Jesus came to save sinners. The first epistle of John, with its imagery of light and darkness is perhaps the most penetrating treatment of sin in the New Testament.

> If we say we have fellowship with him while we walk in darkness, we lie and do not live according to the truth; but if we walk in the light, as he is in the light, we have fellowship with one another, and the blood of Jesus his Son cleanses us from all sin. If we say we have no sin, we deceive ourselves, and the truth is not in us (1 John 1:6-8).

Consequently, forgiveness is a foundational category for grace. Images of a new creation emerging from the old; of light overcoming the darkness; of life overcoming death are traditional ways to talk about conversion. For some the change is abrupt; for others the growth process is gradual and steady. But we must remember that forgiveness for sin is not an exhaustive category for grace. Throughout this study, we have pointed to the need to broaden our understanding of grace to include a more complete range of human experience. Reflection on one's experience of the particular grace of conversion can also lead one to recognize the many other ways in which God's gracious actions touch our lives.

One can talk about sin as death, and identify those things that drain us of energy and life. Sin can also be seen as refusal—saying no to love, to life's blessings and pleasures, or no to being in relationship with God and other persons. Won't we be surprised when, at the gate of heaven, we are held accountable for all the pleasures of life we refused to enjoy? Sin is the choice to exist in isolated self-sufficiency. In the theology of grace presented here, certain forms of sin emerge as especially problematic. These include the choice to remain a child, refusing to become a responsible adult, or to develop one's gifts fully. Thus irresponsible is the choice to limit oneself falsely, to think that the call to holiness, to heroic love, to a contemplative lifestyle is for *other* people. In these situations, one chooses to be safe, to be a pawn, subject to God's whim, rather than owning the role of being a responsible co-creator with God. Another serious sin would be an attitude that takes creation for granted and ends up abusing creation—in the many forms that may take.

Sin is also the choice to live in illusion, to avoid the truth of existence, of gifts, of one's dark side. If grace is understood as that which is the truly *real*, then the choice to live in illusion is a direct refusal of grace. Many persons also experience sin as being trapped, tempted to despair, being held captive. Others speak of sin primarily in terms of fear—fear of self, of others, of taking risks, of speaking out. Such sin is the refusal to trust that God is good and that we are good because loved by God. This results in a life of excessive control, of hanging on, of clinging to self, to others, of grasping for love or life or material things. Sin is giving in to self-hate and to the insecurity that results in a life whose main focus is self-protection at the expense of others. Finally, sin is visible in the cold heart that supports a life of indifference, of apathy, a life devoid of passion and gratitude. One can live life as though life "owed" us—or one can live life in an awareness of the utter giftedness of life itself in its every detail. This latter life is a life of grace, characterized by thanks and praise.

In psychological terms, sin can be described as being on an "ego trip". This means that in any number of blatant and subtle ways, one becomes the center of one's own existence, preoccupied with self in ways that prohibit love of others. When egoism becomes one's primary disposition, discovery of sin feels like being caught, laid bare, shamed. The primary dynamic in this scenario is that one falls short of one's image of oneself. The fruit of this realization is embarrassment, destructive guilt, the sense of being "found out." One's life is drained of energy and filled with despair.

One can also examine the experience of sin in a life that has love, not ego, as its center. In this scenario, sin is understood in the context of the beloved. One is acutely aware of the unconditional love of God and of the honest love of other persons. Sin, then, is viewed as a terrible betrayal of that love. The response is not debilitating guilt, but heartfelt sorrow, followed by repentance and request for forgiveness. Since our God is one whose forgiveness will be extended to "seventy times seven", one is invited to trust that forgiveness will indeed be extended. The fruit of this interaction is a new kind of love—a love that is radically different because it perdures beyond any possible transgression. This love brings in its wake energy, a new enthusiasm for life and for the good, a simple confidence that emerges from the knowledge that one is so loved by God. It is this unbounded love *in spite of any sin* that is at the heart of grace.[18]

Sin as Idolatry

We have spoken at length about the importance of viewing grace in its social-historical context and from the vantage point of experience. The same principle applies to any discussion about sin. Experience and historical realities are key elements in any theology. The women's movement has brought to light specific problems that have developed because of the limited experience upon which our theology is based. Today we are more aware than ever of the sin of excluding the experience of any group in our theological deliberations. We have also become sensitive to the sin of idolatry when we universalize and absolutize the experience of only one segment of the faith community. In order to understand the dynamics of these important discoveries, I have chosen to analyze in more detail the specific case of sin and grace, seen in light of the feminist critique.

Recent research has led us to a new awareness of the ways in which we have been almost exclusively dependent on male experience for our religious categories, and the ways in which

---

[18]A provocative treatment of this theme may be found in *Between Noon and Three: A Parable of Romance, Law, and the Outrage of Grace* by Robert Farrar Capon, (San Francisco: Harper & Row, 1982).

we have universalized these categories. In her ground-breaking book, *Sex, Sin and Grace*,[19] Judith Plaskow critiques the theologies of Reinhold Niebuhr and Paul Tillich in the light ot women's experience. She is building on an essay written fifteen years earlier in 1960, in which Valerie Saiving[20] established and lamented the fact that the meaning of the world and of human experience had been determined almost exclusively from a male perspective. Our values, appropriate behavior, cultural expressions, communication—had been sifted through the male vision (no problem with this in itself), but had then become normative for the entire society.

This realization mandates the re-consideration of experience that includes women's experience. This poses serious problems, since in many cases, the habit of seeing things through a male perspective is so ingrained that women are not able to get in touch with what they really feel or experience. To a great extent, women interiorize the male perspective too well. So begins the long process of recovering women's experience.

A recent, familiar example of this problem is the discussion on Lawrence Kohlberg's theory on the stages of moral development[21] and Carol Gilligan's response in her book, *In A Different Voice*.[22] The effect of universalizing the stages of male moral development is to present women as morally inferior, unable to attain the highest stages of moral maturity. In his books on moral theology,[23] Dan Maguire has done much to reverse this view. He even argues that the more sophisticated development of feeling in women makes women especially sensitive and open to making good moral choices.

A similar problem occurs in our understanding of sin. As a result of the pioneering work of women theologians, we under-

[19]Judith Plaskow, *Sex, Sin and Grace* (Washington, D.C.: University Press of America, 1980).

[20]Valerie Saiving, "The Human Situation: A Feminine View", *Journal of Religion* (April, 1960).

[21]Lawrence Kohlberg, *Stages of Moral Development* (San Francisco: Harper & Row, 1984).

[22]Carol Gilligan, *In A Different Voice* (Cambridge, MA: Harvard University Press, (1982). See also Joann Wolski Conn, *Spirituality and Personal Maturity*, (New York: Paulist Press, 1989).

[23]Daniel Maguire, *The Moral Choice* (New York: Doubleday, 1978), pp. 281-308.

stand that the meaning of sin that has been presented by the churches is primarily a male experience. An example: Pride has always been at the head of the list of sins. It is not hard to figure out that pride is a universal human experience. What we are now beginning to realize, however, is that pride takes on quite different forms depending on culture, age or sex. The egotistical, will-to-power, aggressive, self-promoting expressions of pride are not the ways in which most women experience pride.

The results of this situation are several and all unhelpful for women: 1) Because women do not see themselves (and are not seen by men) in the image of sin presented, it looks as though women are less sinful than men. 2) The corresponding virtue to the sin of pride is humility—a virtue that along with charity has held center stage in the Christian tradition. (At times, one despairs of a wide-spread, accurate understanding of the virtue of humility—which is owning the truth of the totality of one's situation.) Because women are not seen as prideful and self-aggrandizing, they are seen as paragons of humility in the false sense—downcast, self-effacing, unworthy, etc. Therefore, the churches not only fail to identify the nature of women's sin, but they actually turn that sin into a virtue.

To confuse the matter further, another strain in the religious tradition (and in the larger society) sees women as the weaker sex, as prone to evil, as the sinner, the temptress (Eve), the harlot (Gomer), emotionally volatile, and incapable of extra-ordinary virtue or religious experience *by nature*. The ratio of male to female saints is one concrete example of this perception. In either case, whether they are put on a pedestal or in the gutter, women are denied a place as equal, free participants in the drama of redemption.

Women redress this situation by paying attention to their own individual experience in order to discover true patterns of sin and grace. Others speak about sin in more general categories, like the ones discussed above, and then examine the specific ways in which these appear in their experience.

Because of the cultural and ecclesial biases pointed to above, women have to work hard to discover the truth of sin and grace in their lives. They have to want to know the truth about themselves; be willing to view themselves honestly; be willing

to confront the false and destructive ways in which grace and
sin have been understood in the past—ways that are simply
not true for them.

There are many resources that women can tap for assistance
in this process. But the important point is to know and trust
one's own experience. Ultimately it is up to each person to
probe the truth of sin and grace in one's life. Julian of Norwich
is a model. While our experience may be different from hers,
we would do well to imitate the ways in which she trusted her
experience of sin and grace, which went against the traditional,
inherited way of understanding these realities.

From a cultural perspective, grace for women today might
take on the positive dimensions of Pelagianism. Grace would
be experienced as self-confidence; as a deep appreciation for
and celebration of bodiliness; as courage, healthy autonomy,
ownership and use of legitimate power, risk-taking, speaking
one's mind, holy impatience (and holy patience!), holy selfishness, taking responsibility for self and world, giving up messiah
complexes, relinquishing fear or owning it without shame,
refusing to refuse to become a self (a prerequisite for laying
oneself down in love for another).

Concretely, I think of grace visible in the many examples of
women who are organizing and speaking out on any number
of intolerable, evil situations, risking their lives in the process.
Women against drunk drivers; women who have said Enough!
to the drug related violence and loss of life of young people in
our cities; women for peace in Ireland; women protesting the
oppressions in South and Central America and on the West
Bank. Women also point to the grace-filled women in their
own lives who have influenced them for the good, who have
given them courage and a sense of themselves as women of
grace.

Conclusion

This excursus into a feminist understanding of sin and grace
is meant to heighten awareness of the importance of paying
attention to the truth of experience, so that all men and women
may know and trust in the truth of living in the light of God's

grace. Any theology of grace must emerge from the actual, authentic ways in which persons find the presence of God in their lives. As the circle of discourse broadens to include persons of color, women, children, the elderly, persons from other religions, we can be assured that the multiplicity of voices will enhance the celebration of the height, depth, length and breadth of God's glory, God's unbounded graciousness to every creature.

15

In the Company of
the Cosmos

One could argue that this chapter should have preceded the previous chapter on the individual. Such arguments that place community as the primordial human reality are cogent. The term "I" is already qualified by the society in which one lives. The act of conception is a communal experience, and we spend the first nine months of our existence in an incredibly intimate, symbiotic relationship in the womb. The "I" that slowly comes forth into consciousness is the result of constant interraction with others within family and then beyond it. But by placing this chapter here, *after* the chapter on the individual, we are making a statement in cumulative, progressive terms, about the locus of the fullest expression of grace, namely in community. The perfection of grace is not experienced in one's individuality, but in one's associations with others.

In a recent book, *Community and Disunity: Symbols of Grace and Sin,*[1] Jerome Theisen chooses community as the primary symbol of graced reality. He says,

> The divine favor that we call grace is ultimately directed to the formation of a community: a community of people on this earth, a community of believers in Jesus Christ, a community of the dead and newly alive in the presence of the loving God. Community is the ultimate favor of God.

[1]Jerome P. Theisen, O.S.B. *Community and Disunity: Symbols of Grace and Sin* (Collegeville, MN: St. John's University Press, 1985).

Theologically the word community functions as a verbal symbol of the goal of all divine giving and human striving.[2]

It is obvious that the number and kinds of community are legion. But it is possible to speak about grace in communal terms in a way that both encompasses the totality and yet remains true to the all important differences and the specificity of the various communities to which we belong.

The horizon within which this discussion takes place is cosmic in scope. My thesis is that the *primary* community of grace is the cosmos. All other expressions of community must be viewed and understood within this wider horizon. Past viewpoints that saw the faith community as the exclusive locus of God's activity must be left behind. The faith community is crucial inasmuch as it is the place where God's universal generosity is explicitly named and celebrated. But we must not confuse this reality with God's all-embracing presence and activity in our graced world. Gregory Baum puts it well:

> While God's universal will to save and the universality of sufficient grace were acknowledged in all theological treatises, these themes never entered into the center of theological reflection, and so never modified the Christian approach to the world or became an essential part of the church's preaching. In general, the teaching of the Church as well as her legislation and practice gave expression to the sharp division between the Church as the fellowship of grace and the world as the place of God's absence.[3]

As we have seen in the preceding chapter, Walter Brueggemann's recent interpretation of the wisdom literature as a biblical source that celebrates the achievements of culture is a giant step in the direction suggested by Baum. Because we have not always taken the proper care to distinguish between "the world" and "sin", we have often found ourselves, as

---

[2]Ibid., p. x.

[3]Gregory Baum, *Man Becoming: God in Secular Language,* (New York: Herder & Herder, 1970) p. 25.

Christians, with a "we-they" mentality, i.e., we see ourselves as believers with a corner on the market of grace and *over against* the world.

The first order of business in a graced existence is to see ourselves as a faith community that is deeply at one with, and involved in, the wider world community. It is only from *inside* this wider community that we, as believers, will be able truly to see the fullness of the God-given gracefulness of the universe. This new vision will include the awareness that God's grace is not limited to the faith community, but that in fact, it is everywhere around us in places like scientists' laboratories and union halls; at dining room tables and in school rooms; in hospital rooms and hospices; and in ecological and feminist movements, many of which are not motivated by an explicit belief in God.

It is only from *inside* this wider community that one can legitimately raise a critical voice, point to sin, and call to renewal of life. On the inside, one realizes that sin is not "out there" but within every person and in the many communities to which we belong. Rosemary Haughton addresses this issue in terms of God's judgment. She says:

> The Church itself can only be the community of the Spirit by knowing that it is the community of the world, and continuing to work, as worldly, under judgment.[4]

The Christian community which is and has to be worldly, knows itself under judgment and is therefore repentant and reconciled. By undergoing this act of God's judgment, the community exists as a spiritual community that in turn, enables it not only to *be* God's judgment, but also to *utter* God's judgment on the world, which includes its own worldly building. As soon as the church regards its task as *not* subject to judgment, it is guilty of blasphemy by rejecting God's judgments and condemning itself.[5]

---

[4]Rosemary Haughton, *The Theology of Experience* (New York: Newman Press, 1972), p. 56.

[5]Ibid., pp. 56-59.

Similarly, Jesus was free to criticize the Jewish community so harshly, because he was a Jew. He was speaking from inside that community, motivated by love and a profound desire for its well-being. He took for himself no privileged place in terms of an exclusive hold on God's graciousness.

Being awake to the infinite number of expressions of the grace of community will depend on awareness and on one's structures of meaning.[6] One might call this awareness "sacramental", i.e., the persons and events of daily life take on a surplus of meaning. With this awareness, one chooses to see God operative within the structures of everyday living. Nothing, *a priori*, can be excluded as a sacrament of God. We are free to see God's grace showered upon us in every moment of our day—or not at all.

In addition, a renewed sense of the sacramentality of everyday life can only enhance our participation in, and understanding of, the narrower sense of sacrament—the seven specific sacraments of the church. In the sacraments, the community acknowledges and celebrates in word, song and ritual, the never-ending graciousness of God in the world. In the past we have not fully understood the reciprocal flow between world and sacrament. Too often, we saw grace as a one-way street flowing from sacrament to the world. Today we are called to a broader awareness of the meaning of sacrament. Karl Rahner proposes what he calls a "Copernican revolution in Catholic thinking about sacraments". He says, "Instead of seeing in them a spiritual movement outward from the sacramental action to an effect in the world, we should look for a spiritual movement of the world toward the sacrament."[7] Our eyes need to be trained to focus on the graced nature of the world, from which the formal sacraments gain their true meaning.

---

[6]The reader may want to refer to Part I, Chapter 2 above to review what was said there about structures of meaning.

[7]Karl Rahner, "How to Receive a Sacrament and Mean It", *Theology Digest* 19 (Autumn, 1971): 227-234.

Our discussion of grace in a community context will treat: (1) the community of God; (2) the community of the universe; (3) the community of humankind; (4) sin against community; (5) contemplation as an expression of community.

1. The Community of God

Paul concludes his second letter to the Corinthians with the following wish: "The grace of the Lord Jesus Christ and the love of God and the fellowship of the Holy Spirit be with you all" (2 Cor. 13:14). Adumbrated in the Scriptures and later expressed in more precise terminology, the trinity has been a central doctrine of the Christian tradition. As we have seen, the Hebrew Scriptures present God in deeply personal terms. God is the one who is all tied up in the affairs of Israel. This personal dimension of God has been a constant motif throughout Judeo-Christian history. It is not our purpose here to summarize the history and recent developments of this doctrine, but rather to speak of God as community in terms of a paradigmatic model of grace.[8]

In some cases, traditional trinitarian theology, building on a Neo-platonic notion of being, portrayed God in static terms. God was the almighty, absolute, unchanging, unmoved mover. Today this viewpoint is being challenged, in part because it clashes with what we know to be the truth of our own relational experience. Being with and for others is anything but static. It is hard to imagine that God would have created intelligent creatures in a way that was significantly different, or even contrary to Godself. Indeed, the Christian myth has long held that creatures are made in God's image and likeness.

A second argument for this change in our theology of God is the role of Jesus in the Godhead. Jesus of Nazareth is the epitome of loving communal awareness and action. Isn't it

---

[8]Contributions to this recent discussion include: Eberhard Jungel, *The Doctrine of the Trinity: God's Being Is in Becoming* (Grand Rapids, MI: Eerdmans, 1976); Jurgen Moltmann, *The Crucified God* (New York: Harper & Row, 1974); Daniel Day Williams, *The Spirit and Forms of Love* (New York: Harper & Row 1968); Heribert Mühlen, *Der heilige Geist als Person,* 2nd ed. (Munster, 1966); Juan Luis Segundo, *Our Idea of God* (Maryknoll, NY: Orbis Press, 1974); Joseph Bracken, *What Are They Saying About the Trinity?* (New York: Paulist Press, 1979).

natural to include the life, suffering, death and resurrection of Christ in our understanding of the inner life of the triune God? In this case, God would take up into God's self the totality of the loving compassion and suffering experienced by Jesus. God, then, is no longer a cold, distant Being, but rather one who is deeply affected by creation, by the experience of Jesus on the cross, and by our own suffering and joys.

One of the hallmarks of trinitarian theology has been the role of the Spirit as the nexus of love, binding together the first and second persons. The Spirit is the personification of self-giving love. In addition to the love among the persons of the trinity, the tradition speaks of the love that goes forth from them to the world. Experience teaches that a true and intense love naturally overflows from the lovers to others—the love is "diffusive of itself".[9] The Spirit is seen as the distinctive connection between the life-giving love of the trinity and our own empowerment to love. The Spirit is the channel through which we receive the love of God poured forth in our hearts (Rom. 5:5).

One of the most successful portrayals of the dynamic and loving relationships in the trinity is the *Showings* of Julian of Norwich.[10] In Part II, we examined Julian's theology of grace. Perhaps even more distinctive is her theology of the trinity, based on her personal experience of God in her sixteen visions. She presents the love of the trinitarian persons for each other in such compelling and graphic terms that the reader is spontaneously drawn into the divine circle.

> And so Christ is our way, safely leading us in his laws, and Christ in his body mightily bears us up into heaven; for I saw that Christ, having us all in him who shall be saved by him, honourably presents his Father in heaven with us, which present his Father most thankfully receives, and courteously gives to his Son Jesus Christ.

---

[9] The expression that love is "diffusive of itself" can be traced to an influential, anonymous Syrian monk writing about 500. He is known as the Pseudo-Dionysius and his most well known treatise is entitled *The Mystical Theology.*

[10] Thomas Aquinas is also an excellent source.

> This gift and operation is joy to the Father and bliss to the
> Son and delight to the Holy Spirit, and of everything which
> is our duty, it is the greatest delight to our Lord that we
> rejoice in this joy which the blessed Trinity has over our
> salvation.[11]

Julian presents the love of God as real, powerful and overwhelmingly attractive. One has the feeling that even if it were
not possible to move within the ambit of this love, it would be
worth a lifetime simply to be near it, to see it, to enjoy it
vicariously.

Julian knows the official doctrine of the trinity, but her
experience of the dynamism of God compels her to focus on
the communitarian rather than on the unifying aspects of
God. The persons are constantly taking joy and delight in each
other and in humans. For Julian, humans live eternally within
the community of the trinity and the trinity of persons lives
deeply within the human community. The attracting force of
this trinitarian love draws others into it. Julian is shown a
vision of Mary standing at the foot of the cross. Jesus speaks:

> I know well that you wish to see my blessed mother, for
> after myself she is the greatest joy that I could show you,
> and the greatest delight and honour to me. . . . " And be-
> cause of the wonderful, exalted and singular love that he
> has for this sweet maiden, his blessed mother, our Lady St.
> Mary, he reveals her bliss and joy through the sense of these
> sweet words, as if he said, "do you wish to see how I love
> her, so that you could rejoice with me in the love which I
> have in her and she has in me?[12]

If we accept Julian's experience, it is not hard to imagine a
God who wants to reveal how deeply the persons of the trinity
love and rejoice in each other and how much they desire that
we be included in that community.

If what holds true for God holds true for all aspects of the

---

[11]*Showings,* ch. 55.
[12]Ibid., ch. 25.

universe, we find ourselves called to model our own lives of grace on the example of the trinitarian community. But the trinitarian joy portrayed by Julian is no stranger to the cross. On the contrary, the cross of Jesus is caught up into the very life and relationships of the trinity. Daniel Day Williams points out that suffering is a crucial element in all relationships. "The deepest discovery in love is that the other suffers for us, and we discover that we love when we suffer for and with each other."[13] In a dynamic view of the trinity, the persons are continually becoming ever more united to one another, providing the unending source of grace that, if we cooperate, allows us to grow ever more united with one another and with the world. The loving dynamism, care, compassion, self-giving, inclusivity, willingness to suffer, and mutual rejoicing of the three divine persons present a clear and compelling model to emulate, nudging us away from any kind of individualistic self-sufficiency. This trinitarian love is the substance and source of every form of grace.

2. The Community of the Cosmos

The trinity, composed of distinct entities bound together in mutual respect, harmony and love, is reflected in the cosmos. The graced love of God expresses itself in the myriad forms of creation. Certain aspects of the natural world have long been a source for our connection with, and imaging of, a gracious God. One can recall experiences in which one felt close to God and had an inkling of what God must be like—blazing sunsets, the composition of the petals on a rose, snow-capped peaks, roaring oceans or a blooming desert. Nature is a major influence on our image of God. One can also imagine how one's idea of God would be altered by a world of polluted air, dying vegetation and poisoned water. "If the water is polluted it can neither be drunk nor used for baptism, for it no longer bears the symbolism of life but of death."[14] We cannot speak about grace without considering the natural world in which we live.

[13]Daniel Day Williams, *The Spirit and the Forms of Love* (New York: Harper & Row, 1968), p. 183. Cited in Joseph Bracken, *What Are They Saying About the Trinity?* (New York: Paulist Press, 1979), p. 39.

[14]Thomas Berry, "Economics as a Religious Issue," privately distributed paper, p. 12.

Some may object to proposing the universe as our primary community. The utter hugeness of it can be paralyzing. But the experience of many persons today truly reflects a cosmic awareness. Landing on the moon, the continued growth of scientific knowledge about the world, fears about the destruction of the ozone layer and the rain forests, and about the growing number of extinct species—all this is part of contemporary experience. A second reason for speaking from a cosmic perspective is grounded in the very nature of grace. Grace is not something which can be analyzed, but rather grace is a way of qualifying the totality of God's gifts to us. A theology of grace, then, could potentially include anything and everything that is viewed in the light of God. Therefore, it is fitting that believers think about the entire cosmos in terms of the gracious God who created it.[15]

In a paper entitled "Economics as A Religious Issue," Thomas Berry cites religion among the forces that have contributed to our lack of sensitivity to the graced and gifted nature of the world and, in turn, to our abuse of that world. He posits that certain religious attitudes have been instrumental in forming the ways in which we regard the natural world, i.e., as a resource for human utility rather than as a functioning community of mutually supporting life systems within which humans must discover their proper role.[16]

Berry cites four religious attitudes that have contributed to the problem. The first is the biblical commitment to a transcendent personal monotheistic concept of deity that severely

[15]Selected resources include: All writings by Thomas Berry; Claude Y. Stewart, Jr., *Nature in Grace: A Study in the Theology of Nature* (Macon, GA: Mercer University Press, 1983); Ian Barbour, ed. *Earth Might Be Fair: Reflections on Ethics, Religion and Ecology* (Englewood Cliffs, NJ: Prentice-Hall, 1972); John B. Bennett, "Nature—God's Body?" *Philosophy Today* 18 (Fall 1974): 248-254; John Cobb, *God and the World* (Philadelphia: Westminster Press, 1969); Joseph A. Sittler, Jr. *Essays on Nature and Grace* (Philadelphia: Fortress Press, 1972; Brian Swimme, *The Universe Is A Green Dragon: A Cosmic Creation Story* (Santa Fe, NM: Bear & Co. 1984); John Updike, *Facing Nature*, ed. Judith Jores (New York: Knopf, 1985); Rachel Carson, *Silent Spring* (New York: Houghton Mifflin; 1962); Wendell Berry, *The Unsettling of America Culture and Agriculture* (San Francisco: Sierra 1986); Annie Dillard, *Pilgrim at Tinker Creek* (San Francisco: Harper & Row, 1985).

[16]Berry, "*Economics,*" p. 10.

prohibits any worship of divinity resident in nature. In order to distinguish themselves and their God from surrounding religious cultures, Israel despiritualized or desacralized the natural world to some extent. Second, the redemption experience became the dominant mode of Christian consciousness—especially during the Middle Ages—eclipsing attention to creation. Nature was gradually pushed off the screen of Christian awareness. The third position (discussed at some length above) involves the Christian emphasis on the spiritual nature of the human over against the physical nature of other creatures. Perfection or a life of grace was seen in terms of detachment from the phenomenal world. In this view, the natural world becomes primarily an object to be dominated or from which to flee. It is not seen as an integral subjectivity constituting with the human a single earth community within the larger cosmic community. Fourth, Berry cites the heavy emphasis on a millennial expectation beyond the human condition as a factor in Christian disinterest in the natural, material world.[17] Thankfully, a significant minority of the population has become aware of the effects of our destructive practices and is working with great dedication to save the earth. Such persons are a gift of grace to the cosmos and reflect in their actions the caring love of God that we call grace. We are challenged, as part of our life of grace, to join in their efforts.

How are we to recover this broader, cosmic experience of grace? A first step involves awareness and attitudes. It is possible to begin to see ourselves, not in terms of an exclusive anthropomorphism, but rather as one aspect of the larger cosmic reality. Humans are the self-conscious, reflective part of creation. As loving, thinking beings, humans are able to *know* that creation is a gift from God and to be the ones who offer creation back to God in thanks and praise and glory. We have an important, vital function in the universe, but it is not the only one. All animate and inanimate things have their own important, vital functions which need to be respected and protected. We can choose to see the universe as numinous in its deepest center, as well as revelatory of God. It is imperative

---

[17]Ibid., pp. 14-15.

that we recover a sense of awe and reverence for the natural universe.

A second remedy is to reappropriate traditions that reverence nature. Francis of Assisi and Thomas Aquinas, and more recently Teilhard de Chardin come to mind.[18] Everyone is familiar with Francis' attitude toward nature, immortalized in his "Canticle to the Sun" and in innumerable subsequent expressions—film, poetry, stories and garden alabaster statues. In his simplicity and reverence, he saw the smallest creature as peer, as brother or sister. For Francis, even a blade of grass was capable of being charged with the grandeur of God.

In a quite different way, Thomas Aquinas, building on key elements of Aristotelian philosophy, goes to great lengths to affirm the integrity and intrinsic goodness of the natural world. While he would not deny that the natural world reflected the goodness of God, he also wanted to preserve and uphold the intrinsic goodness of things in themselves. The best thing a tree could do to give glory to God was to be a tree—to fulfill the destiny intrinsic to its nature. In Thomas' system, one is invited to look at a tree as a tree and not to rush too quickly to seeing God in the tree.

A second contribution of Thomas to the appreciation of nature as grace was his sensitivity to the value of the infinite variety of the created universe. In Greek philosophy, multiplicity was regarded as an unwelcome detraction from unity. Oneness was the primary image of God and the goal of existence. In contrast, in his discussion about the distinctions in creation, Thomas attributes the differences to God rather than seeing them as destructive of unity. He says:

> For He brought things into being in order that His goodness might be communicated to creatures, and be represented by them; and because His goodness could not be adequately represented by one creature alone, He produced many and diverse creatures, that what was wanting to one in the

---

[18]Beyond the western Christian tradition, one can look to the American Indian and Chinese cultures which continue to nurture reverence toward nature and include nature as a central aspect of their religious consciousness.

representation of the divine goodness might be supplied by another. For goodness, which in God is simple and uniform, in creatures is manifold and divided; and hence the whole universe together participates in the divine goodness more perfectly, and represents it better than any single creature whatever.[19]

Thomas reminds us that grace or the fullness of God is not found primarily in singular, individual entities, but rather in the vast multiplicity of community. The grace of God is eminently reflected in the mutual interaction, respect and love of *all* reality. He invites us to look for grace everywhere and to grow in our appreciation of its infinite variety.

If the physical cosmos is to become a primary locus of grace, it must become for us a spiritual as well as a physical reality. Teilhard de Chardin was a strong spokesperson for this position.[20] A sense of kinship with the world allows us to reverence and take pleasure in its beauties and its workings, and leads us to want to protect them.

The novelist and poet, John Updike, seeks to recover a deep sense of gratitude for the organic mechanisms that sustain us. In a recent volume, *Facing Nature*, there is a sequence of poems entitled "Seven Odes to Seven Natural Processes": Rot, Evaporation, Growth, Fragmentation, Entropy, Crystallization and Healing. For Updike, the otherness of nature, when rightly read, contains the signature of grace. In the ode on Healing, he says:

> A scab
> is a beautiful thing—a coin
> the body has minted, with an invisible
> motto:
> In God We Trust.[21]

---

[19]Thomas Aquinas, *Summa theologiae*, I, q. 47, a. 1.

[20]See Teilhard de Chardin, *The Divine Milieu* (New York: Harper & Row, 1960); *The Phenomenon of Man*, trans. Bernard Wall (New York: Harper & Row, 1959).

[21]John Updike, *Facing Nature*, p. 84.

Our fraternity with the grace of nature is discerned by faith. Only a final trust can espy the graciousness of nature and enable us to receive its blessing.

> The natural world is the maternal source whence we emerge into being as earthlings. The natural world is the life-giving nourishment of our physical, emotional, aesthetic, moral and religious existence. The natural world is the larger sacred community to which we belong. To be alienated from this community is to become destitute in all that makes us human. To damage this community is to diminish our own existence.[22]

The horizon of grace is all-encompassing.

3. *The Community of Humankind*

Most often, community is viewed in terms of persons. Communities are identifiable groups of persons in which one finds identity through affiliation. Examples include the family, the neighborhood, the city, the church. Often geographical proximity is a factor in the formation and maintenance of community. But, again, as we reflect on our experience, we have to admit that in addition to these more local communities, we are now aware more than ever of broader communities such as nations, clusters of nations, hemispheres or continents.

> Any association, regardless of size, in which all of its members care for one another as persons is a community. Consequently, in principle, there is no restriction in size upon community. Indeed ... the ultimate moral ideal and aim is the creation, maintenance and deepening of universal community. In Christian terminology, this would constitute the kingdom of heaven on earth.[23]

In his discussion of Juan Luis Segundo's book, *Our Idea of*

---

[22]Thomas Berry, "Economics", p. 17.

[23]Walter Jeffko, "Community, Society and the State", *The American Benedictine Review* 28 (1977), p. 80. Cited in Theissen, *Community and Disunity*, pp. 88-89.

God, Joseph Bracken calls attention to the inevitable connections between our ideas about God and the ways in which we function with each other. Segundo's hypothesis is that our "falsified and inauthentic ways of dealing with our fellow men and women are closely allied to the traditional concept of God as absolute and self-sufficient."[24]

Of the many manifestations of communal grace, let us examine four: (a) who is our neighbor? (b) the recognition of grace; (c) walking in another's shoes; (d) the gift of self to another. A final element of the fruit of grace in community will be discussed in section five below.

Love is at the heart of communal expressions of grace. Because of God's universal wish for our well-being and happiness, everyone participates in a graced existence. It is impossible to enumerate all the ways in which we experience each other as grace. The main point I want to make about the identity of the neighbor is that it can be anyone. All are graced by the fact of their very existence. The "other" can be a source of grace in herself as well as in the fruits of one's relationship with her.

Grace takes on specific expression in responding to the need of another. The neighbor is anyone who is in need. The choice to respond to that need is a reflection of, and participation in, the graciousness of God. As long as grace is isolated within the realm of personal experience, it will atrophy and die. It is only when the personal experience of grace "bears fruit, when it connects one to the rest of the world in service, that the sense of purpose finds its birth." At the heart of a contemplative existence to which all are called, is the discovery of meaning through the discovery of service.[25] The many faces of solidarity become the living symbol of our shared, graced existence.

One also discovers grace in experiences of abundance—in the beauty, virtue, success, and talents of people; in communication and in physical and spiritual communion. The

---

[24]Joe Bracken, *What Are They Saying About the Trinity?*, (NY: Paulist, 1979), p. 66.

[25]Gerald May, *Will and Spirit* (San Francisco: Harper & Row, 1982), p. 208.

virtue of hospitality is an especially needed balm in an impersonal and indifferent society. Grace gifts us with a welcoming spirit to friend and foe alike.

A second and most important activity of grace is the ability to *see* the grace that surrounds us. God assures us of the divine presence in all aspects of our lives, but too often we lack the ability to recognize it. One of the primary responsibilities of Christians is to be on the lookout for grace, to recognize it and to affirm it. We live in a graced world with graced people. God has taken care of that. Our task is to see. We are reminded of the quote from George Bernanos' novel, *Diary of A Country Priest* with which we began this book. "All is grace." As we shall see below when we examine the expression of grace in literature, sometimes the artist is the best teacher. But as we grow in becoming a community of graced persons, our ability to see all things as grace will grow proportionately.

This ability to recognize grace is facilitated by "crossing over," walking in someone else's shoes. This appears to be a simple act, yet it is demanding. The first requisite is the desire to cross over. One has to *want* to identify with the other, to feel what it is like to be in the other's situation. The imagination plays a crucial role here. I may not be in constant pain, but I can take the time to imagine what it must be like, to use pieces of my own experience as analogues to the experience of another. To the extent that we succeed in this process, we become more able to respond well to the other.

A final expression of communal grace is the experience of giving the gift of self to (or receiving it from) another. One can offer oneself to another through communication that is revelatory of self, through physical and spiritual communion, through one's talents or time, through lifelong commitment, or through death. To offer the gift of self to another—a gift that involves both death to self and recovery of self—is to cooperate in the graced activity of God. It is to live out one dimension of our being that is made in the image and likeness of God.

4. Sin in the Context of Community

As community is the apex of a graced existence, so the

refusal of unifying grace can be said to be the nadir of sin. Theologies in the past have defined sin as "a turning away from God towards creatures." This unhappy wording has caused an immense amount of damage in the community of faith. Our position today is rather that sin is a turning away from God *and* from creatures, and that the two refusals are closely connected. Piet Schoonenberg says of that earlier definition:

> When sin is defined as a turning away from God towards a creature, that formula, with all the fine explanations it may receive, is, by itself, incorrect, and a source of harmful misunderstandings, even of an unchristian conception of asceticism.[26]

Sin is *disordinate* turning toward anything. Grace is the *ordinate* turning toward God and creatures in love. One must also acknowledge the possibility of an *inordinate* turning toward God, i.e., one that is motivated by selfishness or egotism. In fact, entirely too much religion has been a turning toward God at the expense of the world and its peoples. Today we are suffering the consequences of such neglect.

A second viewpoint propagated by past theologies sees sin as a "stain on the soul." Bernard Häring points to the dangers of this concept of sin:

> This view easily allowed us to refuse responsibility, to turn a deaf ear to our calling to be cooperators of the Redeemer of the world and corevealers of his love to mankind and to the world in which man lives. Theologians could have been speaking about sin and original sin in another way that would have taught man to hear the sighs and travails of the created universe, calling for a share in the liberty of the sons of God (cf. Rom. 8:22).[27]

[26]Piet Schoonenberg, *Man and Sin: A Theological View* (Notre Dame, IN: University of Notre Dame Press, 1985), p. 20.

[27]Bernard Häring, *Sin in the Secular Age* (Garden City, NY: Doubleday & Co., 1974), p. 70.

We are called to repent of past ways that have alienated us from the created universe and from one another. We have too infrequently seen sin as a failure to commit ourselves to the development and fulfillment of the world and all its peoples.[28]

This refusal of unifying grace takes on many forms. In terms of our emphasis on grace as effecting mature responsibility, one of the more odious forms of sin against community is the refusal to hand on grace-filled realities from one generation to another.[29] One might ask: How often do I think about the personal responsibility of letting others know how much I value knowing a loving, gracious God or that God is a trustworthy person? Do I presume too easily that others will find out about this gracious God some other way? The audience is legion—children, grandchildren, co-workers, students, friends.

This social refusal may mean that I have said no to grace in my own existence, rendering it impossible to witness to grace. It may mean a failure to teach, to explain, to answer questions, to pass on human and Christian values. It may mean remaining unconscious or mean-spirited in spreading the good news of God's promises and all-embracing generosity. Finally, it may mean giving in to skepticism or cynicism; refusing to trust in a grace that empowers us to forgive and be forgiven, to affirm and be affirmed, to live and love fully.

Second, sin is a refusal to experience the natural world as gift of God. The community sins by taking the world for granted—the air we breathe, the water we drink, the magnificent beauty of mountains and oceans and deserts that we enjoy. We abuse the planet by irresponsible habits of living that are destroying the ecosystem. These habits run the gamut from irresponsible creation and disposal of garbage to poaching endangered species, to ignorance of and indifference to protective legislation.

Third, sin against community takes the form of inertia in the face of dehumanizing determinisms. Since the beginning of time, societies have been organized around exploitative princ-

---

[28]Ibid. Häring posits two theological positions that resulted from this skewed vision—limbo and predestination.

[29]Jerome Theisen, *Community and Disunity*, p. 32.

iples that allow one segment of society to enjoy the good life at the expense of another. These divisions have been predicated on race, sex, bloodline and power. If grace is understood as a godly, liberating force, then our understanding of grace must encompass the human person in her/his total social context. Social sin is blithe possession of an abundance of goods when others suffer from a lack of basic resources.

Sinful social determinisms are so embedded in the very structure and self-interest of any given society that they are very difficult to identify and even more difficult to confront. Liberating grace must involve our growing consciousness of these divisive determinisms. Grace allows us to see oppression for what it is and to work together to overcome it. Grace also allows us to "cross over" into the suffering and deprivation of our sisters and brothers in order to act in creative ways against the social causes of that suffering. It follows, then, that an obvious form of social sin involves an apolitical stance grounded in fear of taking risks, frustration, indifference, or despair.[30]

A fourth form of communal sin is projection. Psychology has helped us understand the inner geography of projection in ways unknown to earlier generations. The sin of projection begins with a refusal to admit the truth that one is a sinner. Denying that I have a harmfully self-interested, murky, dark side to my existence, I am forced to find another outlet for the evil I refuse to acknowledge within. This outlet can be anyone or any group other than oneself. The evil one denies is usually projected on to someone who is different from self— male/female, white/black, old/young—and the person or group is subsequently rejected. Projection wounds the wholeness of the community, setting persons at odds with each other.

Finally, social sin takes the form of radical individualism, self-sufficiency and self-complacency. In this way of life, we live in the illusion that we can "go it alone". This sin involves a profound denial of our need for one another, or for some, the suppression of deep-seated desire for one another. The denial

---

[30]For a discussion of social sin, see Juan Luis Segundo, *Grace and the Human Condition* (Maryknoll, NY: Orbis Books, 1973), p. 37f.

of mutual need forms a protective barrier around us, isolating us from others. The acknowledgment of need provides an opening for us to be for each other, to become bonded in solidarity. American society collectively suffers from this individualistic inclination.[31]

In this context, the old saying "It is more blessed to give than to receive" needs to be reexamined. Although there are important distinctions to be made between the experiences of women and men, in general giving is regarded as virtuous; it has social rewards attached to it and it usually allows one to remain in control. More difficult is the acknowledgment that we are needy and therefore vulnerable. Needing God, needing other persons and needing the world are central pieces in our experience of grace.

In short, sin against the grace of community is the refusal to become what God passionately desires for us, i.e., that we become lovers. We are created in love to live in a loving and life-giving relationship with God, others and the world. The refusal of this grace from God results in the tragic refusal to be this grace for one another.

5. Contemplation as an Expression of Community

Contemplation used to be an elite religious word reserved for those in monasteries, rectories and convents. But since Vatican II, in the Roman Catholic tradition, holiness has begun to be viewed in a more universal, inclusive way. The renewed emphasis on baptism has underlined the adult responsibilities of all Christians to be saints. A second change, inaugurated by Pope John XXIII, was the call to become engaged with the world, to share the hopes and joys, the sufferings and sorrows of the people of this earth, especially those who are poor and oppressed. Our past limited definition of contemplation clashed mightily with this new vision.

We are beginning to realize that the problem lies not so much with the people of God, but rather with the ways in

---

[31]See Robert Bellah et al., *Habits of the Heart* (Berkeley, CA: University of California Press, 1985).

which we have defined contemplation. William Callahan has written a creative and insightful monograph entitled *Noisy Contemplation.* He poses the question, "Can we live an active, noisy, inserted life and still pray deeply?"[32] The goal of "noisy contemplation" is not to usurp the role of prayer "apart" that is fed by silence and reflection. There will always be a need for such prayer in our lives. Rather, "noisy contemplation" seeks to uncover the prayerful, depth dimension of busy, everyday living, and to make contemplation available to everyone.

Noisy contemplation involves being present in love to ourselves and to others as well as to God.

> Partners who gaze at each other with love, parents who look fondly at their children, people who face themselves truthfully and take responsibility for their lives and gifts, people who perceive the injustice done to others and struggle to reverse their suffering, these are all people close to the dynamics of noisy contemplation. They experience bonding in love much like the encounter with God in contemplative praying.[33]

Our daily experience is the "stuff" of this kind of prayer. Prayer becomes not only the raising of our minds and hearts to God, but to ourselves, to our neighbors near and far, and to the world in which we live. Callahan calls noisy contemplation "prayer for crabgrass Christians." It grows anywhere; its roots dig deep and bind the earth. It needs little care, is resistant to drought, wind and sun. It will grow where there is even a crack in the sidewalk and can burst forth in growth when conditions are favorable.[34]

The tools of noisy contemplation include our five senses. Important to a contemplative stance toward the world are senses that are tuned in to pay attention to the world around

[32]William Callahan, *Noisy Contemplation* (Washington, D.C.: Quixote Center, 1983), p. 1. See also "Noisy Contemplation: is Prayer in a Busy Life" *New Theology Review* 2 (1989): 29-39.

[33]Ibid., p. 10.

[34]Ibid.

us. Eyes to see, ears to listen, touch, taste and smell—all bring us into contact with our environment. We can regard the world in a haphazard or indifferent way, or we can view it with some deliberation, with attention and loving appreciation. We are free, in grace, to become present to our world—friends, trees, thunder, symphonies, stories, heat, cold, hugs, garlic, freshly brewed coffee. An inner sense of empathy and compassion enables us to "tap into" the situation of another and offer a consoling word. Imagination and memory can also be put at the service of contemplation.[35]

Contemplative praying calls for openness of heart toward one's experiences—the people and events of our daily life. It is a reverence that can be practiced and nurtured until it becomes integral to living. As we grow in our ability to see all of reality contemplatively, we grow in our awareness that all is grace. Some concrete examples:

— In the morning one can offer the day to God and ask for an open heart with which to contemplate life.
— A look out the window toward the sunrise or sunset can be reminders to keep one's eyes open to the created world.
— A loving glance at a family member or at our rumpled selves in the mirror can set in motion our habit of welcoming people during the day.
— Driving to and from work, walking or travelling alone offer time to build habits of contemplating God, people, nature.
— A loving glance at the work place and at those in it can help one to be open to and reverence what happens there whether it be pleasant or difficult.
— Contemplating the news on TV or in the newspaper involves the "crossing over" of which we spoke earlier. Love calls one to imagine being in the shoes of persons at war, of persons who are hungry, of crime victims, of Nobel prize winners, of politicians or firefighters.
— Pausing to wonder at the crabgrass in the crack in the sidewalk; at airplanes and skyscrapers and bridges; enjoying art, whether it be graffiti or Michelangelo in a museum; laughing with carefree

[35]Ibid.

abandon; celebrating with children under the hose on a hot day—these simple things comprise noisy contemplation.[36]

Noisy contemplation is a kind of prayer that is available and nourishing for ordinary people, no matter where they find themselves. It uses the activity and noise of human living as the foundation for a life of deep prayer that is within reach of anyone who desires it. The grace of contemplation is available in abundance to all. It suffuses the nooks and crannies of daily existence, beckoning us to regard ourselves, others and the world with a gentle, loving and accepting gaze.

The fruit of this contemplation is the same as the fruit of any prayer. One can test the authenticity of one's contemplation, not by keeping tabs on how well we are doing, or by comparing oneself to some outside model, but by watching to see if one's actions begin to reflect the qualities of love, patience, kindness, fidelity for the long haul, peace, tenderness. Action for justice, alleviation of or compassion in suffering, joyful celebration at the fullness of life—these form the litmus test of a life of contemplation.

The Christian story tells us that this is what God wants for us. Do we want it for ourselves? Do we think it is possible? Do we desire and ask for the grace of a contemplative existence that is lived with and for others?

[36]Ibid., pp. 10-13

16

"God Love Admiration":
Grace in Literature

The events of the birth, life, death and resurrection of Jesus of Nazareth—the mediator of our graced lives—carry with them an inexhaustible surplus of meaning. It follows that this abundance of meaning will be expressed in eternally new ways, with a variety of images and interpretations, by Christian people in constantly changing cultures who want to give authentic expression to what the New Testament seeks to proclaim. The New Testament authors looked to the simple experiences of everyday life for language and images to describe their experience of God in Jesus. They talk about redemption in terms of slaves, ransom, the law, farming, and banquets.[1]

With the recent scholarly and popular interest in narrative and story-telling, theologians are being helped to have a greater appreciation for grace as a concrete reality.[2] As we saw in Part I, past theologies of grace have been too abstract, too divorced from the true lived experience of the believing community. Brian McDermott reflects this new turn. "Because grace is embodied, theologians prefer to reflect on its nature and meaning in connection with the bodily realities which render grace present and effective in the world: Jesus and the church."[3]

[1]Edward Schillebeeckx, *Christ,* p. 634.

[2]Among liberation theologians, see Juan Luis Segundo, *Grace and the Human Condition,* Trans. John Drury (Maryknoll, NY: Orbis Books, 1973), pp. 39-43.

[3]Brian McDermott, *What Are They Saying About the Grace of Christ?* (New York: Paulist Press, 1984), p. 59.

One of the objectives of this essay has been to build on the centrality of Jesus, the church and the sacraments as means of grace, by emphasizing the wider context in which we live. It is our graced existence in God and through Christ and the Spirit that gives meaning to church and sacraments. As a community we have been more focused on how church and sacraments feed into and support our lives than on how our lives are the foundation for the meaning of church and sacraments. We need to push our horizons outward, to acknowledge the unlimited possibilities of God's graced activity in a blessed world. God is not bounded by certain institutions or buildings or persons.

The human task, then, is to be on the lookout, to be ready to be surprised by the ways in which God's healing, affirming love may be present in our world. In order to accomplish this, we have to realize that God may choose to give grace in places we may not have looked before. We are invited to choose to see our lives in terms of this graced activity, and to be active cooperators and co-creators with the triune God. Such meaning does not come out of the sky as a *deus ex machina*, but rather from the reverent discernment of the community of faith of which we are all members.

In addition to an expanded awareness of grace in the warp and woof of our own lives and in the lives of others, we may find further enlightenment about the meaning of grace from literature and art.[4] Cornelius Ernst suggests that if Augustine's *Confessions* is the basic text for an experiential reading of the theology of grace and freedom, "it is in the novel that we should look for a modern counterpart to Augustine's sense of the shape of his life taken as a whole."[5] Novels, short stories, poetry, film, painting and sculpture—these forms are particularly apt sources that reveal God's movements of grace. Feminist writers, searching for alternatives to the patriarchal

---

[4]We focus here on literature. Readers may pursue connections with image and art in Margaret Miles, *Image as Insight: Visual Understanding in Western Christianity & Secular Culture* (Boston: Beacon Press, 1985).

[5]*A Theology of Grace*, p. 84. He suggests three titles: Patrick White, *Riders in the Chariot* and *The Vivisector*, and Iris Murdoch, *Bruno's Dream*.

literature of Judaism and Christianity, often turn to literature for myths and symbols that give meaning to women's experience.[6]

If grace is potential newness in all of life, the moment in which love and life break through the constricting bonds of sin, death, and fear, then literature offers the believer a sweeping panorama of the concrete, specific ways in which this struggle and transformation take place. We conclude this essay on grace with a sampling of literature that invites believers to pull back the veil in order to see the gracious activity of God.

When poetry and grace are mentioned in the same breath, the name T.S. Eliot springs to mind. His poetry is a window that looks out upon the many facets of grace. Eliot laments our brokenness in "The Hollow Men"[7] and in "The Love Song of J. Alfred Prufrock,"[8] and petitions for grace in "Ash Wednesday":

> Teach us to care and not to care
> Teach us to sit still
>
> Pray for us sinners now and at the hour of our death
> Pray for us now and at the hour of our death.
> . . .
> Teach us to care and not to care
> Teach us to sit still
> Even among these rocks
> Sister, mother
> And spirit of the river, spirit of the sea,
> Suffer me not to be separated
>
> And let my cry come unto thee.[9]

Eliot captures the graces of nature,

---

[6]See Carol Christ, *Diving Deep and Surfacing: Women Writers on Spiritual Quest* (Boston: Beacon Press, 1986).

[7]T.S. Eliot, *Collected Poems, 1909-1962* (New York: Harcourt, Brace & World, 1970), p. 79.

[8]Ibid., p. 3.

[9]Ibid., p. 86, 95.

Children's voices in the orchard
Between the blossom-and the fruit-time:
Golden head, crimson head,
Between the green tip and the root.
Black wing, brown wing, hover over;
Twenty years and the spring is over:
. . .
Cling, swing,
Spring, sing
Swing up into the apple-tree.[10]

and the connections between the heavenly and the earthly city:

And some say: 'How can we love our neighbor? For love must
be made real in act, as desire unites with desired; we
have only our labour to give and our labour is not
required.'
. . .
You, have you built well, have you forgotten the cornerstone?
Talking of right relations of men, but not of relations of men
to GOD.
'Our citizenship is in Heaven'; yes, but that is the model and
type for your citizenship upon earth.[11]

Eliot sees that the gifts we have received, especially those of
the artist, are intended to be put at the service of others. As
God acts graciously toward the world, we are to act toward
that world with the totality of our existence.

Lord, shall we not bring these gifts to Your service?
Shall we not bring to Your service all our powers
For life, for dignity, grace and order,
And intellectual pleasures of the senses?
The Lord who created must wish us to create
And employ our creation again in His service
Which is already his service in creating.

---

[10]"New Hampshire," p. 138.
[11]"Choruses From 'the Rock'", II, p. 152.

For Man is joined spirit and body,
And therefore must serve as spirit and body.[12]

Volumes have been written on Eliot's "The Four Quartets". In this poem, Eliot describes the pain and the ecstasy of a graced existence. We call attention simply to the refrain he borrows from Julian of Norwich—a refrain that expresses confidence in the power of grace in the face of evil.

Sin is Behovely, but
All shall be well, and
All manner of thing shall be well.
. . .
And all shall be well and
all manner of thing shall be well
By the purification of the motive
In the ground of our beseeching.[13]

The literature that could be discussed profitably in the context of grace is abundant and wide-ranging. In order to limit and focus this material, I have chosen selections in a somewhat random fashion and organized them according to themes that are extremely common and/or that hold promise in terms of a lived theology of grace. These headings include (1) graced nature; (2) the presence of grace in the ordinary; (3) grace as antidote to sin; and (4) grace from women's perspective.

Graced Nature

The poet finds nature an unending source of awe and reverence. The harmony, the power, the color, the intricacy of design from the largest ocean to the smallest insect arouse the poetic muse. The poetry of Emily Dickinson (d. 1886) is replete with nature imagery. The graces of nature lead her to the graces of the spirit. The purple of a Fall landscape evokes the image of a soul conscious of its regal nature.

[12]Ibid., IX, p. 168.
[13]"Little Gidding," pp. 205-207.

Purple—is fashionable twice—
This season of the year
And when a soul perceives itself
To be an Emperor.[14]

For Dickinson, nature stands as an invitation to anyone who hungers for her riches.

These are the Signs to Nature's Inns—
Her invitation broad
To Whosoever famishing
To taste her mystic Bread—

These are the rites of Nature's House
The Hospitality
That opens with an equal width
To beggar and to Bee
. . .[15]

And finally, she equates nature with heaven and with harmony.

"Nature" is what we see—
The Hill—the Afternoon—
Squirrel—Eclipse—the Bumble bee—
Nay—Nature is Heaven—
Nature is what we hear—
The Bobolink—the Sea—
Thunder—the Cricket—
Nay—Nature is Harmony—
Nature is what we know—
Yet have no art to say—
So impotent Our Wisdom is
To her simplicity.[16]

[14]In *The Complete Poems of Emily Dickinson* (Boston: Little, Brown, 1890), p. 458.

[15]Ibid., pp. 488-489.

[16]Ibid., p. 332.

The nineteenth century Jesuit poet, Gerard Manley Hopkins
(d. 1889), also writes of God in nature and is moved to praise:

> Glory be to God for dappled things—
>> For skies of couple-colour as a brinded cow;
>>> For rose-moles all in stipple upon trout that swim;
>> . . .
> All things counter, original, spare, strange;
>> Whatever is fickle, freckled (who knows how?)
>> With swift, slow; sweet, sour; adazzle, dim;
> He fathers-forth whose beauty is past change;
>>> Praise him.[17]

Hopkins also addresses the marring and depletion of nature
by humanity. He could not have known the extent to which
the human community would become capable of destroying
nature, and his viewpoint, therefore, is optimistic. But his
hopefulness can be read as the believers' confidence in the
ultimate victory of grace over the forces of destruction.

> The world is charged with the grandeur of God.
>> It will flame out, like shining from shook foil;
>> It gathers to a greatness, like the ooze of oil
> Crushed. Why do men then now not reck his rod?
> Generations have trod, have trod, have trod;
>> . . .
> And for all this, nature is never spent;
>> There lives the dearest freshness deep down things;
> And though the last lights off the black West went
>> Oh, morning, at the brown brink eastward, springs—
> Because the Holy Ghost over the bent
>> World broods with warm breast and with ah! bright
>> wings.[18]

Walt Whitman (d. 1892), a third American poet of the
nineteenth century, sees himself not only as the recorder of the

---

[17]Gerard Manley Hopkins, "Pied Beauty" in *Poems and Prose of Gerard Manley Hopkins* (Baltimore: Penguin Books Ltd., 1953), pp. 30-31.

[18]"God's Grandeur", Ibid., p. 27.

beauty and dignity of nature but also as one upon whom people depend to trace the path between beauty and their souls.[19] In the poem, "This Compost", Whitman marvels at the cycle of nature in which fresh and beautiful things emerge year after year from the compost of the dead.

> Behold this compost! behold it well!
> Perhaps every mite has once form'd part of a sick person—
> yet behold!
> The grass of spring covers the prairies,
> The bean bursts noiselessly through the mould in the
> garden,
> The delicate spear of the onion pierces upward,
> The apple-buds cluster together on the apple-branches,
> The resurrection of the wheat appears with pale visage out
> of its graves,
> . . .
> What chemistry!
> . . .
> That all is clean forever and forever,
> That the cool drink from the well tastes so good,
> That blackberries are so flavorous and juicy,. . .[20]

The poet says he is terrified at the Earth that gives such divine materials to humans out of such unsavory leavings. From a faith perspective, such renewal of the earth suggests the eternal dying and rising of a graced world, the possibility of renewal breaking forth from decay and death.

Finally, when one thinks of poetry and nature, one thinks of Robert Frost (d. 1963). In addition to capturing in words the beauties of nature, Frost senses the giftedness of nature and its ability to transform. He writes of a rainbow he saw in the company of a friend, the British poet, Edward Thomas. The poem is "Iris by Night."

---

[19]*Leaves of Grass,* Preface to 1855 edition, (Avon, CT: The Heritage Press, 1937), p. xxviii.

[20]Walt Whitman, "This Compost", Ibid., pp. 332-333.

. . .
A wonder! Bow and rainbow as it bent,
Instead of moving with us as we went,
(To keep the pots of gold from being found)
It lifted from its dewy pediment
Its two mote-swimming many-colored ends,
And gathered them together in a ring.
And we stood in it softly circled round
From all division time or foe can bring
In a relation of elected friends.[21]

Frost sees a connection between the encircling ring of the rainbow and the communion he experiences with his friend. A more erotic expression of the relationship between nature and love is found in "A Prayer In Spring":

Oh, give us pleasure in the flowers today;
. . .
Oh, give us pleasure in the orchard while,
Like nothing else by day, like ghosts by night;
And make us happy in the happy bees,
The swarm dilating round the perfect trees.

And make us happy in the darting bird
That suddenly above the bees is heard,
The meteor that thrusts in with needle bill,
And off a blossom in mid air stands still.

For this is love and nothing else is love,
The which it is reserved for God above
To sanctify to what far ends He will,
But which it only needs that we fulfill.[22]

Frost's experience of the giftedness of nature extends to other aspects of life as well. In his famous poem, "Death of the

[21]Robert Frost, "Iris by Night" in *Robert Frost: Contours of Belief* (Athens, Ohio: Ohio University Press, 1984), p. 34.

[22]"A Prayer In Spring" in *Collected Poems of Robert Frost (New York: Henry Holt, 1930), p. 17.*

Hired Man", the image of "home" symbolizes something precious that doesn't have to be "earned"—something like grace.

> 'Home is the place where, when you have to go there,
> They have to take you in.'
> > 'I should have called it
> Something you somehow haven't to deserve.'[23]

In the poem, "Dust of Snow," a simple sprinkling of snow becomes an occasion for unanticipated renewal.

> The way a crow
> Shook down on me
> The dust of snow
> From a hemlock tree
>
> Has given my heart
> A change of mood
> And saved some part
> Of a day I had rued.[24]

All of us have had similar experiences in which a seemingly insignificant, mundane encounter with nature caused new life and new energy to break into our lives. These small, but important and treasured gifts grace one's life in gracious and unexpected ways.

Grace in The Ordinary

The artist is one who "sees" the world as charged with God's graciousness, not only in spectacular sunsets, but in the everyday. Turning to an earlier time, we savor the poetry of William Shakespeare (d. 1616), who presents us to ourselves in powerful language and imagery. In this short exchange from *King Lear*,

[23] *Ibid.*, p. 51.
[24] *Ibid.*, p. 270.

he portrays the gamut of mysterious graces from forgiveness and blessing to butterflies and gossip. Lear speaks to Cordelia,

> We two alone will sing like birds i' the cage:
> When thou dost ask me blessing, I'll kneel down,
> And ask of thee forgiveness: so we'll live,
> And pray, and sing, and tell old tales, and laugh
> At gilded butterflies, and hear poor rogues
> Talk of court news; and we'll talk with them too,
> Who loses and who wins; who's in who's out;
> And take upon's the mystery of things,
> As if we were God's spies.[25]

A second example of "ordinary" grace is found in a short story about hospitality. When one begins to live and view one's existence in terms of grace, the possibility of being surprised by grace is increased a hundredfold. The call to a life of grace is all around us in subtle and blatant forms for those with eyes to see. A short story in *The New Yorker*, "Hostess", proved to be such an experience.[26] As the title suggests, it portrays an aspect of life that is a paradigm for the experience and understanding of grace—hospitality.

The setting is a house trailer. The occasion is a party to celebrate the promotion to crew chief of the hostess' husband, Dale. The guests, all of whom live in the trailer park are a needy lot. One woman drinks too much to drown her hurt feelings caused by her boyfriend's infidelity. Two other guests, Hank and Boyce almost get into a fight over a misunderstanding. The unfaithful boyfriend shows up in need of reconciliation. Melinda is stung by a bee. The unnamed hostess is consumed with attending to the needs of her guests. She is willing and joyful in her response. It seems second nature to her.

At this point the phone rings. A woman's voice mumbles, "She's gone." The hostess recognizes immediately that someone

---

[25] *William Shakespeare, King Lear,* cited in C. Ernst, *A Theology of Grace,* p. 89.

[26] Donald Mangum, "Hostess" *The New Yorker,* September 28, 1987, p. 33. See end of chapter for full text.

has died. She also discovers quickly that the phone call is a wrong number. She relays this information, but instead of hanging up, the woman on the other end of the line just keeps saying, "Oh dear God." Aware of all the happy noise coming from the party, the hostess chooses to attend to the stranger on the line. She says, "Honey, who was it passed away?" The stranger tells her that it was her sister, Beatrice and that none of her people are there.

The hostess says, "Sweetheart, you listen to me," as she reaches to close the window against the noise of her guests. She thinks to herself, "Sweet Christ, dear sweet Christ in Heaven." Then she continues, "Are you listening, angel? You should not be alone right now. You understand what I'm telling you? Now, I'm right here."

The opportunity to be grace for others presents itself at odd and unsuspected moments of each day. Openness to the grace of God produces a readiness to see the need for a graced word or gesture and the willingness to offer that word with love and sensitivity. The moment is obvious and compelling in crisis, less so in the mundane fabric of daily living. The anonymous hostess is a model of one who freely chooses to facilitate, in word and deed, the grace that brings with it the potential for new beginnings.

Our final example in this section is Elizabeth Barrett Browning (d. 1861) who speaks overtly of the danger of separating natural and spiritual things.

> ... Natural things
> And spiritual,—who separates those two
> In art, in morals, or the social drift,
> Tears up the bond of nature and brings death,
> Paints futile pictures, writes unreal verse,
> Leads vulgar days, deals ignorantly with men,
> Is wrong, in short at all points. . . .
> > Without the spiritual, observe,
> The natural's impossible—no form,
> No motion: without sensuous, spiritual
> Is inappreciable,—no beauty or power:
> . . .
> > Earth's crammed with heaven,

And every common bush afire with God;
But only he who sees, takes off his shoes—
The rest sit round it and pluck blackberries,
And daub their natural faces unaware
More and more from the first similitude.
. . .

If a man could feel,
Not one day, in the artist's ecstasy,
But every day, feast, fast, or working-day,
The spiritual significance burn through
The hieroglyphic of material shows,
Henceforward he would pain the globe with wings,
And reverence fish and fowl, the bull, the tree,
And even his very body as a man. . . .[27]

In Browning's view, everything in this world—a leaf, a cup, a stone—is endowed with an outside that everyone can see, and an inside, visible to the artist and the believer, that connects reality with the eternal significance of God.

Grace as Antidote to Sin

Moving from poetry to fiction, we turn to Flannery O'Connor who is well-known for her preoccupation with grace in what she judged to be a grace-less world. She says, "I will admit to certain pre-occupations . . . with belief and with death and grace and the devil." She felt that the more a writer wanted to make the supernatural apparent, the more real she had to make the natural world, for if readers couldn't accept the natural world, there was little hope they would be led to anything beyond it. Her stories are puzzling as stories of grace, since on the surface they seem so filled with evil. But O'Connor's vision, though expressed in a different key, shares with Elizabeth Barrett Browning the connection between the natural and the supernatural. She says,

[27]Elizabeth Barrett Browning, *Aurora Leigh.*

The novelist is required to create the illusion of a whole world with believable people in it, and the chief difference between the novelist who is an orthodox Christian and the novelist who is merely a naturalist is that the Christian novelist lives in a larger universe. He believes that the natural world contains the supernatural. And this doesn't mean that his obligation to portray the natural is less; it means it is greater.[28]

O'Connor sees time in terms of eternity; the struggle against evil as part of the plan for salvation; the "blind malignity of men toward one another as an opening for grace, and flawed and depraved man as the potential 'new man' in Christ."[29] Her desire to awaken a sense of the transcendent in modern readers led her to grab hold of sin "as the last smelling salt that might arouse our dormant sense of the holy."[30] For O'Connor, grace is presented as a dramatic glimpse of a new possibility in the midst of grotesque evil.

In her famous story, "Everything That Rises Must Converge," O'Connor introduces us to Julian, a hard, cynical, first-generation college-educated young man, and his mother, a woman clinging to the old ways of a more gracious South. The convergence in the story takes place on three levels: son against mother; new generation against old; and race against race.[31] Julian is arrogantly self-sufficient, unable to receive his mother's care for him, imperfect as it may be, and also unable to return it. He is viciously spiteful toward her and wishes her ill at every turn. He feels he has turned out well in spite of his mother, even though she has sacrificed to send him to school and is now willingly putting him up until he finds a job and can get out on his own.

[28]Flannery O'Connor, *Mystery & Manners,* eds. Sally and Robert Fitzgerald (New York: Farrar, Straus & Giroux, 1969), p. 175.

[29]Kathleen Feeley, *Flannery O'Connor: Voice of the Peacock* (New York: Fordham University Press, 1982), p. 7.

[30]Harold Fickett and Douglas R. Gilbert, *Flannery O'Connor: Images of Grace* (Grand Rapids, MI: William B. Eerdmans, 1986), p. 110.

[31]See John R. May, *The Pruning Word: The Parables of Flannery O'Connor* (Notre Dame, IN: University of Notre Dame Press, 1976), pp. 94-97.

She asks him to accompany her to the YWCA on the bus.
He obliges reluctantly, and on the bus encounters his mother's
condescension to a Black woman and her small son. In his
mind, he sees himself as tolerant and free of prejudice. He likes
to sit next to Blacks on the bus, arrogantly taking on the
reparation for his mother's sins. However, his mother's kindly
attitude toward others, though condescending, seems virtuous
next to his own intolerance of anyone who lacks his education
and so-called virtue of tolerance. Julian's main agenda, it is
clear, is not to be tolerant of Blacks, but to hurt his mother.

Julian takes seditious pleasure in seeing the Black woman
with the same hat that his mother had just purchased—an
expense for her, but purchased so she wouldn't "meet herself
coming and going."

> The vision of the two hats, identical, broke upon him with
> the radiance of a brilliant sunrise.... He could not believe
> that Fate had thrust upon his mother such a lesson.... For
> a moment he had an uncomfortable sense of her innocence,
> but it lasted only a second before principles rescued him.
> Justice entitled him to laugh. His grin hardened until it said
> to her as plainly as if he were saying aloud: Your punishment
> exactly fits your pettiness. This should teach you a perma-
> nent lesson.

When Julian and his mother get off the bus, the Black woman
gets off as well, and Julian's mother gives the woman's small
son a penny. In an outburst of anger, the Black woman strikes
her with her bulging red pocketbook. The event is the culmination of Julian's incessant provocation of his mother, causing
her blood pressure to rise to the breaking point. The blow
causes a stroke and Julian's mother sinks to the sidewalk.

The stroke stands as a crushing reproach and judgment
against Julian. Julian's desire to "teach his mother a lesson" is
transformed into sorrow and confusion when the impact of his
mother's stroke hits home. She doesn't seem to recognize
Julian and asks for her former Black maid, Caroline. "The
extreme irony of her request stems from the fact that, as a
possible punishment for her, Julian had 'imagined his mother
lying desperately ill and his being able to secure only a Negro

doctor for her.' His mother spontaneously prefers the reassuring presence of her former Black maid to the dubious comfort of her 'stranger' son.["]32

As his mother crumples to the sidewalk, the horror of his sin breaks upon him. The choice is set before him whether to own his sin and enter into the world of sorrow, thus opening up the possibility of repentance, forgiveness, and new life in grace, or stubbornly to cling to his heart of stone. One is led to hope that he will choose the former, and to realize the ways in which the utter darkness of sin can provide the opportunity for new life.

Grace in Women's Experience

Today from every corner of the globe we hear about the struggle for liberation. As we allow grace to free us from sin, the shackles of the oppressed lose their binding power. The poor, the infirm, the imprisoned and the excluded are special candidates for the graces of liberation. They know what it means and depend on its power. We see emerging from many countries a powerful literature that chronicles the journey of women from oppression to new life. The concerns of women cross age, culture, race and economic status. We have spoken of the sins of idolatry and sexism and the ways in which women are struggling to recover their history and true experience. In her poem, "Diving Into the Wreck", Adrienne Rich portrays grace for women today as the recovery of their own stories. The wreck is a ship sunken long ago in the ocean.

> . . .
> I came to explore the wreck.
> The words are purposes.
> The words are maps.
> I came to see the damage that was done
> and the treasures that prevail.
> I stroke the beam of my lamp

32Ibid., p. 96.

slowly along the flank
of something more permanent
than fish or weed

the thing I came for:
the wreck and not the story of the wreck
the thing itself and not the myth

the drowned face always staring
toward the sun
the evidence of damage
worn by salt and sway into this threadbare beauty
the ribs of the disaster
curving their assertion
among the tentative haunters.

This is the place.
And I am here, the mermaid whose dark hair
streams black, the merman in his armored body
We circle silently
about the wreck
we dive into the hold.
I am she: I am he
. . .
We are, I am, you are
by cowardice or courage
the one who find our way
back to this scene
carrying a knife, a camera
a book of myths
in which
our names do not appear.

The woman in the poem has become aware that the truth and glory of her existence have been dulled by a culture that makes women invisible. This knowledge spurs her on to the difficult task of diving into the deep. She sees the damage, the "threadbare beauty", but she also goes to see "the treasures that prevail". These truths become grace. Discovering the wreck, the thing itself and not just the story of the wreck—the myth, is the foundation upon which she will build a future graced existence. The knife, the camera and the book of myths are her tools, the symbols of grace which enable her to reclaim her glory, the image of God in which she has been made.

Two further examples come from the growing corpus of literature by American Black women authors. The first text is from Alice Walker's *The Color Purple*, whose very being and writing is attributed to grace. She dedicates the book as follows:

> To the Spirit:
> without whose assistance
> Neither this book
> Nor I
> Would have been
> Written.

In the first excerpt, Walker speaks through her women characters who underline how much a graced church depends for its authenticity on a graced life:

> I is a sinner, say Shug. Cause I was born. I don't deny it. But once you find out what's out there waiting for us, what else can you be?
>
> Sinners have more good times, I say.
>
> You know why? she ast.
>
> Cause you ain't all the time worrying about God a lot. But once us feel loved by God, us do the best us can to please him with what us like.
>
> You telling me God love you, and you ain't never done nothing for him? I mean, not go to church, sing in the choir, feed the preacher and all like that?
>
> But if God love me, Celie, I don't have to do all that. Unless I want to. There's a lot of other things I can do that I speck God likes.
>
> Like what? I ast.
>
> Oh, she say. I can lay back and just admire stuff. Be happy. Have a good time.
>
> Well, this sound like blasphemy sure nuff.
>
> She say, Celie, tell the truth, have you ever found God in

church? I never did. I just found a bunch of folks hoping for him to show. Any God I ever felt in church I brought in with me. And I think all the other folks did too. They come to church to *share* God, not find God.[33]

In this second selection, Walker portrays the transformation of Shug's image of God from an old white man with a beard to an awareness that God is everything. This discovery leads Shug to a stance of awe and praise before God's handiwork. Her friend Celie soon follows in her footsteps.

She say, My first step from the old white man was trees. Then air. Then birds. Then other people. But one day when I was sitting quiet and feeling like a motherless child, which I was, it come to me: that feeling of being part of everything, not separate at all. I knew that if I cut a tree, my arm would bleed. And I laughed and I cried and I run all around the house. I knew just what it was. In fact, when it happen, you can't miss it. It sort of like you know what, she say, grinning and rubbing high upon my thigh.

Shug! I say.

Oh, she say. God love all them feelings. That's some of the best stuff God did. And when you know God love 'em you enjoys 'em a lot more. You can just relax, go with everything that's going, and praise God by liking what you like.

God don't think it dirty? I ast.

Naw, she say. God made it. Listen, God love everything you love—and a mess of stuff you don't. But more than anything else, God love admiration.

You saying God vain? I ast.

Naw, she say. Not vain, just wanting to share a good thing. I think it pisses God off if you walk by the color purple in a field somewhere and don't notice it. . . .

Well, us talk and talk about God, but I'm still adrift. Trying to chase that old white man out of my head. I been so busy thinking bout him I never truly notice nothing God make. Not a blade of corn (how it do that?) not the color

[33]Alice Walker, *The Color Purple* (New York: Washington Square Press, 1982), p. 176.

purple (where it come from?). Not the little wild flowers. Nothing.[34]

In her novel, *Beloved*,[35] Toni Morrison explores the crucial function of remembering. The principal character, Sethe, is consumed with blocking the painful memories of slavery in a place called Sweet Home. But her mind has a will of its own and the memories intrude on her consciousness. At one point after their escape, Sethe remembers the joyful ministerings of her mother-in-law, Baby Suggs, now dead. In her wisdom, Baby Suggs understands the important role imagination has to play in our experience of grace—a role that is universally applicable, but dramatically indispensable in persons and communities crushed by burdens of oppression.

After situating herself on a huge flat-sided rock, Baby Suggs bowed her head and prayed silently. The company watched her from the trees. They knew she was ready when she put her stick down. Then she shouted, "Let the children come!" and they ran from the trees toward her.

"Let your mothers hear you laugh," she told them, and the woods rang. The adults looked on and could not help smiling.

Then "Let the grown men come," she shouted. They stepped out one by one from among the ringing trees.

"Let your wives and your children see you dance," she told them, and groundlife shuddered under their feet.

Finally she called the women to her. "Cry," she told them. "For the living and the dead. Just cry." And without covering their eyes the women let loose.

It started that way: laughing children, dancing men, crying women and then it got mixed up. Women stopped crying and danced; men sat down and cried; children danced, women laughed, children cried until, exhausted and riven, all and each lay about the Clearing damp and gasping for breath. In the silence that followed, Baby Suggs, holy, offered up to them her great big heart.

She did not tell them to clean up their lives or to go and

[34]Ibid., pp. 178-179.

[35]Toni Morrison, *Beloved* (New York: Alfred A. Knopf, 1987), pp. 88-89.

sin no more. She did not tell them they were the blessed of
the earth, its inheriting meek or its glorybound pure.

She told them that the only grace they could have was
the grace they could imagine. That if they could not see it,
they would not have it.

"Here," she said, "in this here place, we flesh; flesh that
weeps, laughs; flesh that dances on bare feet in grass. Love
it. Love it hard...." Saying no more, she stood up then
and danced with her twisted hip the rest of what her heart
had to say while the others opened their mouths and gave
her the music. Long notes held until the four-part harmony
was perfect enough for their deeply loved flesh.

In this literature we are privileged to glimpse the vision of
woman discovering, owning and celebrating the image of God
within. This is the power of grace. In the experience of our
own liberation—women and men—we come to know the God
whose wish for us is wholeness, freedom and love. There is a
line in James Oppenheim's poem, "Bread and Roses"—"the
rising of the women means the rising of the race." One person's
freedom means freedom for all. As God graces our lives, so in
turn, we become instruments of grace for each other.

Conclusion

Literature uncovers for us the many faces of grace. Grace
takes on as many forms as there are people and times and
human and cosmic events. Faith, trust and hope are the gifts
that enable us to believe that God is everywhere, calling us and
wishing us well. Literature has the potential to awaken in us a
deeper sense of God's graced presence in the very sinews of
our daily existence. It is there for those with eyes to see. The
world *is* charged with the grandeur of God.

One of the hallmarks of great art is its ability to portray the
unifying sense of human destiny, "a joy too deep for tears.
Grace is re-discovery of the comprehensive unity of the initiative of God's love, a unity to which we can only penetrate
stepwise, by a continual conversion, a dying and rising again
with Jesus."[36]

[36]Ernst, *A Theology of Grace*, p. 88.

Hostess
by Donald Mangum

My husband was promoted to crew chief, and with the raise we moved into a double-wide, just up the drive. Half the park came to the housewarming. Well, Meg drank herself to tears and holed up in the toilet, poor thing. "Meg? Hon?" I said from the hall. "You going to live?" She groaned something. It was seeing R.L. with that tramp down in 18 that made her do this to herself. Now there was a whole line of beer drinkers doing the rain dance out in the hall, this being a single-bath unit. I was the hostess, and I had to do something. "Sweetheart," I said, knocking. "I'm going to put you a bowl on the floor in the utility room." The rest of the trailer was carpeted.

Dale, my husband, was in the kitchen with an egg in his hand, squeezing it for all he was worth. Veins stuck out everywhere on his arm. Paul and Eric were laughing. "What's going on in here?" I said.

Dale stopped squeezing and breathed. "I got to admit," he said, "I never knew that about eggs." I could have kicked him when he handed Paul five dollars. I found the bowl I was after, plus a blanket, and took care of Meg.

Then Hank and Boyce almost got into a fight over a remark Hank made about somebody named Linda. They had already squared off outside when it came out that Hank was talking about a Linda *Stillman*, when Boyce thought he meant a Linda *Faye*. Well, by that time everybody was ready for something, so the guys agreed to arm-wrestle. Hank won, but only because Boyce started laughing when Kathy Sueanne sat in Jason's supper and Jason got madder than Kathy Sueanne did because there wasn't any more potato salad left.

You won't believe who showed up then. R.L.! Said he was looking for Meg. "You think she wants to see you, R.L.?" I said. "After what you did to her with that trash Elaine?" So he said he'd only kissed Elaine a couple of times. "Or not even that," he said. "She was the one kissed *me*."

"You know what you can kiss," I said. He stood there looking like some dog you'd just hauled off and kicked for no good reason. "Well, come on," I said, taking him by the shirt. I led him to the utility room to show him the condition he'd driven his darling to. I'm here to say, when R.L. saw that precious thing curled up in front of the hot-water heater he sank to his knees in shame. I just closed the door.

Back in the den, there was this Australian kangaroo giving birth on the television. The little baby kangaroo, which looked sort of like an anchovy with legs, had just made it out of its mama and was crawling around looking for her pouch. The man on the show said it had about ten minutes to get in there and find a teat or it would die. He said a lot of them don't make it. I got so wrought up watching that trembly little fellow that I started cheering him on. So did everyone else. Well, to everyone's relief, the little thing made it. Then Gus wanted to know why everybody over there always called each other Mike. Nobody had any idea.

Eric ate a whole bunch of dry cat food before figuring out what it was and that somebody had put it in the party dish as a joke. He tried to act like it didn't bother him, but he didn't stay too long after that. Melinda went out to her car for cigarettes, and a yellow jacket stung her behind the knee, so when she came in howling, Rod slapped this big wad of chewed tobacco on the spot to draw out the poison, which made her howl even louder, till I washed it off and applied meat tenderizer and let her go lie down in the guest bed for a while.

That's when something strange happened. The phone started ringing, and I ran back to get it in Dale's and my bedroom, which was the closest to quiet in the trailer. I answered and just got this hollow sound at first, like you get with a bad connection over long-distance.

There was a mumble, then a woman's voice said, "She's gone." I didn't recognize the voice, but I was sure what "gone" meant by the way she said it. It meant someone had died. Then she said—and she almost screamed it—"Someone should have been here. Why weren't you and Clarence here?"

Now I don't know a soul in this world named Clarence, and this was clearly a case of the wrong number. "Ma'am," I said as gently as I knew how.

"You'll have to talk louder," she said. "I can hardly hear you."

I curled my hand around my lips and the mouthpiece and said, "Ma'am, you have dialed the wrong number."

"Oh God, I'm sorry," she said. "Oh dear God." And here is

the strange thing. The woman did not hang up. She just kept saying "Dear God" and crying.

I sat there listening to that woman and to all the happy noise coming from everywhere in the trailer and through the window from outside, and when she finally brought it down to a sniffle I said, "Honey, who was it that passed away?"

"My sister," she said. "My sister, Beatrice." And it was like saying the name started her to sobbing again.

"And none of your people are there?" I said.

"Just me," she said.

"Sweetheart, you listen to me," I said, trying to close the window for more quiet. Sweet Christ, I thought. Dear sweet Christ in Heaven. "Are you listening, angel? You should not be alone right now. You understand what I'm telling you?" I said , "Now, I am right here."

The New Yorker
September 28, 1987

17

Conclusion: The Many Faces of Grace

We have come full circle and return to the place from which we began. The experience of grace is *human* experience. The cosmos, human life, and history are the loci of the self-communication of God. Although grace transcends the forms in which it is expressed, it can only be found *in* diverse historical and sociological forms, not beyond or above them.[1]

The experience of grace is also *real*. It is not pseudo-experience or experience that runs parallel to one's genuine concerns and values. To discover where one's heart is is to discover the hub of grace's activity. The grace of the moment, in whatever form, attests to the presence of the Kingdom on earth.

Grace does not replace personality; it works through it. The event of newness brought about by grace can take place in a sudden, dramatic way, or in an unobservable, gradual way. God's gracious care can touch us in the forgiveness of sin, in the suffering that life inevitably brings, in the smile of a child or in the roar of a waterfall. Grace takes on a thousand different faces for men and women, for rich and poor, for caucasians and persons of color, for Europeans and Africans. The unifying element for Christians is a generous loving God who created the world, sent the gift of Godself in Jesus, and who continues to be present and active through the Holy Spirit.

---

[1] E. Schillebeeckx, *The Church with A Human Face: A New and Expanded Theology of Ministry*, trans. John Bowden (New York: Crossroad, 1985) p. 5.

The work of grace is totally God's and totally ours. We do not need to frame the question in a way that opposes God's activity to that of the human community.[2] The freedom and glory of persons is the result and reflection of God's gracious activity. The more one creatively and energetically cooperates with grace, the more is God glorified. One can reflect on the contrast between being an integral part of some endeavor, working with others and having a vital function, and the experience of standing by with nothing very important to do—an onlooker rather than a participant. The former gives one a sense of being valuable, of belonging, of making a contribution to the good, and of the joy of effort, if not always of success. It is odd indeed to think that God's plan of grace would be otherwise. For Christians, the definitive events of grace are creation, the life, death and resurrection of Jesus, and the ongoing presence of the Spirit. We do nothing to deserve these gifts. But we are called upon to carry on the tradition—to acknowledge and accept these gifts freely and to live and act in a grace-full way.

Nor need a positive, optimistic anthropology deny the enormous gravity of sin or the human selfishness and frailty that is its fruit. But the Christian story relates unequivocally that the victory over death has been won in the life, death and resurrection of Jesus. Evil and the suffering it causes are to be fought at every turn both within each person and in the structures of our world, but evil will not be ultimately victorious in the face of God's universal love. Our theology of grace must account for the experience of an Augustine who felt rescued from the overwhelmingly powerful vortex of sin and for a Julian of Norwich for whom sin pales in the face of

---

[2]Juan Luis Segundo makes this point in *Grace and the Human Condition* (New York: Maryknoll, 1973), p. 50. Segundo feels that when such an opposition is set up, people tend to put too much value on human effort. He mentions Pelagius, the desert anchorites, Cassian, and the misunderstanding of Ignatius of Loyola as examples. However, I think his examples represent only a very small and elite portion of the Christian community, albeit a portion that has had enormous influence on the Christian understanding of grace. My hunch is that the problem in the wider community has been the opposite—a sense of God doing everything, leaving to humans a very circumscribed arena of activity, i.e., narrowly focused obligations such as attendance at church on Sunday.

God's grace. In either case, however, grace has the edge. Faith involves trusting in this final victory of goodness without allowing that trust to deteriorate into apathy and indifference to the suffering of the world.

There are no limits to the operations of God's grace. We cannot ignore the presence of grace in nature as well as in history,[3] in our relationships with animals and rain forests as well as with humans, in the experience of success as well as of failure, in the lives of women and persons of color as well as in white men, in the poor as well as in the rich.

The acceptance of forgiveness of sin in Jesus opens the door to a radically new and transformed existence. Grace cannot be situated in a realm that is different from the one in which human projects meet success or failure. Grace confronts death, despair, fear, slavery, literalism and legalism. Grace is also at the root of beauty, color and form, of the loving response, of joy, of communication and communion of every stripe. Grace is to be celebrated in efforts to love our children well, in physical, intellectual, spiritual accomplishments, in being patient with ourselves and others, in facing difficulties with courage and dignity. Ultimately, even in our brokenness, there is no human situation in which God's grace cannot reveal itself.[4]

Tradition and Discernment

We are assisted in our quest for life and meaning by those who have gone before us. The Wisdom literature teaches that responsible cooperation with grace need not be an act of rebellion or unfaith, but an act of passionate commitment to God.[5] Augustine makes us aware of the power and omnipresence of grace. Thomas Aquinas made distinctions that help us avoid pitting God against creation and brought into focus the role of the Holy Spirit in grace. Martin Luther

---

[3]See Joseph Sittler, *Gravity and Grace: Reflections and Provocations*, ed. Linda Marie Delloff (Minneapolis: Augsburg Press, 1986).

[4]Michael Cleary, "The Openness of the Human Person: The Anthropological Foundations of Graced Existence," *Louvain Studies* 10 (Fall, 1984), p. 105.

[5]Walter Brueggemann, "The Trusted Creature," *The Catholic Biblical Quarterly* 31(1969): 491.

reminds us of the real, gratuitous and personal nature of grace. Julian of Norwich invites us to rejoice and celebrate the infinite generosity of a loving God. Ignatius of Loyola reminds us of the possibility of finding God in *all* things.

This distinguished community, in combination with the truth of contemporary experience and the entire community of faith provides the tools by which we discern the presence of authentic grace in our lives distinguishing it from the many counterfeit forms it may take. Grace is above all a community affair. In grace we see ourselves as peers, not only with all peoples, but with the earth itself. Grace leads us to the insight that the goods of the earth belong to *everyone* and to the actions that put flesh and blood on that insight.

The final test by which we judge a life of grace is the fruit that it bears. The exhilaration of living daily within the heart of the divine community is inextricably bound up with the cross. And the graced choice to lay down one's life for another can never be isolated from the intense joy and happiness that are the footprints of grace. We must continue to connect the closeness to God that one feels in friendship or in a spectacular sunset with living simply, feeding the hungry, and raising up those who are downtrodden. And we must connect visiting the sick and imprisoned with the graced joys of a spring rain or the birth of a child. The presence of grace does not mean that one has to abandon one's present life in favor of another that is somehow "supernatural". On the contrary, grace demands that one live the very life one is living, but in a new key that is more and more free, responsible and open to the transforming love of God. Working to change unjust social and political structures is at the heart of such a life.

A certain discomfort may follow upon the discovery of what Segundo calls "the breadth of grace".[6] But the theological imperative is to acknowledge this breadth, to listen, to ponder, and to speak about the experience of grace that is *already taking place* in the world and in the church. The goal of theology is to help believers become more conscious of the

---

[6]Segundo, *Grace and the Human Condition*, p. 127.

giftedness of life so that they notice and nurture more fully the loving presence of God in the world.[7] If one is going to err, let it be in what Walter Brueggemann calls overliving rather than underliving.

To close, I borrow the words of Tom Driver, Paul J. Tillich Professor of Theology and Culture at Union Theological Seminary in New York.

> All my experience is Word of God for me. I hope my readers may be brought to some such awareness of their own experience and thus to feel with their senses the glory that is God. There is no tongue and no word, no joy, pain, good nor evil that does not resound with the presence of God. At least, that is how I figure it.
>
> Look you and see.[8]

This is an exalted, challenging and joyful task. Since the Spirit blows where it will, one must be on the lookout, ready to be surprised by grace. God's glory is creation and the human community fully alive—enjoying God, each other and the earth. God's grace is everywhere.

[7]L. Boff, *Liberating Grace*, trans. John Drury (Maryknoll, NY: Orbis, 1979), p. 5.

[8]Tom Driver, *Patterns of Grace: Human Experience As Word of God* (San Francisco: Harper & Row, 1977), p. xiii.

Index

Subject Index

Adam, 63, 75, 86, 102, 113, 115, 119, 150
adoption, 88, 95
affectivity, 77, 80, 142, 186, 230
American Indian, 6, 18
anthropology, 15, 23, 29, 99-103, 113-19, 137-39, 147, 154, 170-89, 237; See also maturity
Aquinas, Thomas, 3, 8, 35-40, 82-103, 147-48, 200-01, 238
Aristotle, 83-91, 100, 103, 200
artists, 60, 204, 212-13, 215, 221-24, 232
Augustine, 3, 8, 35-40, 65-81, 93, 98, 101, 103, 147-48, 153 177; See also *Confessions*

Baius, 150-51
baptism, 60, 68, 70-72, 141, 208
Barbour, Ian, 198
Baum, Gregory, 4, 191
Bellah, Robert, 30, 208
Bennett, John, 198
Bernanos, George, 204
Bernard of Clairvaux, 82, 84, 168
Berry, Thomas, 197-98, 202
Berry, Wendel, 198
Bible, 7, 40-63, 129, 142, 145; wisdom literature, 178-81
body, 100
Boff, Leonardo, 3, 20, 30, 240
Bonaventure, 85
Bozzo, Edward, 8
Bracken, Joseph, 194, 203
Brown, Peter, 66-72
Browning, Elizabeth Barrett, 223-24
Brueggemann, Walter, 29, 50, 178-181, 238, 240
Buddhism, 6, 18
Burns, J. Patout, 74ff
Burrell, David, 8
Bynum, Carolyn Walker, 108

call, 55-56, 62
Callahan, William, 209-211
Capon, Robert F., 185
Chadwick, Henry, 66
Chardin, Teilhard de, 200-201
charis, 45, 47, 54, 56, 164
charity, 84, 87, 94-95, 148, 152
Christ, Carol, 214
church, 16-17, 35, 89, 212-13, 229-30, 239; See also community
Cloud of Unknowing, 106
Cobb, John, 198
Cochrane, C. N., 66
Colborn, Francis, 4
Colledge, Eric, 105
communion, 9, 95, 164, 204, 220, 238
community, 1, 15, 17, 21-22, 28, 30-31, 43, 54, 89, 99, 124, 140, 178-181, 190-211, 237, 240; global community, 5, 7, 16, 32, 58, 159, 170, 202, 236, 238-239
compassion, 48, 50, 210
Confessions, 72-81, 213, 237-38
Conn, Joann Wolski, 177, 186
contemplation, 208-211
conversion, 64, 70-71, 77, 79-80, 131, 183, 233
cooperation, 159, 175, 181, 205, 213, 237-38
cosmos, 3, 11, 13, 21-22, 59, 65, 114, 162, 166, 174, 179-181, 197-202, 236
covenant, 45, 48-53, 132
cross, 57, 63, 108, 135-37, 142, 239
creation, 7, 51, 57, 61, 69, 72, 75, 85, 89, 100, 114-15, 157, 162-63, 171, 184, 197-202, 237-240; new creation, 71, 90, 95, 139, 146, 171-74

death, 60-64, 183, 219, 224, 238
deification, 93-95, 148, 154
delight, 77-78

devotio moderna, 126, 129
Dickenson, Emily, 216-17
Dillard, Annie, 198
discernment, 239
disciple, 42
divinization, 24, 65, 93, 167
Donovan, Mary Ann, 170

ecology, 198-202, 206, 218
eleos, 47; See also mercy
elevating grace, See grace
Eliot, T.S., 214-16
Ernst, Cornelius, 17-18, 20, 58-59, 75,
    129-32, 157, 164, 172-73, 175, 213,
    222, 233
Evans, Robert F., 67
eucharist, 140
experience, 10-19, passim
exodus, 41, 49

faith alone, 134-135
Fannon, Patrick, 8
favor, 45, 47, 50-54, 141
feminism, 6, 185-89, 213-14, 227-232
forgiveness, 46-52, 61, 74, 135, 138, 142,
    183, 206, 222, 227, 238
Fox, Matthew, 179
Francis of Assisi, 200
Fransen, Piet, 3, 30-31
freedom, 2, 13, 23-24, 42, 45-46, 48, 51,
    57, 61-69, 77, 91-92, 103, 147, 149-53
friendship, 23, 88, 95, 98, 121-22, 135,
    148, 239
Frost, Robert, 219-221

gift, 23, 46-53, 58, 62, 78, 87-88
Gilligan, Carol, 186
Gilson, Etienne, 86
Glazer, John W., 8
God; as Creator, 21-22, 59, 69, 81; as
    friend, 88, 167; as immanent, 110-
    11, 165, 168, 171; as Mother, 107-
    08; as Mystery, 15, 20, 24, 85, 168-
    69; as transcendent, 128-29, 132; as
    Trinity, 95, 108-10, 118-19, 194-97,
    236; image of, 31, 48-50, 58-64, 87-
    89, 108-11, 124-25, 204, 230-32
Goethe, Johann Wolfgang von, 39
grace; description of, 20-25; elevating
    grace, 92-93, 102; errors about, 26-
    32; healing grace, 92-93, 138-139;

nature and grace, 27, 90-92, 150,
    154, 157; supernatural grace, 23, 30,
    92-93, 98, 101-03, 161, 224-25, 239;
    grace as personal, 161, passim; grace
    in literature, 212-235
gratitude, 23, 52-53, 57, 62, 79, 184

habit, 90, 97, 103
Haight, Roger, 72, 97, 145, 154, 156,
    158, 174
hanan, 44-46
Haring, Bernard, 205-06
Haughton, Rosemary, 192
healing, 46, 79-80, 85, 90, 92
Hebrew bible, 40-53; See also bible
hen, 44-45
hesed, 44, 47, 50-51
Hinduism, 6
history, 4, 8-9, 17-18, 25-26, 30-38, 44,
    56, 58, 98, 185, 236; historical con-
    sciousness, 15
Hopkins, Gerard Manley, 218-19
Hosea, 49
hospitality, 204, 217, 222-223

Ignatius of Loyola, 239
imagery, 12, 212-235
imagination, 37, 204, 210, 231-32
imago Dei, 170-71, 229; See also God,
    image of
incarnation, 3, 28, 107, 139, 163-64, 168,
    171; See also Jesus Christ
individualism, 30
Irenaeus, 75, 168, 170

Jansenism, 150-53
Jedin, Hubert, 149
Jesus Christ, 18, 41-42, 56-62, 79, 89-
    90, 138, 163-64, 194-95, 236; See
    also incarnation
joy, 29, 48-49, 51-53, 62, 64, 79, 95,
    108, 110-12, 118, 169, 180, 211, 222,
    232, 238-240
Judaism, 6, 18
Julian of Eclanum, 66, 69, 70
Julian of Norwich, 8, 40, 104-25, 195-
    97, 216, 237, 239
Jungel, Eberhard, 194
justice, 7, 13, 51, 159-60, 174-77, 207,
    211, 227-33, 239
justification, 24, 29, 55, 96, 102, 134-38

Kelly, Brian, 8
Kingdom of God, 88
Kley, Dale Van, 149-52
Kohlberg, Lawrence, 186

Lasch, Christopher, 35
language, 1, 4, 6, 11, 15, 26, 30, 32, 41, 84, 97
law, 55, 58, 61, 63-69, 72, 86, 88
legalism, 29
liberation, 4-5, 93, 174-77, 227, 232
life, 6, 24, 29, 38, 49, 57-68, 75, 89, 160, 170-72, 171-74, 178-81, 211, 238, 240
literature, 212-235
Llewelyn, Robert, 105
Logos, 65
Lonergan, Bernard, 83, 86
Lossky, V., 93
love, 1, 11, 21, 23-24, 27-28, 47, 49-53, 57, 63, 78, 88, 95, 123, 184-85, 203
Lubac, Henri de, 3, 165
Luther, 3, 8, 35, 37-40, 126-43, 145, 147-48, 238

Mackey, James, 4
Macquarrie, John, 3
Maguire, Daniel, 186
Mangum, Donald, 222-23, 233-35
Manichaeism, 73
Mantzaridis, George I., 93
maturity, 32, 38, 68, 101, 103, 177-81, 184, 206
May, Gerald, 159-60, 203
McCool, Gerald, 36-37
McDermott, Brian, 13, 212
McGrath, Alister, 128
meaning, 9, 16-19, 238
Menninger, Karl, 182
mercy, 47-52
Meyer, Charles, R., 8
Meyendorff, John, 93
Miles, Margaret, 213
Molinism, 149-50
Moltmann, Jurgen, 194
Morrison, Toni, 231-32
Muhlen, Heribert, 8, 194
mysticism, 154-55, 164, 217

nature, 27-28, 32, 44, 83, 85, 90-92, 97-98, 102-03, 216-21, 230; See also grace, nature and

New Testament, 40-44, 48, 54-64

Oakley, Francis, 128
O'Connor, Flannery, 224-27
O'Donovan, Leo, 154
Old Testament, 43-53
Ozment, Steven, 128

participation, 24, 65, 88, 91, 94-100, 103, 114, 142-43, 148, 167, 170
Pascal, Blaise, 27, 151-52
Paul, 40, 42, 54-64, 103
peace, 7, 56
Pelagius, 66-72, 177, 237
Pelikan, Jaroslav, 33-35, 145, 148
Plaskow, Judith, 3, 186
Platonism, 37, 41, 74
praise; See gratitude
predestination, 149, 152
Principe, Walter, 92
prophets, 50
providence, 52
Pseudo-Dionysius, 195

questioning, art of, 10-13, 21, 29

Rahner, Karl, 3, 8, 15-16, 28-29, 35, 86, 154-55, 158, 161, 169, 193
reason, 98-99
reconciliation, 63; See also forgiveness
Reformation, 126-30, 144-45, 149
reification, 27, 31
relationship, 12, 18, 21-22, 26, 31, 35, 45-47, 50-53, 58-59, 95, 99, 164-68
repentance, 51, 135; See also forgiveness
resurrection, 57, 63, 93-95, 237
Rich, Adrienne, 227-28
righteousness, 65
Rondet, Henri, 3, 36, 44, 87, 91, 96, 101, 103, 147, 153

sacramentality, 193, 224
Saiving, Valerie, 186
salvation, 24, 142
Schillebeeckx, Edward, 1, 9, 41-42, 45-47, 163-64, 175-76, 212, 236
Schoonenberg, Piet, 205
Segundo, Juan Luis, 3, 39, 194, 202, 207, 212, 237
Shakespeare, William, 221-222
Shea, John, 14

sin, 29, 47-53, 92, 111, 119-23, 137-39,
    157-58, 181-88, 204-08, 224-27; orig-
    inal sin, 69, 70, 73, 85, 100, 147, 149
Singer, Irving, 7
Sittler, Joseph, 157, 198, 238
slavery, 61-62, 64, 238
Spirit, 9, 61-62, 65, 87, 89, 90, 92, 95,
    98, 101, 103, 110, 139-40, 154, 195,
    218, 229, 236, 238, 240
suffering, 237-38; See also justice

Teresa of Avila, 38, 159, 168
Theisen, Jerome, 190-91, 202, 206
Tracy, David, 10-11
tradition, 1, 4, 9, 13, 15, 18, 33-38, 41,
    48, 156-57
transcendent, 28, 164-66, 225; See also
    God, transcendent
transformation, 7, 24, 64, 77, 90, 92,
    135, 141-42, 146, 172, 214, 230
Trent, 8, 29, 40, 144-49

ultimate reality, 10-11
Updike, John, 198, 201

Walker, Alice, 229-31
Williams, Daniel Day, 194, 197
Whitman, Walt, 218-19
wholeness, 24, 30, 32, 79, 100-01, 115,
    232